Safe Teen

Safe Teen

Powerful Alternatives to Violence

Anita Roberts

POLESTAR
An Imprint of Raincoast Books
Vancouver

Raincoast Books gratefully acknowledges the
support of the Government of Canada
through the Book Publishing Industry
Development Program, the Canada Council
and the Department of Canadian Heritage.
We also acknowledge the assistance of the
Province of British Columbia through the
British Columbia Arts Council.

Edited by Lynn Henry and Barbara Kuhne
Cover and book design by
    Gabi Proctor/DesignGeist
Cover image by Stone
Interior art by Anita Roberts
    and Mia Tremblay

First published in 2001 by:
Polestar, an imprint of Raincoast Books
9050 Shaughnessy Street
Vancouver, British Columbia
Canada, V6P 6E5
(604) 323-7100
www.raincoast.com

1 2 3 4 5 6 7 8 9 10

Canadian Cataloguing in Publication Data
Roberts, Anita, 1952-
   Safe teen
   ISBN 1-896095-99-2

   1. Violence—Prevention. 2. School
   violence—Prevention. 3. Teenagers—
   Mental health. 4. Self-help technique for
   teenagers. I. Title.
HM291.R57 2001   155.5'18
   C99-910738-0

Printed and bound in Canada

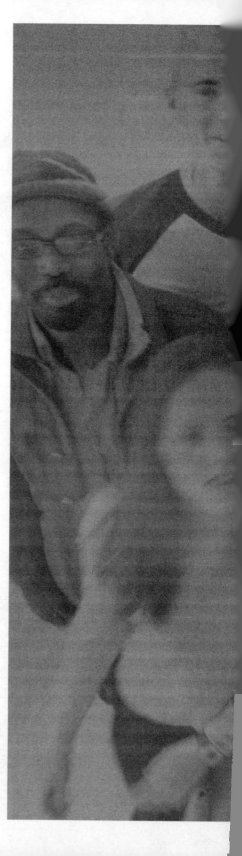

Contents

Acknowledgements

*"Teaching our children
how to make choices
from a place of inner wisdom
can be the best prevention
strategy of all."*

FIRST, THANK YOU to all the SafeTeen facilitators, past and present, for so brilliantly bringing who they are to the work. With thanks to the original team: Kristi Anderson, Laurie Schuerbeke, Aaron White, Leonie Plunkett, Stuart Poyntz, Marcus Youseff, Katrina Pacey. SafeTeen wouldn't be what it is today without you. And to all the other SafeTeen "AGENTS FOR CHANGE"—Dave Hatfield, Teresa Harris, Sherry Simon, Carmine Aguirre, Shonda Wang, Dolphin Kasper, Bill Pozzobon—who go out there every day and make a difference.

A SPECIAL THANKS TO:

Dave Hatfield for your soulful presence, undying enthusiasm and valuable written contributions to this book; Sherry Simon (and your tech-mate, Curtis) for such a cool, cool, cool website! Laurie Schuerbeke—you helped to shape the Heart-Mind-Spirit-Body of this work and your passion for the work sustained me. I will always be grateful for your longterm contribution to SafeTeen; Aaron White for "bravely going where no man has gone before…,"for your absolute commitment to making the Boy's Program work, for your written contribution to this book, for backing up my intuition with your science and for being my travel buddy by plane, boat and dogsled. I couldn't have done it without you; to all the amazing and committed teachers in the schools who have supported—and continue to support—SafeTeen over the years; and to the thousands of teens in the SafeTeen workshops who inspire me to continue this work.

To Michelle Benjamin at Polestar/Raincoast for giving me the nudge to get this book started, and for her faith in my ability to complete it. To my editor Lynn Henry for being the "little boat that could" as she tenaciously laboured with me to put together this 80,000 word puzzle…I'd sail with you again any day! And to editor Barbara Kuhne for her last minute and highly skilled midwifery.

Grateful appreciation goes to my parents, Mildred and Ross Tremblay, for being alive and present and awake so I can have someone to show my book to and say, "TaDa!"

The most enormous gratitude goes to my partner Jeffrey Gourley, whose beautiful food and shoulder rubs I bless him for every single day, and to my daughters Julie Gourley and Bronwyn Gourley for being my home and my heart. And to my son Troy for turning out to be a man I can say I am proud to have raised.

To Lorraine Roberts and Marsha Enamoto, my first self-defense teachers (in 1975). Little did you know at the time the journey you would inspire me to take.

And finally, in a timeless gesture of honor and respect, I place my two hands together and bow to my own spirit's desire to heal.

Introduction

M Y WORK in violence prevention began in 1976 in the form of a self-defence program for girls and women and has transformed over the years to include a complementary and equally important violence prevention program for boys and young men. I want to begin with a relevant piece of my personal journey, and then I will map out how the work that has culminated in this book has evolved over the years.

The Conception of SafeTeen

I was the third girl not-born-a-boy in a family of six girls. Mine was a "normal" 1950s childhood. A devoted but rage-aholic father and a loving but victimized mother combined to create a garden-variety dysfunctional environment with both good times and ordinary times interrupted by episodes of unpredictable crisis and violence.

As female children will do, I observed my mother carefully. I unconsciously knew that she was supposed to determine who I would be when I grew up. She seemed inconsequential beside my father, whose passionate nature and domineering personality made her seem invisible. My memories of my mother from my childhood years are pale and formless. She was utterly powerless in the face of my father's eruptions of rage. When he would go after one of us kids, I remember her hovering on the outskirts of the violent episodes, wailing in despair, her arms flailing like the wings of a broken bird. I loved my mother but it became very clear to me at an early age that I didn't want to be like her.

In my early twenties I began studying karate with a women's martial arts organization. I had no awareness, at that time, of the connection between my fascination with martial arts and the "self-defence" issues in my childhood. My instructors were physically powerful women who seemed so in control of their lives. I was in awe of one woman in particular. She had a quiet strength combined with a fierceness and a skill level that won her the provincial championship in karate for three consecutive years. I wanted to be like her. I wanted to feel that strong and in control, and especially that fearless.

During a casual conversation one day, this fearless woman confessed to me that she was terrified to be at home alone at night. I felt devastated and confused. The warrior woman image I had of her did not fit this damsel-in-distress story. I was deeply disillusioned. Perhaps there was no hope for women to feel safer in the world.

A period of despair was followed by a persistent curiosity. I began to ask questions: Why do females tend to panic and freeze when faced with danger? How is it that a woman can suddenly overcome this paralyzing fear and perform amazing feats of bravery in order to save her children? Do women have good reason to be afraid or are they paranoid?

The more I learned about the facts on violence against women, the more I came to understand that women's "paranoia" is a rational response to a real and potentially life-threatening situation. Women who experience intense fear of assaults are simply women who are acutely aware of the very real dangers around them.

I began to realize that the question shouldn't so much be Why are women afraid, but rather, Why aren't women outraged? And why do women apologize all the time? Why do they take responsibility for acts of violence perpetrated on them? Why do they care so much whether everyone likes them? Why do they so often put others' needs first? Why do they have such difficulty saying "No"?

I felt compelled to understand how women behave in the face of danger. I wanted to know how fear and anger operate for females, and how power and gender impact each other. More than anything, I wanted to know what women could do to be stronger and less fearful in a world where women and children are so frequently the targets of male violence.

These questions informed the direction of my studies. I embarked on an in-depth exploration of the socialization of women and the psychology of assault. Everything that I learned pointed to the same premise: that violence was intrinsically connected to issues of gender and power. Working toward making women safer seemed urgent to me, and this was my focus in the early years. I developed self-defence classes for girls and women based on martial arts, but basic and simple and accessible to females of all ages and abilities. I felt all women had the right to know how to defend themselves, but over time I became more interested in preventing attacks. With this goal in mind I developed an assertiveness model using verbal and body language skills to communicate inner power.

SafeTeen: The Girls' Program

The SafeTeen assertiveness model was developed specifically to prevent and de-escalate violence. The skills are effective whether the threat is by a stranger or by someone we know, whether it is a peer or someone in a position of power and authority. Regardless of the type of violence—verbal, emotional or physical—the assertiveness model provides a concrete set of skills with which to stand up for ourselves. These skills offer females an alternative to the usual advice to "go along with it" or "just ignore him."

Young women between the ages of fourteen and eighteen are the highest risk group for assault. When I shifted to violence prevention as my goal, I began to teach teenage girls. I decided to bring my work into the school setting because I felt I would reach the widest teen audience and I believed the material taught in the workshops should be a vital part of every young woman's education in life skills. In the words of one fifteen-year-old girl, "We learned how to stand up for ourselves and how to fight off some creepy guy. This is the best thing I have ever learned in school but I wish I had it in grade 6 or 7. Before this what was I supposed to do, nail him with my deadly badminton skills?"

SafeTeen: The Boys' Program

The SafeTeen program for girls had been well-established in the secondary schools for ten years when I decided to tackle the often repeated question, "What about the boys?" My early attempts to do co-ed groups failed miserably. The behaviour of the boys in the groups ranged from stony silence to provocative remarks and masturbation gestures in the front row. The behaviour of the girls in the co-ed sessions ranged from giggles to silence. Normally opinionated, lively grade nine to twelve girls clammed up in the co-ed format. It was evident that they didn't feel safe enough to speak up. It became clear that the boys did not feel safe either—they just manifested their insecurity differently. Regardless of how well I understood the gender and power issues or how sensitively I presented the material, I could not bridge the gender gap. I became committed to the task of researching and developing a gender-separate program for boys.

I initiated the program for young men because I believed that men who feel good about themselves won't hurt girls and women. In the beginning, my commitment and passion was still directed primarily toward the safety and empowerment of females. It wasn't until later that I understood the ways in which our boys are in trouble, and I then began to feel a heart-expanding compassion for all the terrified boys out there. Boys who are struggling to live up to the unattainable goal of being a "real man" and who live with the constant anxiety of being exposed as inadequate. Boys who live in fear of letting down their guard for even one moment lest they be violently targeted by other males. Boys who are trying as hard as they can to grow up and be a man while being pressured to give up all that makes them human in the process.

Through my ongoing research it became apparent that boys who become violent tend to oversubscribe to traditional stereotypes of masculinity. I came to believe that in order for boys and young men to examine issues of masculinity they need to feel accepted exactly as they are, without judgement. Only in an atmosphere of unqualified acceptance is there hope for change. This does not mean that educators and parents should have no boundaries regarding behaviours. It simply means that to work with young men on issues of gender and violence we need to create an atmosphere of understanding and compassion. We need to accept the attitudes and language and posturing without judging boys' opinions or comments as bad or wrong.

Given the social conditioning for males and the typical masculine role models for boys, it's not surprising that young males behave the way they do. They are simply channelling all the attitudes and fantasies and cool talk that they have picked up from TV, video games, movies and music videos. The attitudes and opinions they put out are things they are trying on, often as a kind of armour. If we can remember they are not yet fully formed—that they are "adults-in-process"—we won't feel we have to hold them to everything that comes out of their mouths as though it represents who they are. If we can do this, then we can create some space for them to look at what they truly believe. Without that unqualified acceptance, boys simply shut down when we try to engage with them about gender issues.

Over time I learned that to work successfully with boys and young men on these issues we needed to provide a male role model. In order for the young men to "buy" the information and skills offered to them in the SafeTeen program, they need to see a man whom they respect embracing the skills we are teaching. A man who will celebrate with them all the positive things about being male. A man who is able to contain the energy that the young men bring to the topic at hand and who unconditionally accepts what they bring to the moment. A man who will create a safe space for young men to explore gender issues and help them to map out the connections between gender and violence in a way that doesn't leave the boys feeling as though they are being personally blamed. By opening up the whole topic of "manhood" without censure or shame or blame, we allow boys to begin to align themselves with what feels good and true for them instead of attaching themselves to a negative and potentially violent stereotype. If we are able to do this, boys will have the freedom to choose for themselves a new way to be a man.

In 1994 I met Aaron White, an educator who had been working on men's issues for many years. He had begun experimenting with teaching young men how to be more accountable for their behaviours in relation to women. Aaron and I began to work together to build on the curriculum I had developed for boys on issues of gender and power and violence. Over a period of five years, Aaron and I and a growing team of male facilitators continued to fine tune the content and delivery of this new program.

The most challenging aspect of developing the boys' program was coming up with a format that addressed issues of violence without making the boys feel bad about themselves as young men. Given that the vast majority of violence in our society is committed by males and that the leading cause of injury for women in Canada is being assaulted by a man she knows, we were faced with an enormous challenge.

My motivating force for persisting in creating a successful boys' program was hope. I hold a firm belief in the inherent goodness in all children, female and male. The challenge with the young men was to get them to admit their goodness. They seemed determined to posture in ways that supported negative stereotypes about males. Not only did they not feel safe in a co-ed environment, they also felt quite defensive in groups of male peers.

When he first went in to work with boys on these issues, Aaron reported that it was almost impossible to get them to let down their guard and be genuine or honest about their feelings. We needed a vehicle for boys to expose their humanity to each other in a way that felt safe. The solution was designing the program in ways that they can explore questions about intimacy and share their needs and feelings *anonymously.* When they can expose their humanity to each other without risking humiliation, the macho posturing can soften. When the young men feel safer, they open up with each other more and the terrible isolation that many of them feel begins to dissolve.

During one SafeTeen program, a grade ten boy stood up and blurted out, "OK you guys, am I the only virgin in the class?" In response, almost every other boy in the class raised his hand and admitted he was also a virgin. Magic occurs when boys open up to each other in this way. Once they have revealed the truth about themselves, it becomes very difficult for them to revert to the "stud" charade.

By providing a safe environment with a healthy gender role model for boys, we could see that we were making a difference in both the posturing and the belief systems of the young men we were working with. The success of the SafeTeen Boys' Program is due largely to the fact that it tackles male accountability issues through exposing stereotypes in a way that *builds* gender identity rather than destroying it.

We know that men who feel good about themselves don't hurt women. It follows that men who feel good about themselves are also less likely to hurt each other. By transferring the assertiveness model that I had developed for the young women to the program for the young men, SafeTeen: The Boys' Program came into being. A strong focus of the boys' program is to give boys skills to manage fear and anger and to stand up for themselves in relation to other males in non-violent ways. The workshops provide concrete skills for boys to use in asserting themselves from an authentically powerful place, thus giving young men a desperately needed alternative to "give twice as hard as you get" or "just walk away." A powerful alternative to violence.

Safe Teen: The Book

In this book, I am offering a breakdown of the skills taught in the SafeTeen programs as well as an in-depth look at the issues that underscore the work. It is not possible to write the work the way I speak it, and the energy and immediacy of the teenagers themselves cannot be present in the text. In order to communicate the alive quality of the experiential SafeTeen workshops, I've included contemporary scenarios of teens interacting in real-life situations. I have created a cast of characters to represent the young women and men who cannot be physically present, so they can ask their urgent questions and tell you, the reader, their stories.

Part I: HEART introduces a youth-specific assertiveness model that offers teens a way of accessing their own inner power and wisdom. Through concrete verbal and body language skills, the SafeTeen model provides strategies for managing fear and anger as well as giving youth a safe way of standing up for themselves and for what they believe in. This model addresses the roots of violence and demonstrates the difference between being an easy target of violence and being well protected and safe.

Part II: MIND explores the conditioning that informs destructive gender-based patterns of behaviour for both females and males. By shedding light on such sensitive and volatile topics as power, sexuality, relationships, intimacy, sexual harassment and sexual assault, we are able to redefine traditional ideas of masculinity and femininity and open the door to the possibility of change.

Part III: SPIRIT probes deeply into the core of gender and power issues, exposing the bone. This section draws on my lifetime of work focused on healing the great ugly wound in the world that is violence. It holds my hope for a more peaceful world.

Part IV: BODY introduces role-plays, body language skills, boundaries exercises, communications exercises and assertiveness techniques that have been so well-received in the SafeTeen programs. These exercises provide concrete strategies and address issues relevant to the everyday lives of youth: skills for managing fear and anger, how to deal with relationship violence and intimacy issues, how to respond to intimidating or threatening situations; tools to excavate inner strengths and build self-esteem. Designed to encourage young women and men to feel strong and secure in their respective identities, these exercises give teens the opportunity to practise a new way of being in the world and the skills with which to make that choice for themselves.

It is my greatest hope that educators and parents will receive something useful from what I offer in these pages and that they will be able to pass it on to the hearts, minds, spirits and bodies of the adults-in-process in their lives.

Part I: **HEART**

To connect with and nurture the core wisdom that we all have inside us and then to build on it by communicating from that authentic place of strength, this is the upward cycle of empowerment—this is the key to being safe in an increasingly violent world. This is the heart of SafeTeen.

In Part I: HEART, we will learn the SafeTeen assertiveness model—a verbal and body language tool that addresses the roots of violence and offers youth a way of accessing their own inner power and wisdom. This model teaches fear and anger management skills that effectively deal with verbal and physical violence.

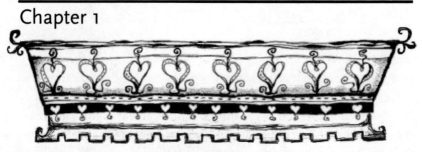

Chapter 1

Easy House / Hard House

I BEGIN HERE, in the opening chapter, with a metaphor that we always use at the beginning of the SafeTeen programs. We use the image of an easy house to break into and a hard house to break into as a tool with which to give the group of teens we are working with a clear and immediate picture of what the focus of the work will be. The image of the two houses describes the difference between being an easy target of violence and being well-protected and safe.

Imagine that you are a burglar. You are scouting out a neighbourhood with the intention of breaking and entering. Now imagine that you see two houses side by side. They are identical in appearance except for the tall fence around the one on the left. When you look closer, you see surveillance cameras mounted all around this house and security alarm systems in place. The doors are well-locked and "Beware of Dog" signs are posted in the windows. You can hear a large dog barking as you walk by.

The second house, the one on the right, has no fence. There is no visible security system of any kind. On closer inspection, you see that one of the windows is open, and as you walk up to the front door no dogs bark, no lights go on and no alarms go off.

You are the burglar. Which house would you break into? This is not a trick question.

It is obvious that the house on the right is an easy house to break into and would be any burglar's first choice. The house on the left—the hard house to break into—would be too risky.

Now let's apply this analogy of the hard house and the easy house to people.

Easy House #1: Caitlyn at the Bus Stop

Caitlyn is sitting at a bus stop. It's early in the morning – barely light out, grey and rainy and she's still feeling sleepy. She hunkers down into her coat and wishes she were back in her warm bed. These early morning band practices really suck, she thinks. As she turtles even further into the hood of her jacket, Caitlyn feels the familiar shift of the wooden slats beneath her as the weight of another person settles down on the bench. She doesn't look up. She keeps her shoulder and her face turned away.

"Excuse me, do you have the time?" a polite male voice asks. Caitlyn has a watch but she can't be bothered to check it. "No, sorry, I don't," she replies and glances up at the man sitting next to her. He is facing her slightly, his legs open, one arm resting on the back of the bench. It's a long bench, why is he sitting way up at my end? she thinks. She scoots over a little and turns her head away, looking up the street to see if the bus is coming.

"Sure is a miserable day. Are you on your way to work?" the man asks her. Caitlyn doesn't want to talk to him but it feels rude not to answer so she tells him she's going to school. She glances up at him again and feels a chill run like tiny spiders up her back—something about the way he's looking at her. Now he's leaning forward, his elbows on his knees and his hands dangling loosely. She notices that he's well-dressed—probably just a nice man on his way to work—but no briefcase—no umbrella either. Somehow it seems strange that he isn't carrying anything. Caitlyn looks up the street once more, hoping to see the bus.

"High school? You look pretty grown up for someone still in high school – isn't it kind of early to be going to school?" he asks her. Caitlyn looks at him again. He's smiling at her and she can't help smiling back. He's running his hands up and down his thighs in an agitated way and then she sees the watch on his arm—that's weird she thinks, why did he ask me for the time? Oh, I'm just being paranoid—maybe his watch isn't working, she thinks. She explains that she's going early because of band practice.

He grins at her. "Oh, I bet you're practising to be one of those Spicy Girls—with your looks you could easily end up in one of those sexy girl bands." Somehow he's moved over even closer to her and his knee is touching hers. She feels her stomach tighten and she pulls into herself. She squeezes her knees together, her hands pressed between them. She's squished over as far as she can go on the bench. "Umm, thanks, but it's not that kind of band," she says nervously. Caitlyn feels trapped. She stands up and looks anxiously up the street again. Maybe if I just ignore him, she thinks...

Easy House #2: Natasha at the Bus Stop

Natasha is sitting at a bus stop. She just missed the bus she was supposed to catch, which means she'll be late getting home. She knows she'll get grounded for being late and she's in a rotten mood. It wasn't her fault —it was Kyle—he got angry every time she told him she had to go. He didn't even walk her to the bus. The more she thinks about it, the more frustrated she feels. It feels as though she's constantly in trouble. Someone is always yelling at her and she's been grounded every weekend for the past three months. Sometimes it feels like the whole world is against her. She sits slumped over, her arms folded tightly across her chest and her head down. She's squeezing her eyelids together hard, trying not to cry.

Natasha is surprised when she feels someone bump up against her. She opens her eyes and sees this older guy sitting right next to her. His leg is touching hers. When she glances up at him he winks at her and gives her a creepy smile. One of his front teeth is missing and he stinks

of cigarettes. Suddenly she feels furious. Natasha doesn't think first—she shoves him with her elbow and says, "Move over, loser."

"What did you call me?" he says as he stands up and looks down at her. "Leave me alone, loser," she replies. She feels too angry to be afraid. She just doesn't care.

"You little bitch! You think you're so tough?" he says leaning over her, his hands on the bench on either side of her, pinning her in, his face inches from hers.

A Hard House: Daniella at the Bus Stop

Daniella is at a bus stop. It seems to Daniella that she spends half her life either on the bus or waiting for a bus. She has had to take three buses to get to school ever since her family moved. She likes the new house but there's no way she is changing schools in the middle of the year. All her friends since grade six are at her school and she plans to graduate with them next year. She has to leave early every morning and in the winter it's dark when she leaves and it's dark again by the time she gets home. Sometimes she's scared but she doesn't complain because she knows her parents would just make her change schools. Riding the bus isn't so bad really; she can get extra homework done and read to pass the time.

The hardest part was the creepy guys who would sometimes try to sit next to her—even when there were tons of empty seats. Daniella soon learned to put her knapsack on the seat next to her—and on the bus stop bench when she was waiting, too. This deterred most of them—she could see them thinking about it and then changing their minds. Daniella felt good about coming up with that one. Although when the bus was crowded she couldn't hog the seat and she'd have to move her bag for whoever wanted to sit down. She hated it how some guys just thought they could invade her space. They sat with their legs wide open so she had to sit with her knees pressed close together to avoid touching them. It made her so mad.

At least when she was on the bus she could ask the bus driver for help, which she did one time when this drunk guy wouldn't leave her alone. Waiting at the bus stop, especially when it was dark out, that's when it was scary.

This morning it was cold and Daniella wished she had worn a sweater under her jacket. She hoped the bus would get there soon. There were so few people out at this time of day, so she paid attention when a man came around the corner and approached the bus stop. She looked right at him and then slid her knapsack onto the bench beside her just as he sat down. Sitting up straight and looking straight ahead, she could see that he was looking at her.

Daniella looked back at him and his eyes scanned up and down her body and he smiled at her. She hated it when guys did that! It made her feel as though they were stripping her clothes away and looking at her naked body. She didn't smile back. She just kept looking him in the eye. He looked away for a moment and then looked back at her. He let his eyes scan her body again and then said, "Hey, you got the time?" Daniella kept her gaze firmly on him and said in a strong but calm voice, "I don't like the way you're looking at me."

The man put his hands up in a gesture of surrender and said, "Whoa babe, I'm just asking for the time!" Daniella replied calmly, "Well, I don't like the way you're looking at me." Daniella couldn't believe it when his gaze swept over her again and with a crooked half smile he said, "So, what do you want to do about it? It's a free country, last I heard." Daniella thought, What a jerk! She felt like he was never going to give up. She felt a bit panicky inside and wanted to look up the street to see if the bus was coming but a voice in her head told her not to look away. She kept her gaze steady and she remained calm. She couldn't think of anything else to say so she said one more time. "Like I said, I don't like the way you're looking at me." At this, the man got up and Daniella stood up too. As she stood, she picked up her bag and held it in front of her. She thought, If he makes a move toward me I'm throwing this bag at him as hard as I can and I'm out of here! She knew there was a gas station open on the next block and she planned to run in that direction. But the man just shrugged his shoulders and as he turned away he mumbled "Bitch" under his breath.

Daniella watched him walk away and when he glanced back at her she was still looking calmly back at him. She didn't feel calm. The urge to yell "Asshole" was really strong. She kept watching in the direction he had gone until he disappeared behind some trees up ahead. She felt exhilarated but relieved when the bus finally pulled up.

At the next stop, the same man got on the bus. He must have walked up to the next stop and waited there, she thought. For a moment Daniella was afraid. She felt like turning her face toward the window but she kept her gaze straight ahead and she could see from the corner of her eye that he didn't even look at her as he walked to the back of the bus. When she got off at her stop, she checked to make sure he didn't get off and follow her. Oh my god, she thought, I'm so glad I didn't swear at him back there! All the way to the school, she let herself say, "Asshole! Asshole! Asshole!" under her breath and the minute she got there she told her best friend about the jerk at the bus stop. They went into the washroom together and Daniella yelled "ASSHOLE!" as loud as she could until they were both laughing so hard they really did have to pee.

Can you see how Daniella made herself a hard house to break into? Later on we will be able to go back and identify all the skills that Daniella used to make herself both physically and emotionally safer in this situation.

Nice Girls and Boys Live in Easy Houses

When children express many of the behaviours that could later be crucial in defending themselves from violence and abuse, such as speaking up, not obeying or getting angry, they are often called bad and rude. Although generally true for all children, to be bad or rude is a far worse offence for a little girl than for a boy child. There is an expectation that boys will be spunky. There is a belief that boys have an innate fierceness that is natural and to be preserved and honoured, while high-spirited behaviour in girls is considered abhorrent and aberrant. The commonly accepted gender rule is "Boys will be boys" and "Girls will be nice."

This traditional female conditioning teaches girls to be easy targets of intimidation and assault—easy houses to break into. As well, this conditioning makes it almost impossible for girls and women to avoid dangerous situations and provides them with no skills to protect themselves when they are in danger. Boys who are sensitive and gentle are easy targets in much the same way girls are. Physically small boys or boys who are not adept at sports may also be seen as easy targets for abuse. Other people will pick on them because they see them as emotionally vulnerable and different.

Martyrs Live in Easy Houses

Nice girls and boys can grow up to be martyrs. Because all females have been conditioned to be nice girls, this is a very common inner demon that many women have to battle. Martyrs are usually truly compassionate people who feel deeply for other people but are unable to direct that compassion toward themselves.

Martyrs will go out of their way to over-meet others' needs so that they always have some in the bank. Martyrs tend to focus too much on the offenders' feelings. They say things like, "What about him? What about his feelings? I just couldn't say that—it would hurt his feelings." Even in situations where they are being blatantly violated, martyrs cannot seem to consider themselves first.

The martyr will over-empathize: "But deep down he's really a nice guy, what if he didn't mean anything by it?" The martyr will deny that it is a problem. She will say, "Oh it's not that big of a deal. It didn't bother me. I just thought it was funny," or perhaps, "He's such a low-life—who cares what he thinks." The martyr may pretend that s/he is above it but the violation doesn't go away. The martyr's anger turns inward. Other people, especially abusive people, know they can take advantage of a martyr.

Smiley Girls Live in Easy Houses

Our conditioning as females teaches us to trust in the goodness of others. It teaches us to be open and caring and nurturing. We are taught that we should be positive, generous in spirit and deed, and to make the best of things. We are taught to forgive and forget. We are taught not to rock the boat. More than anything, we are taught to be cheerful and happy. We are taught to smile. In fact, we are expected to smile all the time. If a female is not smiling she is often asked, "What's wrong? Are you OK? Where's your smile?"—as though a part of her is missing if she isn't smiling. The message to girls being it is not OK to step out of the "smiley girl" role, even for one moment. Most girls and women will tell you that they feel angry when this happens. Even if they don't understand why, they sense that being forced to smile at all times is an infringement on their rights—it is a denial of their full power. If a girl is trying to say "No" and she is smiling at the same time, she will be giving a mixed message and she will be less likely to have her boundary respected. Anytime she tries to stand up for herself with a smile on her face, some of the power of her message will be erased.

"You can't be nice and make a revolution at the same time."
—GLORIA STEINEM

Sorry Girls Live in Easy Houses

Girls and women apologize far too much for their own good, and far more often than boys and men. It is as though we are apologizing for our very existence on this planet. To say "sorry" frequently and in situations where it is not necessary communicates an insecure emotional posture, one that says, "I question my right to exist." Other people will respond to that message accordingly. When we apologize unnecessarily, abusive people will feel powerful around us and we become easy targets. Healthy people may feel uncomfortable and avoid being around us. Most importantly, current research tells us that people who apologize a lot get picked on more often than people who are not so apologetic. Even the corporate world is responding by training both management and staff to apologize less. It has been found that customers will complain less when customer service is courteous but assertive.

Please-like-me People Live in Easy Houses

Needing to be liked is a powerful motivating force in the human psyche. Both males and females can get caught up in this dynamic; however, gender conditioning makes approval-seeking behaviour particularly common for females. Even in situations where the female doesn't like or respect the people she is dealing with, she may resist standing up for her rights because the small, approval-seeking child-self can't bear it that someone (anyone) doesn't like her.

The young girl-child learns that she will be perceived as unfeminine if she steps out of the "please-like-me" box. To be seen this way is an enormous threat to her survival. If she is not likeable—and not feminine and therefore "unattractive"—she will never be chosen as a mate. Girls understand this at a very early age and they learn to be cute and coy as a way of getting their needs met. Duplicity and manipulation become their survival skills. Females have a tendency to dance around a confrontational situation, refusing to deal with it directly, because they are afraid they will be labeled "a bitch." When women behave as doormats, other people will walk all over them.

"I myself have never been able to find out precisely what feminism is. I only know that people call me feminist whenever I express sentiments that differentiate me from a doormat."
—Rebecca West (1918)

"Instead of being the doormat, get up and be the door."
—Lillian Allen (1994)

No-Fear People Live in Easy Houses

The "No-Fear" posture is particularly common among males. Females sometimes adopt this posture as a survival skill but usually not until adolescence. Boy children learn very early on that they will be perceived as weak and therefore unmasculine if they step out of the "No-Fear" box. For a male to be exposed as weak is a threat to his survival. He could be physically harmed by other males and he may not be successful with females. Boys understand this at a very early age and learn to pretend to know all the answers and hide their perceived inadequacies. Instead of allowing themselves to feel fear, males just get angry. They will spend their lives proving their manhood and pretending they have no fear, even in life-threatening situations.

Bullies Live in Easy Houses

Powerless people tend to have short anger fuses. Their buttons are easy to push and they can blow up with very little provocation. Because it's a powerful feeling to create an explosion, other people will be tempted to goad them into "losing it." That's why a smaller person who is likely to lose in a confrontation with a bigger kid may persistently provoke the big kid. Even knowing the outcome, they are willing to risk being hurt in order to feel the power of pushing those buttons and to get the satisfaction out of having caused the loss of control. They may also be banking on the further satisfaction of seeing the bigger person get into trouble. Also, boys and girls who are bullies themselves will often be targeted by bigger, tougher bullies. The tough attitude is seen as a challenge. This is a very common way for fights to start among both male and female adolescents.

We call this type of angry and reactive behaviour "easy house" behaviour because the people who act this way often get into trouble with teachers, employers and the law. Then, because they are feeling powerless and like victims, they are likely to continue victimizing others. The cycle of violence continues.

As we can see, there are many ways of being an easy house to break into. In the following chapters all these topics will be discussed in more detail and, most importantly, we will learn skills for becoming a hard house to break into.

Chapter 2

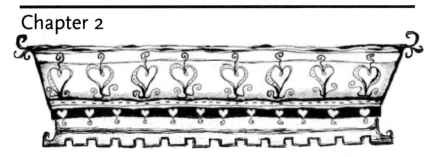

Becoming a Hard House to Break Into

I N THIS CHAPTER, we'll talk about what assertiveness is and why it works as an effective strategy in violence prevention. We'll learn how assertive behaviour is different from aggressive behaviour. We'll take an in-depth look at power dynamics in order to understand why some people hurt others.

Along with specific verbal and body language skills, we'll learn how to contact inner strength, manage fear and anger, respond effectively to intimidation and harassment and defuse potentially dangerous situations.

What Is Assertiveness?

Assertiveness is a way of standing strong and choosing a powerful way not to engage in violence. In other words, assertiveness gives us a way to walk away from violence with our dignity intact and without increasing the likelihood of future victimization. The strength, clarity and non-reactive quality of assertive behaviour makes it a highly effective method of de-escalating potentially violent situations.

Assertiveness is a learned behaviour that reflects authentic power, utilizes effective communication skills and inspires us to be centred and non-reactive.

To be assertive is to defend one's rights in a centred and direct manner, with a clear verbal message supported by strong body language. Ideally, both the voice and the body should be neutral. To show any fear or anger, however justified, can trigger a reactive response in the person you are dealing with and escalate the situation. The more grounded in an authentic inner strength and an unequivocal belief that one has the right to defends one's personal space or beliefs, the more effective the result. Assertiveness is shown in a calm and clear "no" or a hand raised in a gesture that says, "Stop." Or a direct gaze with a message that says, "That's enough" or a verbal message that calmly states, "I don't like what is happening here." Even in a situation where you feel the violation has been extreme, a clear verbal statement such as, "I am feeling very angry," can be enough. Letting the words out in this neutral and non-emotional way is effective because you are less likely to "dive in to" the emotion and "lose it" at a time when it may not be safe or productive to do so. By staying connected to the body, keeping the breath moving and staying neutral, you will remain calm and can have a calming effect on the emotions of others as well. Most importantly, the neutral stance does not give the other person anything to hook into as a way of justifying any abusive behaviour on their part. You are communicating a message of authentic power and this can have a profound effect.

In learning to be assertive we are transforming ourselves. A new emotional posture emerges, one that says, "I have a right to be here." When we practise assertive behaviours, we stand taller and walk with more confidence. Our more powerful physical presence says, "I am not afraid." When we are connected to our inner strength and have the tools to communicate that strength clearly, we can move through our lives with more safety and freedom.

The "Cave or Kill" Dynamic

It is common to think that we only have two choices when we feel threatened: one choice is to be passive and not stand up at all, and the other is to be aggressive and fight. If we are limited to this "Cave or Kill" dynamic, we may feel that in order to survive we have to choose either violence or victimization.

Assertiveness skills introduce us to a new choice: a calm place in between anger and fear; a way of standing strong without resorting to violence and with less fear of being violated. Assertiveness skills are a powerful alternative to violence and victimization.

Acting Angry Can Be Dangerous

If we are easily triggered into anger, other people will sense our lack of control and will commonly behave in one of two ways. Fearful people will feel anxious and "walk on eggshells" around us, which can trigger us into being abusive. Others will seek out and "push our buttons," potentially provoking us into rages to which they will then react with their own anger. In both instances, the situation is likely to escalate into violence.

Feeling angry is okay. Acting angry can be dangerous. An angry feeling is a natural and healthy response to being violated. It is important to let the anger inform us, to trust the message and to affirm it. "If I am feeling angry, I am being violated." It is important to acknowledge the anger but not let the anger control us. Angry behaviours are often rooted in feelings of powerlessness. If we don't feel we have any control in a situation where we are being violated, we may fly into a rage, putting ourselves and others at risk while trying to establish control. With assertiveness skills we can do more than just manage our anger. Assertiveness gives us a way of validating our anger and using the energy our anger provides us with to stand up for ourselves and what we believe in, without hurting ourselves or others.

Acting Afraid Can Be Dangerous

When we are too fearful to stand up for ourselves or what we believe in, our self-esteem is at risk. When we suffer violations and humiliations without defending ourselves in any way, we are communicating to ourselves and the world that we are "victims." Other people may sense our fearfulness, and abusive people may be drawn to us as easy targets for their frustrations.

When we are very fearful, we may need to connect with our anger as a way of balancing our fear and grounding ourselves in our right to defend ourselves.

Feeling afraid is okay. Acting afraid can be dangerous. Feeling fear may be an appropriate response to a threatening situation. It is important to acknowledge that the fear is there, but not allow the fear to control us. Assertiveness skills give us a way of managing our fear so we can walk away more safely and with our dignity intact.

Exposing the Bully: Tough on the Outside, Tiny on the Inside

The reason assertiveness is an effective strategy in potentially dangerous situations is because people who hurt other people want power. They want it because they feel powerless, because they have had their own power taken from them at some time in their lives. Powerless people may seem powerful on the outside. They may be successful, rich, good athletes, attractive. From the outside, it looks like they have everything going for them. Why would someone who has so much need to put other people down? Because all the outer-world power in the universe doesn't make up for the lack of self-worth at the core of our being. It is common for people who feel this inner emptiness to try to compensate for it by building up their image. They are trying to convince others—and themselves—that they are powerful.

Authentic Power Versus False Power

Authentic power comes from inside—from a genuine sense of worthiness—and it is a genuine part of who we are. We may have a strong self-concept from having our value as a person affirmed by a healthy childhood environment or we may have earned it from surviving hardship and experiencing our own trials and successes. Regardless, real power is not stolen from someone else.

False power is stolen—it comes from other people and it's usually about hurting or humiliating others. False power gives us a temporary sense of being in control. It is a momentary "rush" or "hit" that soon fades and leaves us feeling hungry for more.

Most of us can remember a time when we felt powerless and tried to get power from someone else. Children often feel powerless in an adult world. It is common for siblings to vie for power and they can become very adept at honing in on each other's vulnerabilities. Most of us can remember the feeling of "winning" one of these power battles with a sibling or playmate. A time when perhaps we made someone cry or get angry and we experienced that "Ha, gotcha!" feeling.

A power hit can give us a sense of euphoria but when it fades we feel empty again and need another "fix." As with drugs, in order to feel the rush again, we need to do it again.

When we can recognize that someone is coming from this false power place, we can choose to respond not to the big "look how tough I am" performance (like a blowfish, all puffed up) but to the tiny, insecure, power-hungry person on the inside. If we respond neutrally and firmly, the person doesn't get their power hit and they will be exposed. Not exposed in a naked-in-public kind of way—more as though someone has quietly placed a mirror in front of them and they can see themselves. When their bluff is called in this way, it is likely that they will feel extremely uncomfortable and unable to continue with the charade. As well, because they don't feel challenged, it is unlikely that they will feel compelled to continue the harassing behaviour. Imagine how it would be if the sibling you were trying to torment just looked at you and said, "Oh, this again—you know, I can see what you're doing and I don't want to play this game anymore." When you notice yourself behaving in bullying and power-hungry ways, you are exposing your "tiny person." People who feel good about themselves don't hurt other people.

Remember: Tough Person on the outside = Tiny Person on the inside. When a person, female or male, is behaving in an abusive, intimidating and controlling manner, regardless of how big and tough they may seem on the outside, they are exposing their "tiny person" to you.

The Neighbour's Son
BY MILDRED TREMBLAY

Sly tormentor, two paths of constant snot
running down like larvae.
I tangled with him once
only. He snatched my licorice whip.
I kicked; he laughed,
caught my foot
held it
for as long as it took.

When I think of him now, I think
of the way I danced for him:

a one-legged doll.

Bully Magnets and Power-hungry People

Have you ever known a boy who was bullied at one school, moved to a different school and was targeted as a victim again at the new school? The boy may begin to believe that there is something inherently wrong with him or that he is asking for it in some way. In desperation, parents may begin to wonder what the child is doing to bring it on himself. What about the young woman who gets out of an abusive relationship only to find herself in another one shortly after? She may begin to believe she is somehow creating the abuse. Other people may accuse her of provoking the abuse and even liking it.

The people in these two examples are innocent. They are not asking for the abuse. However, it is possible that there are things they are doing without being aware of it. They may be exhibiting specific behaviours that could communicate to potential abusers that they are easy targets. There are also things they can learn to do that could deter abusive people.

How Does an Abuser Decide Who to Abuse?

How does an abuser know who will fight back and who will be easily intimidated? The inner powerlessness of bullies requires that they pick on people that they perceive as easy targets. Abusive people often feel an emptiness inside that can be likened to a kind of hunger. Abusive people are predators: they are "power-hungry" and they are hunting for people they can feed on. These people often develop very accurate radar systems that can scan a crowd and hone in on the people who are giving out "easy target" signals.

For the most part, the signals are sent out through body language. Sometimes the signals are obvious. For instance, a very sensitive boy who doesn't like the rough play of the other boys and cries easily is a common target. Sometimes the signals are more subtle. A young woman who has low self-esteem because she is being abused at home would be like a magnet to an abusive boyfriend. The signals she gives out may be things like laughing too readily at every joke he makes and not making eye contact when she's talking to him. The abusers will be subconsciously drawn to these people, almost as though they are "bully magnets."

As well, anyone who looks or acts "different" could be at risk for being bullied. For example, physically challenged people, racial minorities, gay people and overweight people are common targets of harassment and bullying. Unfortunately this is a phenomenon that builds on itself. People who have been targeted in the past tend to develop insecurities and low self-esteem and therefore will suffer even more abuse—and so on, in a seemingly hopeless cycle. All these factors and many more contribute to what we call, in the SafeTeen program, a person who is an "easy house to break into."

Easy House Behaviours

In the following account, Dr. Aaron White, who has presented the SafeTeen Boys' Program for many years, gives examples of easy house behaviours from a SafeTeen workshop:

Fourteen-year-old Dustin was hard to miss. It wasn't his size that you noticed, for he was physically on the small side. It was his voice. For despite his small size—or maybe because of it—Dustin's loud, boisterous voice was the first thing I heard as I walked into the SafeTeen workshop room. He was a puffed up, macho little guy, and it was almost comical the way he strutted around the room. He was a flurry of hyperactivity, even when sitting down. During the first part of the workshop I observed Dustin verbally taunting other boys in the room, threatening to beat up one boy, and throwing paper wads when he thought I wasn't looking. By the time I met him, he had already been in over a dozen fights with other boys. Dustin seemed unable to avoid a fight; he felt compelled to fight any boy who challenged him. It was obvious that one day, perhaps very soon, Dustin would accept the challenge of an older, stronger, even meaner boy, and that he would then be at risk of being seriously injured or even killed. Because of his belief that he had to fight to be a man, Dustin was an easy house to break into. Another boy could get him to fight just by pushing a few predictable buttons.

Shawn was easy to overlook. A shy, fifteen-year-old Inuit boy who sat scrunched in a silent shell in the back of the room, Shawn was an inviting target for boys like Dustin. He was an easy house to break into. Head ducked, no eye contact. Turtling. I felt that I wanted to pick him for a role-play instantly. Let him experience his inner strength. Let the other boys see him acting strong. I decided to give him time, see if he would volunteer. I knew why he wouldn't want to volunteer for a role-play; the last thing he wanted was any more attention drawn to him. And I knew there was also the risk that he might be publicly humiliated as soon as he stood up. Finally I couldn't stand it any longer and I asked him to do a role-play. When he shook his head, "No," I asked him to respond again, but this time by saying "No" in a loud, clear voice. He did, and I repeated my request that he do a role-play. He looked at me with a bit of steel in his eye and said "No" in a firm voice. I felt a small rush of pleasure and pride. Celebrate small victories.

"My research investigating the causes of peer sexual harassment among adolescents indicates that males who gender harass their male peers are much more likely to commit more serious types of harassment—and even assault—against female students."
—Dr. Aaron White

How Can the Abuse Cycle Be Broken?

Our race, physical size and ability, age and appearance are things that we cannot or do not wish to change. However, we *can* change how vulnerable we are. Many "easy house" behaviours are learned behaviours and they can be unlearned. We can learn how to connect with inner strength and be in control of the signals we are communicating to others. We can learn to read people and situations more accurately and to trust our instincts. We can learn to stand up for ourselves and what we believe in safely and respectfully.

*By unlearning "easy house" behaviours and building self-esteem,
we become a "hard house to break into."*

Through assertiveness skills and self-esteem building exercises, even people who have been chronically bullied or abused or battered can learn how to stand strong. We can learn how to give off strong signals even when we're not feeling strong, and we can build on the strength we do have until what we are *doing* and who we *are* inside integrate into a stronger, more assertive person.

> *As much as abusive people are drawn toward insecure behaviour, the bully will typically steer clear of people who are giving out signals that communicate strength. When a person has a strong presence and communicates directly and clearly, it is as though they are saying "The lights are on, the alarms are set, there's somebody home."*

Bullying is Emotional Terrorism, Not a Spectator Sport

Educating our children about the effects of bullying is important. Educating parents about destructive behaviours among siblings that have up until now been considered "normal" sibling rivalry is also important. Putting systems into place within schools—and families —that counter bullying and provide adult intervention is also necessary. However, empowering our children to stand up for themselves is crucial for their survival on a day-to-day basis. It's the kids who don't make it through today because they didn't know what to say that we are losing.

According to Shelley Hymel, associate dean of education at the University of British Columbia, who has researched children's social relations for twenty years, about 10 percent of B.C. kids report going to school every day in serious danger of being a target. Hymel notes that anti-bullying programs can reduce episodes by about 50 percent. A large number of kids do not seem to get the idea that what amounts to emotional terrorism is not acceptable behaviour. In a survey of one B.C. school district, it was found that 15 percent of grade 6 to 12 students admitted to regular use of bully tactics and that the middle school years (grades 7, 8 and 9) are the worst. In the early grades, the teens are honing their skills, becoming adept at negotiating the schoolyard system of cliques and hierarchies in preparation for the big leagues (high school).

"With girls, it's all about friendship politics."—a ten-year-old girl.

"Sometimes you just go nuts because you want to be in the 'in-crowd'…" —an eleven-year-old boy.

The most powerful of human urges, the need to belong, reaches a peak during adolescence. Like contestants on the TV show "Survivor," kids learn quickly that a series of false moves can lead to their exclusion from the group—heir worst nightmare. And aggressive behaviours can earn them much needed points. Hymel says she has seen bullies turn into victims in record time. The research of other experts has shown that there are three very natural group processes that characterize human groups at any age:

Stage I: group differentiation: maximizing the difference between your group and other groups.

Stage II: group assimilation: individuals within a group tend to develop common attitudes and behaviours, increasing similarities within the group.

Stage III: within group hierarchies: individuals within groups tend to develop status hierarchies—for instance, putting someone else down to make sure you stay on top.

The other factor that plays a monumental role in bullying behaviour is the "audience." Bullying behaviours become almost a sport and the spectators find it exciting, contagious and—unfortunately—educational. This is one place where they learn to be bullies.

(Stats and quotes reprinted from the article "Stop the Bullying,"
Vancouver *Province*, 15 January, 2001.)

What if Being Assertive Makes the Situation Worse?

In every classroom from Bainbridge Island, Washington to Kugluktuk, Northwest Territories, teens who have watched a demonstration of the "Hard House to Break Into" have said, "Yeah, that looks good—but what if the person gets really mad and then kills me?"—or some version of that.

The fear that being assertive will make the other person more angry is very common. In fact, the fear that speaking up will make the situation worse is what prevents us from being assertive in many instances. Most people will identify feeling simultaneously exhilarated *and* terrified at the thought of standing up for themselves in a potentially dangerous situation. This is because while it's empowering to imagine ourselves strong and unafraid, many of us have experienced trying to stand up for ourselves with devastating results. Perhaps it was as a child trying to stand up to an angry and abusive parent. Or it could have been as a teenage boy trying to stand up to a school bully or as a young woman trying to stand up to an abusive boyfriend.

It may be that the end result was far from what we had hoped for. It may be that our worst fears were realized and the person we attempted to stand up to did get even more angry, the situation escalated and we got hurt. If this has been our experience, in effect we've been punished for trying to stand up for ourselves. It's no wonder that so many of us quickly learn to placate, avoid, ignore, repress—do anything but confront. The fear of making the situation worse can be very strong and can stand in the way of learning and practising assertiveness skills. The key to overcoming this fear is to understand that the majority of us, when we do finally stand up for ourselves, do so in an aggressive manner. Aggressiveness is fundamentally different from assertiveness and usually produces a defensive and aggressive reaction. Once we are able to identify the difference between the two, we can begin to practise our "hard house" skills with less fear.

How Is Assertiveness Different from Aggressiveness?

The primary difference between assertive behaviour and aggressive behaviour is where the behaviour stems from within us. Aggressiveness is reactive and defensive in nature. It is often rooted in anger and powerlessness. The energy behind aggressiveness is volatile and agitated. Aggressiveness is about winning and dominating. Aggressive behaviours usually include elements such as loud voice, blaming, name-calling and swearing, and body language such as tight jaw, angry face, tensed body, wide stance, hands on hips or folded across chest, chin forward and fists clenched.

Assertiveness, on the other hand, is rooted in authentic power and healthy self-concept. It is pro-active and non-defensive. The energy behind assertiveness is calm and neutral. Assertiveness is about communication and self-empowerment. Assertive behaviours include calm voice, clear and direct messages, non-blaming and non-reactive tone, consistent eye contact, and strong and well-balanced but relaxed body language.

Assertiveness is not magic. Sometimes a person is already so angry, or so intoxicated, or so mentally unstable that nothing anyone can do will de-escalate him/her. Although in most cases assertiveness skills are a good tool for making the situation a safer one, it may become clear that violence is unavoidable. If we feel we are seriously at risk, the wisest choice may be to run or, if necessary, to fight.

Choosing to release our anger in order to physically defend ourselves is very different from being out of control with our anger.

Remember: Choosing to run away—or walk away—could be a safe and wise choice. This is not "wimping out."

Assertiveness is not a weapon. Assertive verbal and body language skills are very powerful tools and they are not for controlling or hurting or humiliating other people. They are not for winning. The purpose of assertiveness skills is self-empowerment and personal safety. For example, if a teenage girl walks past a group of young men and they call out rude sexual remarks and she makes strong assertive eye contact with them, it is possible that the men will stop making remarks and become uncomfortable. This is clearly a successful result. However, if the guys just get louder, does this mean the skills didn't work? No—this is also a successful result (although somewhat less satisfying) because the point wasn't to make them stop harassing her. The point wasn't to "win." In making eye contact in an assertive manner, the young woman was able to communicate to herself and to the harassers that she is a strong person. In so doing, she has affirmed her own self-esteem and clearly communicated that she is not an easy target. She may have prevented the situation from escalating and even prevented further harassment from those particular guys. Regardless of the reaction to her assertive behaviour, she is stronger and safer for it.

Let's look at a real-life situation where assertiveness skills could be used.

Jay and Katrina: The Beach Party

Jay and Katrina have been going out together for about two months. It's a Saturday night and they are hanging out at the beach with a group of their schoolmates. It's the first beach party of the summer and everyone is celebrating the school year finally being over. Katrina is having a good time until partway through the evening, when a boy she doesn't know sits down beside her.

Katrina has seen this guy around and he gives her a creepy feeling. He's older than most of the group she and Jay hang with. The boy sits too close. Katrina looks around for Jay but it's getting dark and she can't see him anywhere. The older boy makes some comments about her looks.

He's making her feel really uncomfortable but she doesn't want to make a scene. She says, "Umm, thanks," and looks down and away. He leans in toward her and says, "Where's your smile?" She smiles even though she's annoyed. Katrina looks around for Jay once more. She turns away a little and tries to ignore the boy but he leans in closer and starts whispering sexual things in her ear. She shrinks away from him and laughs nervously. Still no Jay. She tells him in a jokey way that she already has a boyfriend. "I'm not surprised—a good-looking babe like you—but he's not here right now so I don't see the problem with a friendly little kiss..." He puts his hand behind her head, pulls her toward him and tries to kiss her.

Suddenly Jay appears. He grabs Katrina by the arm and pulls her to her feet. Katrina jerks her arm away from him and stumbles back in the sand. Jay is yelling at her and calling her names. She starts crying and yells back that she didn't do anything and tells him "that creep" was hitting on her.

Then Jay turns his anger on the other boy. He shoves him and swears at him. The older boy picks up a heavy piece of wood and, holding it like a baseball bat, he starts daring Jay to "bring it on." He calls Jay a "wuss." Katrina screams at Jay to forget it and pleads with him to walk away and leave with her. Jay is afraid but the crowd of kids circles around them yelling, "Fight! Fight! Fight!" and Jay feels he can't back down.

Understanding the Beach Party Scenario
Let's take a look at what was going on for Jay.

At the moment when Jay saw another boy leaning intimately toward his girlfriend, what do you think he was feeling?

The emotion on the surface—and the one that Jay was showing—was anger. Underneath anger there is almost always another, more vulnerable feeling. In this case it was probably jealousy. When we feel jealousy it usually means we are afraid. In that moment Jay would have been experiencing fear of losing his girlfriend. He may also have been feeling fear of humiliation—fear that his peers would laugh at him and think he wasn't man enough to defend what they saw as his "territory."

Why would Jay show only anger when he was feeling fear too?

As a boy growing up, Jay was probably not allowed to express his vulnerable feelings. In a traditional male upbringing, he would have been taught to cover up any feelings of fear or sadness or even confusion. The only feeling he would have been permitted to have is anger. But what was Jay supposed to do with all his feelings? Just walk away?

Anger is a legitimate feeling. It's how you express angry feelings that can be destructive and dangerous. First of all, Jay directed his anger toward Katrina and put his relationship with her at risk by touching her in anger. Then he turned his anger toward the older boy, who reacted with his own anger. Once this cycle has started it is very difficult to stop. The crowd cheering them on didn't help things either.

Feeling angry is okay. Acting angry can lead to violence.

Can you see how Jay felt his only choice was to "cave" or "kill"?

In order to preserve his dignity and prove his manhood, Jay felt he *had* to fight.

Now let's take a look at what was going on for Katrina:

Why did Katrina smile when she was feeling annoyed?

Katrina didn't want to make a scene. Partly because she didn't want to draw attention to herself and partly because she has been strongly conditioned not to "rock the boat." She feels she has to be polite and concerned with others' feelings even when her own personal space is being threatened. What Katrina didn't see is that when a guy invades her space in this way, the boat is already rocking! *He* is rocking the boat! Any assertive behaviour on her part would merely be an attempt to steady her boat.

When Katrina shrank away and laughed nervously, what do you think she was feeling?

On the surface, Katrina was showing nervousness and discomfort. These are fear-based emotions. Her smiling and nervous laughter at the guy's rude remarks didn't communicate a boundary. In fact she communicated the opposite of what she felt and wanted. Katrina didn't think his remarks were funny and she didn't want him leaning over her and whispering in her ear. She didn't like how close he was sitting and in fact she didn't want to talk to him at all. What she was feeling beneath her discomfort was powerlessness and anger. She may also have felt embarrassed and offended by his sexual remarks.

Why did Katrina keep looking around for Jay?

Katrina didn't believe she was capable of rescuing herself; she felt her only "out" was to have Jay show up and "claim" her. Katrina believed that telling the guy she already had a boyfriend would stop him because he would see that she was in effect another man's property.

She didn't know how to stop him herself. Also Katrina knows Jay is the jealous type; she may have been looking around because she was worried that Jay would see the guy coming on to her and think she was flirting with him.

Can you see how Katrina's "easy target" behaviour indirectly contributed to the fight?

Although it was not Katrina's fault that the guy came on to her—and she didn't ask for the sexual harassment in any way—her inability to handle the situation herself and her fear of rocking the boat contributed to Jay playing out his role as rescuer. When she told Jay the guy was hitting on her, she set herself up as the helpless victim. This set Jay up to play his part as protector and defender of his "territory."

For an exercise on "rocking the boat," see page 268.

In Chapter 3 we will be introduced to the SafeTeen assertiveness model. It will become evident that we can choose to respond to most dangerous and intimidating situations with either fear, anger or wisdom. We will then apply the new skills to Jay and Katrina and take a look at how they could have handled themselves more safely and assertively at the beach party.

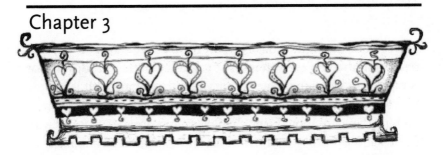

Chapter 3

Getting to Know the Child, the Warrior and the Wise Person

W HEN WE ARE faced with emotional or physical danger, we have three basic choices. We can respond with fear, with anger or with wisdom. Wisdom isn't something we learn in school or achieve by trying hard. It is simply what happens when we become aware of our anger and our fear and find a way to work with them. When we can validate our anger and focus the energy it brings and when we can acknowledge our fear and learn how to manage it, we are left with wisdom.

I have attributed a persona to each of these options: Fear = the Child; Anger = the Warrior; Wisdom = the Wise Person.

In the SafeTeen Girls' Program we call them the Child, the Bitch and the Wise Woman. In the SafeTeen Boys' Program we call them the Child, the Tough Guy and the Solid Guy.

The Child

Who is the Child? Regardless of how strong and mature we may feel in our everyday lives, each one of us has a part of us that is insecure.

The Child is the "little" you. The part of you that is at times shy and uncomfortable and even afraid. The Child is also the part of you that is capable of being spontaneous, playful, silly and joyful. It is important for us to honour and celebrate this part of ourselves. There is nothing shameful about being childlike in appropriate situations with friends and family we trust. However, when we are in emotionally or physically dangerous situations it is possible that our "small self" will come forward to try to deal with the conflict.

In general, females are more likely than males to resort to childlike behaviours when in threatening situations. This is partially due to the fact that female children are traditionally so strongly disciplined for expressing anger. Most girls and even adult women can relate to having a lump in the throat or the urge to cry when they feel angry, resulting in an inability to speak.

Girls are also not encouraged to be direct, to ask for what they want or to say "No." They are more likely than boys to be seen as rude and selfish when they are taking care of their own needs. Conversely, they are given an abundance of permission to be fearful, tearful and indirect. Girls soon learn that they are more likely to get their needs met by being manipulative, coy and duplicitous. Females are more likely than males to develop a very strong need for external approval. They tend to care a great deal about being liked while males care more about being respected. As well, females are commonly reactive—they wait their turn, look for cues, respond as opposed to initiating, put their hands up as opposed to calling out. They are less likely to take control of anything—from a basic conversation to a life-threatening situation. These childlike behaviours and postures often remain the same for females throughout their lives. It's as though males get to grow up and become the "drivers" in life and females are forever the small children just along for the ride.

Regardless of the pervasive societal conditioning that boys receive to be aggressive, unfeeling, fearless and in control, many boys are innately more passive than aggressive. Sensitive, gentle-natured boys tend to show their vulnerable emotions and are often subject to intense and persistent cruelty and humiliation because they are seen as less than male—in other words, they are seen as female. They are called "wuss," "fag," "sissy," "wimp," "pussy" and "girl." They are often picked on, bullied and beaten up. These "child-identified" boys desperately need assertiveness skills in order to survive emotionally and perhaps even physically. These are the boys who get run over by the bigger, tougher boys who are in the driver's seat.

The Child's Body Language

Fidgeting; blushing; restlessness; toes turned inward; stuttering; inability to project the voice; appeasing and questioning voice tone; over-politeness; intermittent or lack of eye contact; chin down; head averted; hands clasped in front, rigidly by the sides or behind the back; hand wringing; obsessive playing with hair; nail biting.

Imagine walking by a bus stop late at night and seeing a small child sitting there by her/himself. Would this seem like a safe place for a child to be? Do you think this child would be able to cope with a scary or abusive situation? Would you want to take charge, rescue the child and get her/him to a safe place?

Remember: When we are in difficult or threatening situations, it can be very useful to imagine putting our small self in a safe place so that a more capable and protected part of us can cope. Honour and celebrate your child but keep her/him safe.

For "Getting to Know Your Child" and "Creating a Safe Place" exercises, see page 246.

The Female Warrior: "The Bitch"

Who is the Bitch? She is the Inner Warrior. How many girls and women have never been called "a bitch"? When we ask females in grades 4 through 12 this question, 99 percent of the time no hands go up. Most females discover at a very early age that whenever they express anger they are likely to be called "bitch." Even expressing frustration, disagreement or a strong opinion can result in being labelled "bitch". In other words, whenever a female's behaviour is not passive, nice and polite, she may be called "bitch". The word "bitch" is probably used more often than any other word to insult females of all ages. It is generally considered a very negative and disrespectful word. In SafeTeen, we have reclaimed the word "bitch" to give it a positive meaning.

We recognize the Bitch as the part of us that stands up and speaks up. She is also the part of us who will fight to defend us. This is the part of us that uses her anger to cope. Research tells us that in the case of violent attacks, women who get in touch with their anger before they get in touch with their fear get away more often. This tells us that it is safer to respond to an aggressive attack with the Bitch than trying to handle it with your Child. However, responding with Bitch initially, before the incident has become physically violent, is likely to lead to an escalation of the situation and to increase the possibility of violence. Clearly this is not the wisest choice—especially if the person you are confronting is physically larger or has power over you in some other way.

Remember: The Bitch in us is very, very brave but not very wise!

When we realize who the Bitch in us is, we can honour her for her power and courage and fierceness. We can even celebrate this part of us for the life-sustaining role she plays. She is our power, our anger, our last defence. We will not know we have a right to defend ourselves without her. Bitch is our "HOW DARE YOU!" voice. Her job is to defend the Child. In fact, it would be wise to take her with us—our own personal Xena, Warrior Woman, wherever we go. The key is not to have the Bitch take control. Because she doesn't stop and think before she acts, she may not discriminate between a situation that requires physical resistance in order to survive and one in which violence could be avoided. She has no fear. She will fight anyone, anytime. Bitch is the part of us that has the Immortality Syndrome. She does not understand that she can die. Because of this she may take unnecessary risks and even create opportunities to prove her bravery and fearlessness, such as participating in high-risk behaviours like wild parties, unsafe sex and drugs and alcohol. Once we realize this we can be clear that we want to keep her available for emergencies, but not in the forefront. It is best to have her standing guard in the background. It is as though we can imagine saying, "I honour your courage, I might need you later, but for now, back, Bitch, back."

bitch. 2. Sl., derog, a malicious, spiteful or coarse woman
(Collins Concise Dictionary)

One woman reclaims the word "bitch":

When I stand up for myself and my beliefs, they call me a bitch.

When I stand up for those I love, they call me a bitch.

When I speak my mind, think my own thoughts, or do things my own way, they call me a bitch.

Being a bitch means I won't compromise what's in my heart.

It means I live my life MY way. It means I won't allow anyone to step on me.

When I refuse to tolerate injustice and speak up against it, I am defined as a bitch.

The same thing happens when I take time for myself instead of being everyone's maid, or when I act a little selfish.

I am proud to be a bitch!

It means I have the courage and strength to allow myself to be who I truly am and won't become anyone else's idea of what they think I "should" be.

I am outspoken, opinionated, and determined.

I want what I want, and there is nothing wrong with that!

So try to stomp on me, try to douse my inner flame, try to squash every ounce of beauty I hold within me.

You won't succeed. And if that makes me a bitch, so be it. I embrace the title and am proud to bear it.

B - Babe

I - In

T - Total

C - Control of

H - Herself

The Female Warrior's Body Language

Bitch typically stands with her hands folded across her chest or perhaps with her hands on her hips or thumbs hooked into pockets. Her chin is out, shoulders back and her legs are widely planted, feet turned out. Bitch glares but doesn't maintain consistent eye contact. She will jab her finger in someone's face or "flip someone the bird" with little or no provocation. Bitch is usually frowning, jaw clenched, and lips drawn tightly. Sometimes when she is in a challenging mood she has a "smart-ass" smile on her face, one eyebrow cocked as if to say, "Oh yeah, you think you're scaring me? Come on, let's go." She's tough. She's cool. She's looking for trouble.

Girls and Violence: When Bitch Takes Over

When boys are violent, well, "Boys will be boys." When girls are violent it seems there is often a reaction of surprise. It is as though we are saying, How could this be? Girls are supposed to be nurturing and life-sustaining. Beyond the initial surprise, people respond to violence from girls with shock and despair.

It is worth noting how much media attention each isolated incident of female violence engenders. For example, males violently assault

their female partners so frequently that this is the leading cause of injury for women in Canada and the United States. Males kill their spouses and children all the time. Every week two women in Canada and seventy women in the United States die at the hands of their current husbands or boyfriends. But when a woman assaults her husband or kills her child it is the lead story on radio and television news, on the front pages of the newspapers and the covers of national magazines. It is as though every incident of female violence is a vindication of the male species: "See? It's not just males. Females are violent too!"

In a world where the vast majority of violence is committed by males (with females their frequent targets), why are we so shocked and dismayed at the upsurge of female violence? Is it really so surprising that females are angry? Is it so surprising that girls are resorting more often to violence as a way of resolving disputes? Our young women are sick of feeling powerless and they are tired of being the victims. They are looking around and seeing the power displays of male attitude and body language. They know how intimidating it can be to be on the other end of that. Not seeing any other role models, they are choosing to "act like men." In effect, they are choosing violence over victimization.

"Girls are definitely cracking more heads than they used to. Some girls think we have to. We live in a male-dominated society. Theories about girl violence abound. Some claim that girls are just looking for the attention that their traditional roles don't afford them. I think it is the climax of the consumer age. We need money to buy stuff. Have no money? Well, there's always a place to steal it from, whether it's an old lady or a 7-Eleven.

We've even bought into the image supplied to us by advertising, film and television. Tough girls are cool. Tough girls are sexy. Tough girls are ready to scrap and kick some shit.

We're not supposed to let people walk over us. But no one told us HOW not to. We never learned that to be assertive doesn't mean to be violent. We went the easy way, the way that gets attention, reaction, and works.

> *Let us be strong. We don't want to let people walk all over us or treat us badly. We need to be taught a new way of being assertive. I don't want to be violent. I just want to be able to stand up for myself in an effective way. A way people will respond to. Give me a voice so I don't need to use my fists.*
>
> *Strength is new for girls, power is new for girls. Girls learned they could use violence to gain power. Power can be nice feeling. Feeling strong is nice feeling. Just give me a better way to feel it."*
>
> —ALEXIA CORSILLO, 18, FROM ONE L.O.V.E.
> A LEAVE OUT VIOLENCE PUBLICATION, VOL. 2 #1.

"Give me a voice so I don't have to use my fists." This statement speaks so perfectly to the reason female violence is on the rise—and why assertiveness skills are needed.

The inner Bitch is being awakened in young women all over the world. This phenomenon could be likened to an evolutionary survival mechanism that is possibly as natural and arguably as necessary to the survival of the female as a species as the lengthening of tooth and claw in the animal world.

The Bitch is a powerful force within us—the key is to learn how to work with this powerful force.

Let's see what happens when Bitch takes over. Think back to Natasha at the bus stop in Chapter 1. She was cornered by a guy who was hassling her.

Jaz and Natasha: Cat Fight

Natasha knew she was lucky. She knew if the bus hadn't come when it did, she would have been toast. She kept getting flashes of the guy at the bus stop that night. The smell of him as he leaned over her, his face inches from hers, breathing stale cigarette breath onto her—and the evil sound of his voice as he said, "You little bitch—you think you're so tough?"

If only I'd gotten on the bus! she thought. When the bus had pulled up, the guy had backed off and she had run. Without even thinking she'd run back to Kyle's house.

Natasha's heart was pounding when she got to Kyle's. There were still lots of people there—it seemed she was always the only one who had to leave early. Natasha felt a flash of anger at her parents for being so strict—and then she felt even more angry when she remembered what a jerk Kyle had been. It was his fault she was late and if he'd walked her to the bus none of this would have happened. Once he heard about the guy at the bus stop he would feel so guilty. She went into the kitchen looking for him. Maybe she could tell her parents she was almost attacked and they wouldn't ground her... No, she knew that would only make things worse—they wouldn't let her out at all if she told them about it. And now she was really going to be late. Her dad would kill her. Natasha felt frustration and powerlessness surge through her. And then she saw Kyle.

Kyle was standing in the kitchen leaning against the counter, and leaning up against him was a girl. Natasha knew this girl. Her name was Jaz. She was really gorgeous and she had a "rep" for being a huge flirt. Natasha just stood there for a moment, staring at them. Jaz was standing on her toes, stretching up and whispering something in Kyle's ear. Her whole body was pressed up against him. Kyle threw his head back and laughed.

Natasha felt something inside of her snap. She strode across the room screaming "You SLUT!" She grabbed Jaz by the hair and with all her strength yanked her down to the kitchen floor. What followed after that was a blur in Natasha's mind. She remembers Jaz swearing and digging her nails into her arm until she let go of her hair. It wasn't until Jaz stood up and turned to face her that Natasha realized how drunk Jaz was. Jaz's eye make-up was smeared and her eyes were unfocused.

Suddenly everyone was standing around them chanting and yelling, "Cat Fight! Cat Fight!" That's when Jaz laughed in a crazy way and reached over to the counter and picked up a small sharp knife. Waving it back and forth in front of her she said, "You want to go? Come on you wussy little bitch, you want to fight?"

Understanding the Cat Fight Scenario
Let's take a look at what was going on for Natasha.

Who do you think Natasha was angry with?

By the time Natasha got back to the party, she was angry at her parents for being so strict and at Kyle for not supporting her in getting home on time and then for not walking her to the bus stop. The creepy guy at the bus stop had scared her, but before she felt afraid, she had felt angry toward him.

Why didn't Natasha express her anger toward the people she was mad at?

Natasha didn't take time to think or to make a plan. She just reacted from all the powerless and angry feelings that had built up inside. Jaz seemed to be the easiest person for her to take her anger out on. She may have felt it would be impossible to speak up to her parents about their strict curfew, especially that night when she was already in trouble for being late. She may have felt unable to express her anger directly to Kyle because she feared losing him. She did try to let the creepy guy know she was pissed off but things just got worse and then it was way too scary.

Why did Natasha direct all her anger onto Jaz?

When Natasha saw Jaz draped all over her boyfriend, the big pile of anger that was building up inside was triggered. It was easier to target Jaz in more ways than one. When Natasha chooses to blame the other girl, she doesn't have to see that her boyfriend is choosing to be with someone else. She can see him as the victim of the other girl's attentions. With Jaz, there was less to lose, and less to be afraid of—or so Natasha thought.

Did Natasha have a right to be angry?

Natasha had lots of reasons to be angry. Her anger was legitimate. Acting on that anger in a violent way is what got her into trouble. When Natasha walked in that room with all her intense feelings boiling around inside her, she probably felt her only choice was to hang her head and run out crying or fight the other girl. Natasha didn't have the skills to deal with the situation in a powerful but non-violent way so her Bitch took over.

Honour your Bitch, validate her anger, and tell her firmly,
"Back, Bitch, back."

For exercises to get in touch with your Inner Warrior, see page 250.

The Male Warrior: "The Tough Guy"

Most males will be familiar with the concept of the fighter that lives in them. In SafeTeen, we call this persona "Tough Guy." Tough Guy's job is to defend and protect. Some males are more in touch with this part of themselves than others. Some males are overidentified with their Tough Guy persona. When this is the case, two guys can get into a physical fight over nothing. Most of us have seen two males challenge each other and then it escalates into yelling and threats and even physical violence within seconds. The conflict could be about anything: a comment, a perceived look or even accidental physical contact such as bumping into someone in the hall at school. After some violent confrontations between two guys, neither of them is even able to say how it started.

When asked, most males will openly state that there are some things worth fighting over. They claim their right to defend themselves and those they care about. A minority of males claim that they like to fight and will take any opportunity to do so. However, most males will admit that in most instances they would prefer not to fight—particularly when it's over trivial or non-existent issues.

Males are more likely than females to resort to anger and violence as a method of coping. This is partially because male children are persistently humiliated for expressing fear but are given permission to express anger. Traditional parenting practices, peer pressure and media culture have all encouraged males to use physical violence to prove themselves as "real" men and to establish their place in the "pecking order."

When two guys get into a fight for no apparent reason, their Tough Guys are in control. Tough Guys believe that their only choice is to fight or back down and lose face, so they feel they have to fight. Most males will identify with this dichotomy and say they feel they have no choice. In their experience, to refuse to fight means communicating that they are afraid.

Most adolescent males will tell us that the advice "just walk away" is useless. First of all they say that to walk away when another guy is challenging them to a fight would give them a reputation as a wimp.

Instinctively, most guys know that to be labelled as "wuss" or "fag" means they will be targeted for future harassment and violence. Secondly, they say that to turn their back on someone who is angry and threatening to beat them up is not safe. In both these instances, their instincts and past experiences are informing them and they are accurate on both counts.

The Male Warrior's Body Language

Very much like Bitch, Tough Guy stands in a fighter stance. He struts in a rooster-like fashion and displays an almost comical amount of bravado in his body language. Unlike Bitch, Tough Guy juts out his chest — and slams his chest into another guy he is confronting. Tough Guy glares and engages in staring contests. To lose eye contact can mean he has backed down. To hold it too long can mean he has made a challenge to fight. The eye contact Tough Guy makes is usually accompanied by either a frown, a smart-ass smirk or a stony hard face with a very tight mouth and jaw. Tough Guy will never admit fear. Like Bitch, he's trouble waiting to happen.

Let's see what happens when the Tough Guy takes over.

Jay and Paul: The Chair

Jay is trying to finish his assignment before the bell rings. If he can get it done, he won't have any homework for the weekend. Jay's dad is stopping by after school to pick him up and take him camping. He hasn't seen his dad since his parents split up two months ago and Jay wants to get home right after school so that he's ready on time.

Jay's classmate, Paul, is kicking the back of Jay's chair with his foot. Jay has told him to "Quit it" but Paul is being a jerk and keeps doing it. Jay knows Paul is just trying to bug him and he tries to ignore it, but he just can't concentrate. Jay tries moving his chair forward out of Paul's reach but Paul just slides his own chair forward and keeps on thumping his foot on the leg of Jay's chair. His pencil jerks across the page with every thump. Jay glares at Paul and mouths, "F__ off!" and Paul gives him the finger and laughs. Jay turns back to his work. A few seconds later Paul starts up the kicking again.

Finally Jay loses it. He throws his textbook at Paul and yells at him to "F__ off!" Without asking any questions, the teacher gives Jay a detention. Jay can't believe it. Now he'll be late getting home and his dad will be on his case for being in trouble at school again. Why does this always happen to me? he thinks. It's not fair. I didn't start it.

Jay is feeling so furious, he can't even try to explain. He feels sure the teacher won't listen and his classmates will call him a tattle-tale if he even tries. Frustrated and angry, he tips his desk over. Jabbing his finger in Paul's face he says, "Later buddy—you're dead." The teacher orders Jay out of the class and down to the office and threatens to have him suspended. Jay calls her a "bitch" as he storms out of the classroom.

Understanding the Chair Scenario
Let's take a look at what was going on for Jay.

Jay tried to deal with the situation in a few different ways before he lost it. What strategies did he employ?

In Jay's first attempt at stopping his classmate's aggravating behaviour he said, "Quit it." When that didn't work, he tried ignoring it and he also tried moving his chair out of range. None of these attempts by Jay to stop the harassment and get on with his work were successful. In fact they just seemed to make things worse.

Why didn't these strategies work?

First of all, Jay's choice of words, along with his non-assertive body language, were much like a little kid who is feeling annoyed and powerless. Attempting to move his chair was also very much like something a little kid would do. Jay's classmate was feeling more and more powerful and rather than being discouraged he was encouraged to continue his behaviour.

Jay did finally try to stand up for himself. Why didn't that work?

Jay did a very typical thing at this point. Feeling frustrated, he went from passive behaviour into aggressive behaviour. He glared and swore at his harasser. Now his classmate was really feeling the power. He not only could distract and annoy Jay, he could make him angry. He was definitely not going to stop now. He began kicking the chair once more and, predictably, Jay lost it.

Can you see how Jay felt his choices were to be either passive or aggressive? What are the results of having such limited choices?

Jay acted out his anger and even though he didn't initiate the situation, he was the one to get into trouble. Now he is even more angry and more likely to lose control in the future. Feeling powerless to deal with a minor conflict like someone kicking his chair, Jay ended up being late for his time with his dad and facing a suspension from school. He may also feel he has to follow up on his threat and may end up in a fight with the boy he threatened.

This is a familiar path for boys. Neither Jay nor his classmate was necessarily intending to end up in a fight—or in trouble at school. It is as though they start down this road and then things escalate and they don't know a way out.

Tough Guy deserves to be honoured for his role as defender and protector. But when Tough Guy takes over he hurts us and sometimes other people.

Remember: Tough Guy needs to be told firmly to take a back seat and let a more grounded, wise person make the decisions about how to behave when faced with conflict.

Wise Woman/Solid Guy

Now that we have met Child, Bitch and Tough Guy, we need to be introduced to the part of us that will step in and keep us safe once we get the Warrior to stand back. This is the part of us that is wise—the part of us that knows things we do not know we know. For females we call this wise part of us Wise Woman. For males, we call him Solid Guy.

Listening to Your Wise Person

The ability to perceive a truth about a situation as though invisible antennae were probing around and sending us silent messages is a powerful and accurate assessment tool. Females and males can practise and develop this ability to listen to the inner wise voice. In SafeTeen we call this listening to your Wise Person.

Most teenagers will identify times when they were about to go somewhere or perhaps were feeling pressured by their peers to do something and a voice in their head was saying, "Bad idea! I wouldn't do that if I were you!" Often they will just brush that voice aside and carry on with the activity. If they are able to listen with the awareness that the voice they are hearing represents their inner wisdom and then choose to alter their behaviour accordingly, they will be safer. This does not mean that teens who listen to their Wise Person will never go out to parties or be in potentially dangerous situations. When teens trust their Wise Person's voice and understand where it's coming from they may choose to continue with the activity, but they can carry an increased awareness with them, which will result in increased safety. The more space we give to the voice of the Wise Person and the more often we "tune in," the stronger that voice becomes.

For example, a teenage girl could say to herself, "I still want to go to the party and I still want to meet up with the guy I just met but that voice was there for a reason. I am not just being paranoid. I'm going to make sure I go with a group of friends and that I have a safe ride there and a safe ride back so I can leave whenever I want." A teen boy could choose to ride to a party with his friends but if he suspects there will be drinking, he could plan ahead and bring enough money for a cab home.

Teenagers desperately need the guiding force of their Wise Person to help them navigate safely through the rough terrain of adolescence.

Letting Go of Our "Survival Skills"

For both females and males, much practice is needed to get in touch with and implement our Wise Person skills. It's not that the skills are complicated or difficult to learn—they are actually very simple. The biggest barrier to practising Wise Woman/Solid Guy skills is that most of us learned to rely on the Child or Warrior persona as our survival skills.

A survival skill is a pattern of behaving that we learn as children in order to survive neglect or emotional, spiritual or physical abuse. As children some of us learned to appease, manipulate and placate to get what we needed. Some of us held onto anger to cloak the pain and vulnerability we were feeling. And some of us did a little of each.

Do not underestimate how difficult it can be to let go of a survival skill. To put these skills aside—skills that we may have felt at one time we would die without—can feel like leaving ourselves completely defenceless. Learning to let go of the old ways of negotiating our way through life and embracing a new way can be very frightening. We have to create opportunities to practise, in safe places with people we trust, over a period of time, slowly building up our confidence in the new skills. We need to experience success with the new skills in order to believe in them. Through a series of body language exercises and role-plays we can become familiar with this new and very powerful part of ourselves.

Wise Woman

Wise Woman is the name we give to female inner wisdom. The Wise Woman is the manifestation of our self-esteem. She doesn't doubt she has the right to be treated with respect and has no need to treat others with disrespect. Wise Woman knows what to say and how to say it in order to most effectively de-escalate potentially dangerous situations. Wise Woman is the part of us that will keep the Child safe and the Warrior back.

As well, Wise Woman is the part of females that is deeply intuitive. Wise Woman knows things without knowing how she knows them. Females will readily identify with this aspect of themselves. Many girls and women, when telling a personal story of a scary incident, will identify the moment when they "felt" something was wrong. Unfortunately, this feeling is often dismissed as silly or paranoid. Feeling that something is wrong is a good enough reason to take an action to make ourselves safer.

We have to teach our young women to trust their inner knowing.

The concept of Wise Woman is readily embraced by girls and women of all ages. The practice of Wise Woman, however, is an enormous challenge. For females to let go of "wanting to be liked" and to embrace being respected, to stop worrying so much about being rude, to feel less afraid of standing up for themselves, this is the challenge. Young women need to see strong, confident, women—women with whom they can identify—women of all sizes and races. Women who are cool and funny and compassionate. Women who are successful in the world and women who are mothers. They need to see all types of women model assertive behaviour. Young women need to see "powerful" and "female" as synonymous.

Becoming Wise Woman

Wise Woman is not afraid to stand strong, in opposition to other people. She is not afraid to risk disapproval or even of being disliked. Each time she is faced with confrontation, she asks herself, "Would I rather be liked or respected?" Wise Woman does not seek approval or depend on outside evaluations of herself as worthy. She is able to validate her own worthiness and see her imperfections as inevitable and accept them without judgement.

When a girl or woman realizes that her boundaries are in place, her fear has become her ally, her anger is her protector and the word "No" flows effortlessly from her lips, she becomes Wise Woman. It is as though all the moments of courage and struggle have accumulated and being a Wise Woman is no longer something she is purposefully doing but has become who she is.

Solid Guy

Solid Guy is the name we give to the part of males that can stand strong without aggression. Solid Guy is the manifestation of a strong inner core. A sense of solid belief in self. The Solid Guy has no desire to win and no need to retreat. He is the part of males that knows how to stand strong without resorting to violence. The Solid Guy is the part of him that will keep the Child safe and the Warrior under control.

The Solid Guy is the part of males that isn't afraid to admit that he is afraid. He doesn't feel ashamed of having vulnerable feelings. Solid Guy knows that he doesn't have anything to prove. We have to teach our young men that there is a new way of being a man—and that being strong has less to do with how much he can bench press and more to do with being capable of being open and real and fully human.

The concept of Solid Guy often seems wimpy to boys who are convinced that their very survival depends on extreme and often violent displays of bravado. In order to be convinced of the effectiveness of Solid Guy, young men need to be exposed to men who will talk about their feelings, their relationships, their fears—in a way that's natural and comfortable. They need to see the skills modelled by a man they respect. They need to be able to explore the issues and try out the skills in an open atmosphere, in the company of their male peers, in a way that's safe.

"Boys are caught up in the certainty that to be a man means to not be afraid. To never be concerned or worried. To never feel doubt, indecision, uncertainty. After all, the men in the movies don't ever look afraid, they never are unsure of what to do in a dangerous situation or of how to handle a beautiful woman. Given the continual messages of masculine invulnerability and cocksuredness boys are exposed to in the media, it is no wonder that they grow up to be adult men who drive their wives crazy by not being able to stop and ask for directions when they are lost. The cult of movie masculinity is so strong that many boys wear T-shirts that proudly proclaim 'No Fear.' Part of the SafeTeen message is getting boys to own up to their emotions, to admit to being afraid at times, to admit that they cry. We adults have to hold teens to their humanness; we mustn't let boys forget that they have the full range of human emotions."

—DR. AARON WHITE

Solid Guy doesn't get to his power by trying hard. He doesn't get there by using discipline and pushing himself. He gets there by opening to a softer place. By slowing down long enough to feel. When he stops working so hard there will be a void and he may feel fear. He will learn he can survive the fear without getting angry. When he stops defending himself he will realize he is not always under attack. When he opens up doors and windows in his fortress he can let light and other people in.

He will be less alone. He will be less afraid because he will see that he doesn't have to go out all raw and pink like a snail from its shell.

Solid Guy knows how to stand strong without getting angry. Because he is less angry, he doesn't feel the need to go to war over every little thing. He takes himself less seriously and knows how to play. Every interaction doesn't have to be about winning or losing. When Solid Guy is faced with a confrontation he knows to ask himself, "Do I want to win or learn?" When Solid Guy can let go of having to know everything all the time, he can stop feeling inadequate. He can be free of the "never good enough" voice in his own head and he can stop trying so hard. Finally, when he realizes he has nothing to prove, he can ask to be accepted and honoured for who he is.

Solid Guy doesn't come into his power all at once. He starts in small steps, trying out new ground and learning to trust himself. He learns to feel strong when he is open and finds relief in tears. When he is connected to his solid self, he can stop doing and start being. He finds that from this place, he can still be powerful but he doesn't have to be violent. One day he realizes that every relationship isn't a contest and his life doesn't have to be a war, and he surrenders to a softer place inside himself. When this happens, instead of feeling vulnerable and weak, he feels grounded and strong. He feels solid.

The Wise Person's Body Language

Communications experts tell us that over 75 percent of communication is established through body language. The tone of voice and the actual words—in that order—make up the remaining 25 percent. It is alarming to realize that we may be sending out signals and messages all the time without even realizing it. And other people are picking up on or "reading" these communications either subconsciously or perhaps even consciously. This is why Child postures and Warrior postures can clearly work against us. Once we become aware of our body language and are able to control the messages we are sending, we will have a powerful new tool at our command.

Assertive Eye Contact

The old cliché "the eyes are the windows to the soul" holds great truth in an assertiveness context. It is through eye contact—or lack of it—that the most powerful and immediate messages about who we are can be communicated. There are so many different ways we can look someone in the eye. The tension surrounding the eyes and eyebrows, tension around the mouth and the set of the jaw can all either support or detract from the message we wish to communicate.

Assertive eye contact has two key elements:
• Relaxed gaze: When making assertive eye contact, it is essential that the "energy" or emotional content behind the gaze is neutral.
• Steady gaze: When making assertive eye contact, it is essential that the gaze is unflinching and does not communicate any fear or uncertainty.

Wise Person Speaks Up
There are times when just strong eye contact is enough. There are also times when it is necessary to speak up. When we access our Wise Person, we don't find ourselves fuming after a confrontational incident because we didn't say the right thing or (even worse) because we didn't say anything at all. Wise Woman/Solid Guy always knows what to say. All we have to do is take a breath, go inside and ask ourselves, "What is going on here that I don't like?" Once we have identified the specific behaviour that we find offensive, we can simply name it directly and assertively. The Wise Person speaks to the behaviour, not the person. The Wise Person doesn't over-apologize and isn't overly polite. S/he doesn't feel rude or guilty for speaking up because s/he knows we have the right to stand up for ourselves, those we care about and what we believe in—respectfully and assertively.

For exercises on "Getting to Know Your Wise Woman/Solid Guy," see page 252.

Resolution to the Beach Party Scenario

Now that we have met the Child, the Warrior and the Wise Person, let's take a look at how Jay and Katrina could have handled themselves more assertively at the beach party (in Chapter 2). You'll remember that Jay saw an older guy coming on to Katrina and he responded by yelling at Katrina and getting into a fight with the guy.

Jay's perspective: *What could Jay have done differently? Can you see how he could have used his Solid Guy skills?*

Jay didn't have to respond with anger. He could have been assertive. First of all Jay needed to take a time-out to manage his anger. By taking some deep breaths and taking a moment to assess the situation, he could have given himself time to calm down and be less reactive. Then he could have acknowledged both his anger (Tough Guy) and his fear (Child) by telling himself, "I feel like breaking that guy's balls but he's got a bad reputation for fighting dirty, he's tougher than I am and I'll probably get wasted if I try. I don't really want to fight him because I'm afraid of getting hurt."

Most importantly, this incident has more to do with Jay and Katrina than with Jay and the other guy. Trust is one of the most important things in a relationship. If Jay cares about his relationship with Katrina, he could have made a decision to check things out with her before he jumped to conclusions. To deal with this situation with his Solid Guy, Jay could have approached his girlfriend. In a calm manner, and briefly making strong but neutral eye contact with the older guy, he could have asked her if she'd talk with him for a minute. Once out of earshot, Jay could have asked her to clarify what was going on. Together, they could have chosen to leave. If they did not feel like leaving they could have agreed to stick close by each other for the rest of the night—both for Katrina's safety (but only if this is what she feels she needs) and to give the other guy a clear message about the commitment in their relationship.

Does it seem that Jay wouldn't really be standing up to the guy if he did this?

It is very common for assertiveness to feel like it's not enough. We are used to seeing our heroes and heroines in the movies deliver scathing verbal assassinations that leave the other person speechless and humiliated. (Or they just pull out a gun, say something clever and shoot.) In the movies, people don't really get beat-up or die. In real life it can be dangerous to humiliate another person, especially if that person is drunk, irrational or clearly angry. Some people are just not worth telling off. If you have an opportunity to walk around a land-mine instead of stepping right on it, walking around it is a wise and intelligent choice. By not exposing his jealousy (Child) or his anger (Tough Guy), Jay has made a choice to be safer and more in control. The older guy will see him as someone who is not easily provoked.

At the same time he will see that Jay is a man who is not afraid to look him in the eye. He will see that Jay is not one of those people who will just stand by and do nothing. Instead of fake bravado, Jay has communicated authentic power.

Isn't there something Jay could have said that would let the guy know to back off his girlfriend in the future?

Katrina is Jay's girlfriend, not his territory to be defended as though she belonged to him. He may not always be around to "protect" her. Jay's Tough Guy may have a hard time letting go of his protector role but it is up to Katrina to learn how to stand up for herself assertively in situations where her boundaries are being invaded. Jay's job is to take care of his own feelings in the situation and to re-establish trust between himself and Katrina. Jay's Solid Guy would be clear with Katrina that he doesn't feel it's his job to fight off other guys. He could tell her that he would feel more comfortable if she were more assertive with other guys when they hit on her. He could offer to support her in learning how to stand up for herself more assertively in the future. Jay's Tough Guy could even show Katrina some cool self-defence moves!

What is the assertive message that Jay's Solid Guy is communicating when he handles the situation in this new way?

By making eye contact with the other guy and then moving on to hang out with his girlfriend in a supportive and caring way, Jay would be relaying an authentically powerful message. In effect, he would be saying, "I see what you're doing, I have a good and trusting relationship with my girlfriend and I don't feel threatened by you."

What are the assertiveness skills that Jay could have used?
breathing
time-out to assess the situation
acknowledging his vulnerable feelings and getting his Child to a
    safe place
acknowledging his anger and getting Tough Guy under control
strong but neutral eye contact
honest and direct communication

Katrina's perspective: *What could Katrina have done differently? Can you see how she could have used her Wise Woman skills?*

If Katrina had been able to be assertive with the guy who was invading her space in the first place, Jay would not even have had to get involved. In other words, Katrina could have "rescued" herself. Beginning with a deep breath and grounding herself, Katrina could have put her Child in a safe place and made sure her Bitch was standing back but at the ready. With good eye contact and without smiling, laughing or responding to his questions, Katrina then could have clearly stated what she didn't like about what the older guy was doing. By being assertive Kat is letting the guy know without a doubt that she is not an "easy house to break into." Chances are he will give up.

How could Katrina have handled Jay's angry reaction differently?

Assertiveness is not magic. Even if she had used all her Wise Woman skills perfectly, it is possible that the guy—especially if he had been drinking—would have persisted. Jay may have seen the interaction and misinterpreted what he was seeing. In this case, Katrina may not have been able to prevent Jay's angry reaction but she could have dealt assertively with Jay and how he directed his anger toward her. She could have kept the other guy out of it. When Jay grabbed her, she could have calmly but firmly pulled her arm away and said, "Jay, I don't like how angry you are right now and I don't want you to touch me. I want you to stay away from me until you calm down." Later, when Jay was calm, Kat could tell him again that she did not want him to touch her ever again when he was angry. She could tell him that she plans to break up with him if he ever does it again. Once she was reassured that he understood and agreed to this boundary, she could explain to him the details of what had happened and how she had felt. No longer in the heat of the moment and with nothing to prove in front of his friends, it is unlikely that Jay would go looking for the guy to pick a fight.

What are the assertiveness skills that Katrina could have used?
breathing
acknowledging her vulnerable feelings and getting her Child to
    a safe place
acknowledging her anger and getting her Bitch back
calling on her Wise Woman
strong but neutral eye contact
repeating her clear statements
establishing clear "Touch Boundaries."

Assertiveness Techniques for Wise Woman/Solid Guy

We have watched Jay and Katrina get into trouble at a beach party and Jay and Paul get in trouble at school. We have seen Caitlyn and Natasha narrowly escape a close call at a bus stop and later we saw Natasha get into a serious fight with Jaz. We also saw Daniella stand up for herself at a bus stop. In the next section we will look closely at the specific assertiveness techniques that Daniella used and the other teens could have used to make their lives a little easier and themselves a lot safer.

The Broken Record
Wise Woman/Solid Guy doesn't have to think of dozens of clever things to say. S/he chooses a message and sticks to it. When we feel we

are not being heard, we can repeat our message up to three times regardless of what the other person is saying. By repeating the original message, we are saying, in effect, "I meant what I said." The Broken Record technique gives us something to ground ourselves with and helps us to not respond to the words or tone of the person who is harassing us.

Teaching Tip: Avoid saying the message a fourth time. It loses power after the third time. Pace yourself. Let the other person unwind a little. Pause in between statements—in other words, don't use them all up too soon—you only have three! Do not try to talk over or interrupt; just wait for an opening and maintain the eye contact and neutral expression.

Piggybacking

What if the person is doing or saying more than one thing that we find offensive? Sometimes it is simplest just to choose the most offensive behaviour and speak to that. However, there are times when a person begins with one behaviour and then adds another. For instance, if a man began by "scanning" a woman's body, the woman could tell him she didn't like the way he was looking at her. If he then reached out and touched her, she has her first message to repeat plus a behaviour to speak to. She could "piggyback" one message on top of another, saying, "I don't like the way you're looking at me and I don't want you to touch me."

If a person is doing many offensive things, it becomes impossible to list them all in one clear statement. In that case, firmly repeating a general statement such as " I don't like what you're doing" is sufficient.

The Look

What if the person doesn't go away after you've repeated your message the third time? After the third message, a calm steady gaze and strong body language backs up our message and says clearly once again, "I meant what I said." In the SafeTeen program, we call this "The Look." The Look is a neutral matter-of-fact gaze. Steady eye contact with a focused silence. The eye contact is made in a slow and deliberate manner and is held just until we sense the other person has received the message. Once the other person has glanced away it is important to release the direct gaze—as though we are communicating our strength and then getting on with our day. Continuing with the eye contact could be perceived as challenging in some situations.

As well as being an effective way of backing up a verbal message, silence coupled with assertive eye contact can be used when it feels too intimidating to deal with a situation verbally or when our mind goes blank and we just can't think of what to say. It could be used, for example, when dealing with a person in a position of power and authority. The Look is also effective when there's more than one person to deal with or they are too far away to use verbal skills effectively—for instance, a gang of teens across the street or someone driving by in a car.

The STOP Hand
When someone is invading our personal space—standing too close or touching us in some way—it can strengthen our verbal message to put one hand up in a STOP gesture. Even without a verbal message, this body language is a clear and strong communication that we want the other person to back off. The hand should be firm, fingers closed and held around shoulder height. It is important to put the hand up at a

distance from our body to define where our personal space is. When the Child in us uses her/his STOP hand, the fingers fold down and the hand drops before the message has been communicated three times. The Child also tends to keep her/his hand close to her/his body and the hand either "cringes" when we are approached or jerks back, fingers spread wide in a startled gesture. The Warrior in us brings the hand up fast, fingers curled into a fist and blocks the touch by striking the other person's arm away. The Wise Person's STOP hand is just like the Wise Person's whole body—calm, firmly upright, and standing her/his ground until the message gets through.

The Bully Mirror
Rather than reacting to what a person is saying, it can be very powerful to expose the behaviour of someone who is bullying or harassing us. We can look past the words they are using to try to hurt us and look through to the insecure part of them that needs to put us down. By refusing to defend ourselves and instead making a neutral statement about what we see, we are holding a mirror up for them to see themselves. When we do this we expose the small person on the inside. Here's an example of how the Mirror can be used:

Bully: "Hey fat girl!"
Target: "That's name-calling. Name-calling is bullying."

Remember: It's important not to use this skill in a taunting or humiliating way. If we do, we will only be exposing our own small self and potentially putting ourselves at risk for more bullying and even physical violence.

XYZ
This technique is effective in an ongoing relationship when we wish to communicate more than a simple statement and we hope some learning can take place. The XYZ structure works like this: "When you do/say (X), I feel (Y) and I need/want (Z)." For example, "When you make racist jokes, I feel offended and I want you to stop making them around me."

Affirming Positive Intention

Sometimes people we care about do or say things that offend us or hurt our feeling or cross our boundaries. Sometimes people genuinely don't realize they are offending us because they are not aware of areas where we may be sensitive. Although in cases of harassment the person's intent is not a legal defence, it can be useful to consider the person's intent when deciding how to most effectively communicate our feelings.

Affirming Positive Intention can be an extremely useful skill because it defuses defensiveness and gets the message across without damaging the relationship. It is important that we ask ourselves if we genuinely wish to consider the other person's feelings and if we actually trust their intentions are good. For instance, if someone we know is too physically affectionate but we are certain that they are not meaning to be invasive, we can affirm their positive intention before we state our boundary: "I've noticed you are a very affectionate person. I also know that you are a sensitive person and you will understand that I'm not so comfortable with all the hugging." Or if a person we know compliments us and we know they intend to boost our self-esteem but we feel uncomfortable with comments about our personal appearance from this person, we could say, "I know you mean to make me feel good—and I need you to know that I feel uncomfortable when you make comments about my appearance. I know you wouldn't purposefully offend me and you would want to know how I feel."

It is often more effective to use the word *and* rather than the word *but*. The word *but* tends to erase the positive message preceding the boundary. The word *and* serves as a bridge between the two statements.

There is no doubt that some discomfort will occur in most instances when we choose to assert a personal boundary. A good question to ask ourselves is, *Whose* discomfort is at stake? *Whose* feelings are more important? And if we choose *not* to speak up, the behaviour will likely continue; then how will we feel?

Being assertive does not always have to be confrontational and serious. Once we learn the basic skills we can integrate them into who we are. We can be funny and assertive. In our daily lives we can be assertive and friendly. In an intimate relationship we can be assertive and loving. For example, we could say to our partner, "I love you and this relationship is really important to me—I just don't want to have sex right now."

As you read the following scenarios, see if you can identify what the behaviours are that indicate that the characters' Child personas are present. See if you can rescript the scenarios the way the Wise Person would have handled them.

In the first scenario we will be introduced to Jamal. Jamal is a gentle-natured boy who is a frequent target for bullying by the other boys in his school.

Jamal: Leaving the Beach Party

Jamal is scared. He is at a beach party with a group of kids from school and a fight has broken out. Somehow, Jamal has been jostled by the crowd to the inner edge of the circle. He can see that one of the guys has a big piece of wood and he's swinging it at the other guy's head. He doesn't want to watch and he's terrified that someone will get seriously hurt. One guy's nose is already bleeding. All the other guys and even some of the girls are screaming, "Fight! Fight!"

Jamal wants to leave and he edges around to where he sees an opening in the circle. He squeezes through the crowd to the back and starts backing away toward the trail leading up to the road. That's when one of the guys spots him. Jamal knows this guy. His name is Jack and he's always bugging Jamal at school. He teases him and calls him "fag" because Jamal isn't good at sports. "Hey, wussy," Jack yells at him now, "what's the matter, can't you stand the sight of blood?" Jamal looks down and scuffs the toe of his sneaker back and forth in the sand. He doesn't look at the guy but he says in a small voice, "No, I just have to go." Now two of Jack's pals are standing with him and one of them says, "What's the matter, Jamal, you have to go home? Are you late for your bedtime story? Are you a mama's boy?" Jamal can feel his face flush red. He feels furious at these boys and for a moment he pictures himself pulling a gun out and blowing their heads off. He can see it in his mind clear as day. You want to see blood? he thinks. I'll show you blood!

At that moment, Jack starts toward him. "C'mon and watch the fight, Jamal, don't jam-out Jamal..." Jamal's anger disappears as he feels fear rush through his body. He starts backing away, stumbles over a log and, arms flailing wildly, falls flat on his back. The three guys burst out laughing and before he knows what's happening they have dragged him up onto his feet and are pushing and pulling him toward the crowd where the fight is still going on. "Don't," Jamal whines. "Cut it out ..." He is desperately fighting tears. "Oh god," he prays silently, "please don't let me cry. If I cry, I'm dead."

What do you think? Can you picture Jamal's body language throughout this incident? Does backing away from Jack seem like a safe thing to do? Can you imagine what the tone of voice was that Jamal used when he resisted? What do you imagine will happen if Jamal can't control his tears? Can you sense the power the other guys would be feeling in this situation? Did you recognize Jamal's "easy house to break into" behaviour?

Jamal is afraid. He has no hope of winning in a physical fight and he doesn't know that there is another way to stand up for himself. When he backs away fearfully he is showing his vulnerable child-self. His pleading tone exposes his Child even more. Like most boys, Jamal knows without a doubt that crying is the most dangerous thing he can do in this type of situation.

Jamal is also angry. Because he has no way to express his anger, he represses it. His violent fantasies tell us that he has probably been pushing his anger down for a long time and it's not far below the surface.

In the next scenario we meet up with Katrina once more. Again, see if you can identify her Child behaviour and rescript the scenario the way her Wise Woman could have handled it.

Katrina: After the Beach Party

Kat is really upset. She couldn't stop her boyfriend, Jay, from getting into a fight and she'd left the party because she didn't want to watch him get hurt. She felt angry at him and angry at all the other kids for cheering the fight on. She knew that if everyone had ignored them, the two guys would probably have just put on a big show and then quit. It's dark out and Kat is walking up the road toward the bus stop. She is walking slowly with her head down and her arms folded across her chest. She's thinking of breaking up with Jay. Kat feels like crying and wonders how long she'll have to wait for the bus. She so badly wants to be at home and in her room right now. When she turns around to look up the road to see if the bus is coming, she sees a guy walking behind her. It's a warm night but Kat feels a chill and gets goosebumps up and down her arms. Something about the guy... No, she thinks, I'm just being paranoid. She picks up her pace a little.

The guy is walking fast and he soon catches up to her. She looks over her shoulder as she hears him approach and moves over a little to let him pass. But he doesn't pass her. He walks along with her and she can feel him next to her—too close. Kat feels her stomach tighten with anxiety. She moves over to the side of the road as much as she can. She glances anxiously at him and then past him looking up the road again for the bus. In a quiet voice he says "Hi." She looks quickly up at his face and she sees it's someone she knows—sort of. One of the guys from the party. Well, she doesn't know him exactly but she's seen him around. Kat feels stupid then for having felt afraid. She tells herself she's just jumpy because of the scene with Jay at the party. "Hi," she says. "Sorry, I didn't recognize you at first." She glances up at him and then quickly looks away.

The boy is staring intently at her. Katrina doesn't look at him but she can see in her peripheral vision that he is looking at her. She lets her gaze fall down to the ground as she walks. She can see the lower half of his body—his long legs striding along beside her. He is wearing big baggy pants and she notices his hand, which is in the pocket of his pants, is moving up and down on his thigh—or is it rubbing higher up? Now Kat is getting a really bad feeling inside. She can see the bus stop just up ahead. She walks a little faster but he easily keeps up. She thinks she feels the boy's other hand—the one closest to her—brush her leg and she walks closer to the bush at the side of the road. She can feel the twigs scratching at her legs.

The bus stop is just a post by the side of the road but there's a gas station nearby. Even though it's closed Kat is grateful for the light from the neon sign. She stops and stands facing the road. Her arms are still folded across her chest. She doesn't look at him. "Yeah," he says in the same quiet voice, "I saw you back there at the party. You're the chick whose boyfriend was freaking out. My name's Jack—so what's your name? " Kat doesn't want to tell him but it seems rude not to answer so she makes up a name. "That's a pretty name," he says and then he tells her she shouldn't be walking alone at night. He tells her she's a really pretty girl. Kat feels her face go red. She knows she's smiling and she hears herself saying "Umm, thanks." He is standing next to her and she can see his hand in his pocket is moving in a slow, rhythmic way but she's afraid to really look at what he's doing. She moves away from him but he just steps in closer again. Kat is scared. She turns her back on him. She stands there, staring up the road, praying for the bus to come. She can feel him behind her. *What do you think? Does turning her back on him seem like a safe thing to do? What do you imagine will happen next? Can you sense the power the guy would be feeling in this situation? Do you think, right at this moment, the guy will say to himself, "Cool, this feels awesome, think I'll go home now and watch some TV...".*?

Katrina is trying to ignore the boy. She is using a survival skill that is very familiar to most girls and women. Most girls are instructed to "just ignore him," usually by their well-intentioned mothers who were taught the same thing by their own mothers. As a prevention skill, ignoring may work with timid guys but it is not a useful strategy in most threatening situations. When a woman ignores a situation, the message she is giving is, "I don't know how to deal with this." In SafeTeen we call this the Ostrich Syndrome. When we picture the ostrich, its head stuck in the sand, the absurdity of the strategy becomes painfully clear.

Can you picture Kat's body language throughout this incident? Did you notice how she discounted her feelings and how she didn't trust the voice in her mind that told her she wasn't safe? Why do you think Kat felt stupid for feeling afraid when she realized she sort of knew the guy? Did you recognize Kat's "easy house to break into" body language?

Jack: Underneath the Tough Guy

Jack hates going home. He spends as little time at home as possible. It's Friday night, and as usual his dad is well into his bottle of scotch and as usual he's going on and on about Jack getting a job. Jack is just standing by the door waiting for him to finish so he can leave. There's a party at the beach tonight and he wants to score some beer before he goes. He agrees to look for a job tomorrow. He just agrees to everything his dad says—that usually shuts him up. But tonight he's not so easy to appease. Jack shifts from foot to foot and finally he says in a strained voice, "Okay, okay, I'll check the paper tomorrow, can I go now?" Suddenly Jack's dad loses it. He jumps up from his chair and grabs Jack around the throat and slams him up against the wall. He calls him a no-good punk and tells him for the thousandth time that he'll grow up to be nothing, a nobody. Jack is choking, he can't breathe, he tries to push his dad off of him but his dad is bigger and stronger. Finally, his dad releases the grip he has on his throat, opens the door and pushes him out onto the porch. "You want to go? Good. Go. And don't bother coming back until you can pull your own weight around here you good-for-nothing," his dad says in a voice filled with disgust. Then he spits on the porch floor and slams the door behind him, going back inside. As Jack stumbles down the steps he chokes back tears of rage.

A few beers later, Jack feels better. He's not thinking about his dad anymore and he's having a good time at the party. A good fight has broken out and Jack is pumped just watching it. The smaller guy is getting creamed! Then he sees a guy from his class leaving the crowd that has gathered—he sees him trying to make his way to the back. Probably can't stomach the blood, Jack thinks. This guy is such a wuss. One time he actually made him cry! This is one of Jack's favourite games. The guy's name is Jamal. Stupid raghead name, Jack thinks. Jamal makes Jack sick. He grabs a couple of his buddies and goes after him. Jack and his two friends grab Jamal and throw him into the middle of the fight. He falls flat on his face in the sand and getting up he scoots backwards on his butt like a little sand crab trying to get out of the way of the two fighters. Jack laughs and moves around to push Jamal back into the centre.

Suddenly someone is standing in front of Jack, arms by his sides and blocking his way. Startled, he looks at the guy who just looks calmly back at him. "What's your problem?" the guy says in a quiet voice. "You got no one your own size to pick on?" Jack tells the guy to f__ off and get the hell out of his way. The guy is about Jack's size and Jack figures he and his buddies could take him if it came to that. Jack looks around but can't see his two friends. Oh shit, he thinks. He looks back at the guy in front of him and feels uneasy when he sees the calm expression on his face. He feels even more uncomfortable when the guy repeats, "What's your problem? Why are you picking on people smaller than you?" Jack doesn't know what to say. He tells the guy to go f__ himself and heads up the beach toward the trail leading to the road. He glances around for his buddies but they are still nowhere in sight. The guy is still standing there, calmly looking at him. It gives Jack the creeps. He wants to give him the finger before he heads up the trail but thinks better of it.

As he climbs up the trail Jack feels like shit. He doesn't even know where he's going to go—he can't go home tonight, that's for sure. Jack feels rage swell up inside as he thinks of his dad again. Just then he sees a girl walking up the road ahead of him. She looks familiar. Jack's seen her around, can't remember her name but she's quiet, blonde—he likes her type. The girl looks nervously over her shoulder and Jack feels a pleasant rush of power surge through him. He picks up his pace.

Can you feel what is going on for Jack on the inside? Can you sense the powerless person inside who has low self-esteem? Did you recognize the Solid Guy skills that the guy who confronted Jack about his bullying used? Can you see why these skills would work with someone like Jack? Can you see how Jack will be drawn to the girl on the road and how her vulnerability makes him feel powerful?

Using Assertiveness Skills

It is all very well to learn some simple and effective assertiveness techniques; however, in real-life situations we may find ourselves overwhelmed with fear or consumed by anger. We could be taken off guard or emotionally confused. The following "What if" questions are common ones when we are first learning to be assertive.

What if your mind is blank?

What if you are feeling panic and your mind and body feel paralyzed? Just take that first calming breath and make eye contact and wait for the fear to subside and your mind to clear so that you can find the right words. Very often just the silence and eye contact gives such a strong message on its own that the person confronting you will de-escalate and even retreat. If the desire to surrender to the fear (cry, collapse, look away, apologize, etc.) is very strong, right then, in that moment, tell your child-self it is not safe to be there. Imagine quickly sending the Child to your safe place. Make a promise to your child-self that you will come to get her/him later. Sometimes acknowledging the anxiety in the moment can help delay the fearful reaction. It is important to keep your promises, even to yourself. Once the threatening situation has been defused, when you are no longer at risk, find a safe place and perhaps a safe person to support you and express your vulnerable feelings.

What if the situation so offends you that your anger feels out of control?

Just take that first calming breath, recognize and acknowledge your right to feel angry and make a commitment right there and then to voice that anger later. Tell your Warrior it is not safe for her/him to be there because you are at risk of escalating into a physical situation with someone bigger and stronger than you are (or someone smaller and weaker). In other words, tell Bitch/Tough Guy: "I promise I'll let you out later." And then later, when neither you nor anyone else is at risk, and when you have a safe place and preferably a safe person to support you, allow yourself to express those legitimate angry feelings.

What if you are taken by surprise, can't pull yourself together quickly enough, "lose it" halfway through the encounter and cry or yell?

You can recover your composure and start again—even in the middle of losing it. Knowing that you didn't deal with a situation as well as you could have, you can make a commitment to come back to it and try again (or resolve to try again the next time a similar situation presents itself). It is never too late. Try to give yourself credit for what you did right. Mistakes are an unavoidable and potentially valuable part of the learning process.

What if you feel you are "losing it" regardless of how hard you are trying to use your new skills?

You can take a time-out. If you are on the telephone you can say, "I have to go. I'm too angry to talk to you right now. I'll have to get back to you." If you are face to face you can say the same thing or as an emergency strategy you can say you need to use the washroom. Once you get there you can breathe and ground yourself.

Remember: Being assertive does not come naturally or easily for most of us. You may feel like you are faking it at first. In the beginning you will be aware that you are using your body language to mask what you are really feeling inside. It is helpful to know that using the skills and experiencing success with them builds on itself. After a while it no longer feels like you are using a technique. With practice, it no longer feels like something you are doing—it becomes who you are.

Remember: Assertiveness is not a weapon. It is not something to shoot other people down with. Being assertive is not about winning. Assertiveness is a communication skill, a self-empowerment tool and above all a personal safety strategy. When we practise assertiveness, we communicate to ourselves and to the world that we are not an easy target and that we deserve to be treated with respect.

When asked what was the most important thing they learned in the SafeTeen workshop, some boys wrote:

"I learned how to be solid when confronting someone that's likely to hurt or harass you."

"About how to get what you want without insulting the other side and without hurting one another."

"Learned the many things involved in intimate relationships, such as love, companionship, etc."

Some teenage girls responded:

"Learned how important it is for women to get respect from other women."

"How to be more confident, strong and wise when I'm in a bad situation."

"Assertiveness. It was awesome!"

"How to say 'No' and mean it."

For role-plays to develop assertiveness skills, see page 261.

Chapter 4

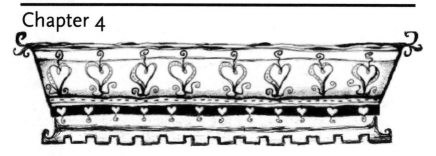

Fear and Anger

FEAR AND ANGER are the two emotions that will most likely be triggered when we face threats to our inner or outer selves. Understanding fear and anger and how they operate as survival mechanisms can help us make healthy and even life-saving choices.

Understanding Fear

Fear is a survival mechanism. It functions as a way of warning us that danger is present. Fear is also an extremely powerful emotion. Most people can identify with the fear fantasy—or perhaps have had fear dreams—of being unable to fight or run or scream when under physical attack. Some of us may even have experienced being paralyzed by fear. Certainly most of us have had the experience of being unable to find the words to defend ourselves when under verbal attack. To overcome what is in effect a fear of fear, it is useful to understand what fear is, what its biological function is and how it can work for us or against us.

Fear and the Body

When we experience fear, we feel it in the body. The physical sensations of fear, such as sweating, trembling and increased heart rate, are due to a chemical release in the bloodstream. The hormone adrenaline is released as a survival mechanism. Adrenaline is experienced as a rush of energy and its function is to help us to fight or run with more power and speed than usual. We need to learn to recognize the physical symptoms of adrenaline and then we need to learn strategies that we trust so that we can channel the energy into effective action. The action required may be as simple as making direct eye contact with a person or locking the car door. Or it may be to push someone firmly away and run or, in a life-threatening situation, to fight back with all our physical force.

Fear and the Mind

When we are in a threatening situation and we reach into our minds for an answer to the question "What should I do?" and we draw a blank, we can become overwhelmed by our fear. The unchannelled energy that has been triggered by the adrenaline can result in an out-of-control physical reaction that we call panic or hysteria. If the information that we do have is ineffectual (such as "just ignore it") or contradictory (fight back/definitely don't fight back), we can feel paralyzed. When we are conditioned to believe that we will be unable to respond effectively ("you are a wimp/loser"), we may feel hopeless and give up. We may fear that we will be incapacitated when faced with danger, but we can unlearn such fears.

Fear is your friend. Fear tells you danger is present.

We may not be able to escape our fear but we can transform it. We can incorporate the experience of fear into our daily lives as a tool, a useful companion. We can carry it with us as the survival skill that it is meant to be. If we can learn how to reframe our experience of fear and rescript our learned responses to it, we can feel more confident about how we will respond in a crisis.

Children, adolescents and adults can all experience fear differently. Females and males can also experience and react to fear differently.

Children and Fear

A peculiar phenomenon about childhood is the ability that children have to be in the moment. Most of us have seen a child go from crying to laughing in a heartbeat. Because of this ability, it's possible for children to be ostensibly free from fear, particularly if they have been fortunate enough to escape being abused. Even children who experience abuse can be free from fear afterwards or in between episodes because of their ability to stay in the moment, go into denial and sustain a fantasy world. Children tend to push their fears underground, which is why they often manifest as nightmares or irrational or abstract fears such as fear of the dark. As well, children have less of the big picture: they tend to be more sheltered and unaware of all the terror and violence in the world.

Adolescents and Fear

In the years of adolescence, we are armoured by a uniquely adolescent phenomenon sometimes called the Immortality Syndrome. While in this developmental phase we seem unable to grasp that anything bad will ever happen to us. Teens will fiercely resist anything that threatens their newly won freedom and they may use anger to block their fear. They often throw themselves wildly at life with little regard to their own safety or the safety of others, taking risks that later in life will make them cringe. This "no-fear" phase can strike much fear into the hearts of parents.

Individual Responses to Fear

As individuals, our mechanisms for coping with fear are usually rooted in either the child mind or the Immortality Syndrome. Which posture we choose will depend on personal nature, individual experience and gender role modeling. Five common ways of dealing with fear are:

denial, shielding with anger, coping, living in terror, and knowing no fear. Let's take a closer look at these.

Denial: A person who has not been rudely awakened by an act of violence may be able to remain in "child-mind," the naive state of fearlessness many children inhabit. When we adopt a posture of childlike naivete with respect to danger we may be in, we are not using our inner radar. When we are not tuned in we are less likely to be assessing people or situations to determine our safety and may not be prepared if something threatening happens.

Shielding with anger: The individual who stays attached to this adolescent posture feels angry that s/he has to restrict her/his life because of the threat of violence. This person's anger becomes a shield between themselves and their fear. When we operate in a state of stubborn anger we may be putting ourselves at unnecessary risk.

Coping: Because feeling fear in its full intensity all the time would be intolerable and psychologically paralyzing, it is very common for some people to experience fear as a consistent, low-grade anxiety that they carry with them every day. Like the hum of a fridge, it is everpresent but not in the forefront of the person's awareness. And much like the hum of the fridge, it would drive them mad to have their attention called to it constantly. It's much more comfortable to exercise a subconscious vigilance. Without really thinking about it, they map out their daily activities and plan their nights according to the always present possibility of violence.

Living in terror: Some people are unable to screen out the fear of violence. This is particularly true for females. Many girls and women live in a child's nightmare state of terror on a daily and nightly basis. They cannot go out at night alone, live alone or sleep alone. Even spending an evening at home alone can be difficult. Although the restriction on their lives is an enormous violation, they don't experience healthy outrage. People who live with this level of fear live severely restricted and dependent lives.

Knowing no fear: Because fear is the emotion that masculinity traditionally censors most strongly, this strategy is most common among males. If little boys express fear they are risking physical injury, ongoing bullying and name-calling. The names they are called most often are things like "fag" or "wuss" or "girl". What a little boy learns from this is that if he shows fear, he will lose his gender identity. He will no longer be male and he will never grow up to be a man. For his physical and psychological survival, the little boy must stop himself from expressing fear at all costs. This means he will engage in high-risk behaviours in order to prove he is not afraid. Eventually the boy becomes a young man who is no longer just hiding his fear, he can no longer feel it.

Working with Fear
Why do females always panic and freeze in dangerous situations? Females don't always panic and freeze when faced with danger. However, this is a common enough female response to warrant the question. It is well-documented that animals—male or female—will defend themselves when cornered. When antelope run or monkeys scream, they are using strategies for survival. Some animals remain very still or feign death, but this too is a strategy, not an inability to respond. The female of any species has as much ability to defend herself as the male—and in some cases, the female is better at it. This is particularly true when she is defending her young. So it can seem that female human beings are the only living creatures on this planet that don't instinctively defend themselves.

The Mother Bear Syndrome

Ask a female what she would be willing to do in order to save herself in the event of a violent attack and it is common for her to hesitate. She may question her ability to be able to fight effectively and she may express reluctance to hurt or maim her attacker. Ask the same female what she would be willing to do to protect her child and she will reply without hesitation and with a fierce confidence, "Anything." We call this the Mother Bear Syndrome.

Examples of the Mother Bear Syndrome are not difficult to find. One newspaper reported on a camping trip where a woman awoke in the night to find a cougar dragging a child from one of the tents. Without hesitation, the woman jumped onto the huge cat's back, got it into a headlock and forced it to release the child. The cougar ran off into the dark and the woman ran after it, shouting. Suddenly she realized what she was doing and she stopped and returned to the camp. The woman herself couldn't believe what she had just done. In this case, the child was not even her own.

Another newspaper article describes a woman waking in the night and hearing an intruder in her house. The woman's teenage daughter was asleep in the next room. The woman said it was the thought of her daughter that inspired her to action. Both mother and daughter were avid archers. The woman grabbed her bow and strung an arrow. When the man entered her bedroom, she shot him in the leg. She then yelled for her daughter, handed her the bow with a new arrow strung and ready, and instructed her to keep him there while she called the police. When the police arrived, they saw two women holding a wounded man at bay with bows and arrows!

It is possible that the women in these two stories overcame their conditioning to be passive and fearful because their conditioning to protect their young was stronger than their fear. Therefore it stands to reason that if girls and women learn to value themselves, they will think of themselves as worth protecting. Females' traditional responses to fear are conditioned or learned responses. If we can learn something, we can usually also unlearn it. We can replace the useless advice and mixed messages about how to deal with violence with effective assertiveness strategies and self-defence skills.

The "Nice Lion" Syndrome

When girls and women feel something is wrong, they often discount their feelings. Even though they may get many signals telling them they are in danger, they have a tendency to ignore those signals. They tell themselves that this couldn't be happening to them, or that the person in question seems so nice. In his book Protecting the Gift, *Gavin DeBecker talks about something he calls "wild mind." He urges women to allow this more primitive state of mind to take over when they're in danger and he says, "You don't have to wait for motherhood." With humour, he reminds us that when a wild animal spots a predator, it doesn't say to itself, "Not that lion, that lion looks nice."*

Giving girls and women an understanding of how and why fear operates in threatening situations and teaching them to rescript their conditioned responses are the first steps in teaching women to defend themselves when needed. Teaching concrete verbal, body-language and physical options for coping with dangerous situations can create changes that will enable girls and women to make more informed, more effective and ultimately safer choices. Most importantly, we need to affirm female rights and nurture a strong and healthy self-concept in girls so that they learn to value themselves and trust their own inner wisdom.

For exercises on working with fear, see page 271.

Women don't get angry—they just get afraid. Most females can identify a time when, feeling very angry and determined to stand up for themselves, they confronted the person in question and found themselves struggling with the inability to speak and the humiliation of tears. When one considers the pervasive attacks on dignity and self-esteem girls and women suffer every day due to sexual harassment, coupled with the enormous restrictions on their lives because of the dangers of violent assault, it becomes apparent that it is actually inappropriate for females not to feel anger. More importantly, for a female to experience fear to the exclusion of anger means she will not be armed to verbally or physically defend herself.

Men don't get afraid, they just get angry. When men bang their shins on a coffee table, they curse instead of saying "Ow! That hurt!"

Although this reaction is not exclusive to males, it is more typically a male response. When males experience fear, grief, confusion, vulnerability or physical pain, they commonly express anger. Whether it's a stubbed toe or a loved one leaving them, males will typically skip over any vulnerable feelings and leap into anger as a way of not feeling the pain or fear. Although this is an effective strategy for avoiding vulnerability, the result is often hurtful to others or themselves. Fear of feeling vulnerable can lead to medicating with drugs and alcohol and engaging in high-risk behaviours such as fast driving and fighting. As well, a person who can't feel his own fear or pain will have very little empathy for others. How can we expect a young man to understand and care about his girlfriend's feelings if he doesn't know or care about his own?

Understanding Anger

Anger is an emotion. Just like all our other emotions, it is natural and serves a purpose. Anger is a positive survival mechanism. It exists to signal that our boundaries have been violated. If we did not experience anger, we would not know when to defend ourselves. To feel anger when we have been violated is appropriate and healthy. The graphic violent images we may have in our minds when we are very angry can be disturbing to us. Some of us have had the experience of verbally or physically acting on an angry thought without actually making the intention to do so and regretting it later.

What Is Healthy Anger?
Healthy anger is not attached to a history of other repressed incidents. When anger is healthy, it is fresh and in the moment. We call this "clean" anger. There is nothing bad or ugly about anger when it's healthy. It is not destructive or dangerous. Healthy anger just says, "Stop" or "No" or "I didn't like that" or "I don't want that" or "Go away" or simply, "I am feeling angry."

What Is Unhealthy Anger?
Anger is not normally explosive or out of control unless it is repressed. Imagine yourself feeling angry. Now imagine someone telling you to calm down, get over it, "stuff it" or "put a lid on it." Can you feel how the anger just gets more intense? How it gets bigger and bigger the more you are told you don't have a right to be angry? Now imagine taking the huge anger you are feeling and picture stuffing it into a container of some kind, stuffing it in, forcing it in and cramming a lid on it. Can you feel how the anger simmers away in there, just waiting for a reason—any reason at all—to burst out? When anger is repressed, a very small incident can trigger a very big explosion!

When we suppress our anger, we may have the illusion that we are controlling it. In fact, the repressed anger usually represents issues that are not being dealt with. Neither the issues nor the feelings really go away. They are only temporarily out of the spotlight.

Repressed anger is like a furious monster, lurking in the dark. It wants out and it's waiting and watching for an opportunity.

Have you ever "lost it"? When we lose it, we are often as surprised as anyone else. The "it" in this case refers to our self-control. The space between having an angry image in our minds and lashing out in violence can be less than a heartbeat, faster than thought. The truth is, when we suppress our feelings we are rarely in control and it is only a matter of time before the feelings become bigger than we are.

For an exercise for transforming anger, see page 272.

For an exercise to release anger, see page 272.

Understanding unhealthy anger can help us to choose safe and healthy ways of expressing our anger. *Unhealthy* anger is usually either "acted out" or "acted in."

"Acting Out" Anger

It is far more common for males than females to act out their anger. The acting-out male commonly overidentifies with traditional male behaviour and is tough, aggressive and scornful of wimpy behaviour. The acting-out male is setting himself up to constantly have to prove himself a big man by dominating women or fighting other guys. It is interesting to note that in recent years we have seen an increase in females acting out—particularly adolescent females. The acting-out female teen has rejected the traditional feminine conditioning, refusing to identify with the powerlessness that she sees in other girls and women. She has overidentified with traditionally masculine behaviour and behaves much in the same way as macho males do. This is her way of refusing to be a victim.

Acting out is a teenage girl's way of refusing to be a victim.

Acting-out behaviour provides a temporary feeling of being in control and a false sense of strength. However, when the female or the male acts out aggressively, s/he often incites an aggressive response. The person in the power position (the person who is in charge or who has authority or who is simply more powerful physically or socially) is likely to feel challenged by the aggressive behaviour. If we act out of anger when dealing with a person who wields some form of power other than physical power over us, the result can be hurtful in a different way. For example, a coach may cut an athlete from the team or a boss could fire an employee. Although both females and males may be using anger to protect themselves from being vulnerable, acting out anger usually has the opposite result.

For example, when a girl tries to stand up to an abusive boyfriend by yelling at him, she typically meets with an even more aggressive response, the situation escalates and she gets hurt. Although it is true that people who connect with their anger before they connect with their fear get away from violent attacks more often, most violent attacks begin with verbal escalation. If we act out of anger when dealing with a person who is larger than we are, the result can be dangerous because the most common reaction to anger is more anger. If we want to defuse a potentially dangerous situation, the last thing we want is for the other person to feel challenged. When a person feels challenged they may feel they have to prove their dominance with physical violence.

If the girl doesn't stand up to her boyfriend, she will probably feel angry. If she takes her frustration out by getting into a fight with a bigger, tougher girl (or a group of girls) at school, she could get hurt.

Another example would be an adolescent boy trying to stand up to an abusive parent. The boy may feel it is hopeless to stand up to his father, so he suppresses his anger, only to act it out later at school by mouthing off to a teacher or starting a fight with another boy. Even if he picks on a smaller boy, he is risking getting expelled from school. Either way, he loses.

"Acting In" Anger

When people suppress their anger they are in effect turning it inward. Although some males "act in" their anger, it is more common for females to turn their anger inward. In our culture overtly angry behaviour is far less tolerated from girls than it is from boys. Children who suppress their angry feelings because they are not permitted a healthy expression of anger can become adolescents whose repressed anger is manifested in self-hatred and self-destructive behaviours.

The teenage girl who tries to stand up to her angry boyfriend and gets hurt learns "If I try to defend myself I will just make this person more angry and then I'll get hurt even more—maybe even killed." The anger then turns into fear, which becomes a hopeless cycle. Being unable to stand up for herself increases her low self-esteem and self-hatred. She is being treated like garbage and she begins to feel like garbage. Eventually, she will begin to treat herself like garbage.

Overeating, undereating, high-risk and reckless behaviours, slashing, piercing (although some piercing is purely about fashion, obsessive piercing can also be an expression of self-mutilation), prostitution, abuse of drugs or alcohol, depression and suicide are all examples of acting in anger. The end result is powerlessness and violence.

Acting in and acting out anger are learned survival techniques that are usually formed early on in life. They are likely to be carried over into adult life unless we learn the skills to cope with anger in a healthy way.

Working with Anger

We commonly hear advice on how to "manage" anger: Be less angry; control your anger; what are you so angry about? Most of these messages are about getting rid of our anger. We will never succeed if we see our anger as something that doesn't belong—something to be rid of. In SafeTeen we offer ways of working with our anger.

"If your expressed rage results in someone shooting you it won't matter that you die with healthy arteries."
—CAROL TAVRIS, AUTHOR OF *ANGER, THE MISUNDERSTOOD EMOTION*

Many people have theorized that repressed anger can make us physically sick. However the solution isn't just to release your anger whenever you feel like it. The solution is to learn how to rewrite our learned scripts about anger and learn assertive ways of expressing our angry feelings.

Two common scripts are:
1. "It's not ever OK to be angry."
2. "Anger is the only way to survive."

Some new scripts could go like this:
1. "I have a right to feel my anger."
2. "My anger has a purpose. It exists to indicate that my boundaries have been violated."
3. "I can learn to express my anger in strong and non-violent ways."

By learning concrete skills to channel the energy of anger and transform it into assertive verbal communication, we can alter the old patterns of acting in or acting out anger. When we learn how anger operates and learn skills to stand strong without using violence, we are far less likely to be harmed or to harm ourselves or others.

Feeling Anger/Doing Anger
Feeling anger is different from acting violently. Thinking about anger is different from "doing" anger. However, feeding the angry thoughts can lead to violent behaviours. There is a difference between telling ourselves that we have a right to feel angry and building a case against others for causing our anger.

Other people don't make you angry—your anger lives inside you. You are always accountable—no matter what the other person did—for your own angry feelings and any behaviours that result from them.

Anger is not violence or abuse, nor is it an excuse for violence or abuse. Your anger's job is to protect you, not to put down or abuse other people. If a person uses their anger to abuse others, it is a clear sign of low self-esteem. Behind abusive anger there is usually power-lessness, hurt or fear.

If you have good self-esteem you are less likely to feel powerless and therefore less likely to be abusive with your anger. However, even people with very high self-esteem feel angry sometimes. Anger is just one of the human emotions and is a strong and vital part of us when it is healthy.

Remember: Anger is an emotion—a voice inside that is there to protect you. Anger is good. Anger is powerful. Anger is healthy and necessary for survival. Anger is a motivating force.

Suppressing Anger

If you bury anger instead of expressing it, it will rise from the dead. If you bottle it, it will explode. If you push it down far enough it will leak out and poison you. If it does not make you physically ill, certainly it will make you emotionally unwell. Sometimes we are forced to sup-press our anger (for example, a child may be forced to apologize for something they do not feel is their fault). Or we may choose to sup-press it because we feel it is unsafe or unwise to express it (a student may not express her/his anger to a teacher for fear of getting a low grade or being kicked out of class). When we suppress it, the anger does not go away. It stays inside and, like a patient demon, it waits for an opportunity to strike.

For exercises on safe and unsafe anger actions, see page 274.

Anger "Triggers"

An anger trigger is something said or done that sets off a strong anger reaction. You may have heard the expression "pushed my buttons." It can feel as though there is an actual anger button that can be pushed by a certain comment or word or tone of voice, triggering an immediate or sudden anger reaction. For example, if you are a young guy who is often treated at home as though he is stupid and perhaps even called things like "stupid," "dumb," "retarded" and "idiot," and one day your girlfriend calls you an idiot—even in a kidding around kind of way—you might feel an amount of anger that seems inappropriate to that situation. When the feeling is very sudden and strong and seems out of proportion to the incident at hand you can bet that you have been triggered. It can be very useful to identify what some of our anger triggers are. When we know what they are, we can try to steer clear of triggering situations or at least understand why we feel so suddenly angry.

To find your triggers, ask questions such as these:
1. What things/actions/words/gestures/voice tones make you especially angry?
2. When and where do you feel most angry?
3. Where do you feel anger? At school? At home? At work?
4. Who do you feel angry around? Authority figures? Males? Females? Children?

Expressing Anger

Once we know how our anger is triggered, we have more control over how we react to those triggers. We can also tell the important people in our lives what triggers our anger so they can avoid stumbling blindly onto our personal landmines. However, it is not possible to be completely in control of others or situations, and we may still need to express our anger in healthy ways. That is where assertiveness skills come in.

When we feel angry and decide to do something about it, we usually have the choice of taking a safe or unsafe action. Anger by its very nature demands that you do something. It can feel as though an energy has been released that says, "Stand up! Speak up! Resist!" The action required does not have to be violent or even overtly physical. Just writing your feelings down can be enough. Telling a safe person your angry story can help. Telling the person you are mad at that you are angry is a very powerful action. The following rules keep everyone safe:

1. No hurting self.
2. No hurting others.
3. No hurting property.

When you are feeling angry, chances are you have been violated.
Feeling angry is OK. Acting angry can be dangerous.

Tips for Working with Anger
Anger, like most emotions, begins, builds in intensity, peaks and then recedes, much like a wave. Very intense anger can flare up and down more like sharp mountain peaks and valleys. The key is to know the feeling will decrease in intensity and eventually pass. Like surfers, our job is to ride the wave in to shore.

Here are some more ways to work with anger:

1. Time Out
When we storm out, slamming the door behind us, and then walk around in circles thinking ourselves into even more of a rage, often we are just running away. It can feel much more powerful to take time out: leave calmly, making good eye contact right until you click the

door quietly behind you. Once we are away from the situation, we can release the energy by running or yelling or breathing.

2. Make a Strong Statement

Anger demands action. A physical action is not necessary, just an action toward righting what is wrong. Making a strong statement about feeling angry before we leave and then stating that we are choosing to take a time-out is an effective action. To practise, stand up and make a statement about something that has happened in your life (or in someone else's life) that you feel angry about. End your statement with "…and I feel really angry about that," in a strong, clear voice.

3. Count Down

People often advise us to count to ten—but this is often not enough to stop the enormous energy of the anger from erupting out of control. Counting backwards from one hundred is probably more realistic, and combining the counting with a time-out is even better. We need to give the anger time to get from our bodies (the fight response) to our brains, where we can choose how we want to behave.

4. Bomb Defuser

One way to defuse anger is to acknowledge it—and your right to feel it—immediately. For example, "I am feeling angry. I am feeling angry for a reason." We can also create a non-violent affirming message to ground ourselves with—a positive statement about ourselves that we can use to centre ourselves until we can choose a safe action.

Repeating our message until the anger passes can help us feel more in control. Examples of acknowledgements and affirmations are:

"I am feeling angry and I am not a violent person."

"I am feeling angry and I do not hurt myself or others when I am angry."

"I am feeling angry and I don't believe in hitting."

5. Breathe Through

We can also move through anger by sitting still and breathing through it. By taking deep breaths and focusing on the physical sensations as they move through our bodies instead of focusing on the angry thoughts, often we will get in touch with the underlying feelings of powerlessness or sadness or fear. As we breathe and pay attention to the feelings it can help just to name what we are aware of feeling: anger, anger…fear…more anger…BIG anger, etc. Once again, riding the wave and trusting it will pass.

Remember: We need to make a commitment ahead of time to choose non-violence. Then we will be more likely to actually use skills like counting down or taking time-outs.

Katrina and Jasmine: The Betrayal

Kat and Jaz have been close friends since grade 6. They are now in grade 10. Jaz is very popular with guys and has had lots of different boyfriends. She is thin and pretty and really outgoing. Kat is quiet and shy. She's tall and big-boned and although she's a good athlete, she's constantly worried about being too fat. Sometimes Kat is uncomfortable with how much her friend flirts and at times she is a bit envious of all the attention Jaz gets from guys. Kat has just started going out with Jay. She spends hours on the phone telling her friend Jaz all the details of their time together. Jay is Kat's first boyfriend, and although she really likes him a lot she doesn't feel ready to start a sexual relationship.

One day a classmate announces that her parents are going away for the weekend and she's having a party. Kat has a bad flu and can't go. She's disappointed but a little relieved because it's a sleepover and she knows a bunch of guys, including Jay, are planning to crash the party. She talks with her friend Jaz the night of the party and tells her jokingly to "keep an eye on Jay."

The next day Kat finds out from another girl that Jaz and Jay were making out at the party. Kat stays away from school for two weeks, dragging out her flu symptoms as long as she can. She avoids talking to Jaz on the phone and when she does talk to her she's distant but she doesn't say anything about that night. When she goes back to school she won't look her friend in the eye. Finally, Jaz confesses to making out with Jay. She tells Kat that she feels really guilty and the only reason it happened was because she was really drunk. She tells her it didn't mean anything and that she barely remembers it. Jaz reminds Kat that she has a drinking problem, and that Kat promised she would support her and not judge her. She begs her friend to forgive her. Kat tells her it's no big deal and to just forget it.

Kat doesn't mention anything about any of this to Jay at all. The next weekend when she and Jay are making out in his car, she goes all the way with him. She feels really depressed afterwards, and the weekend after that she breaks up with him. The weekend after breaking up, Kat tries to kill herself. Kat loses her virginity, her boyfriend, her best friend and almost her life.

Why didn't Kat confront her best friend?

As a girl, Kat was brought up to believe that it wasn't OK to express anger. She was uncomfortable with her anger toward her friend so she just tried to push the feelings away. Her angry thoughts and feelings made her feel like a bad person. Kat was brought up to always think of others first. She felt guilty about how bad Jaz was feeling. She worried about her friend's drinking problem and thought to be a good friend she had to forgive her. She pretended to forgive her friend because she just wanted things to go back to the way they were, before any of this had happened. But every time she saw Jaz, she wanted to scream at her that she was a drunk and a slut. Keeping her angry feelings inside was making her feel crazy but it was just too painful to think of losing her best friend. Can you see that Kat felt she only had two choices—to lose her best friend or to suppress her anger?

Why didn't Kat confront her boyfriend?

Kat was afraid to express her anger toward her boyfriend because she was afraid she would lose him. She didn't have much confidence around guys anyway, and her self-esteem was especially fragile right at this time. She thought Jay secretly wanted to be with Jaz. Kat was certain that if she allowed herself to get angry at him he would leave her.

Why did Kat sleep with her boyfriend when she knew she wasn't ready?

The thing Kat was most afraid of was that Jay would leave her for Jaz. She thought she had to compete with her friend. That's why she slept with Jay. She thought that it would secure their relationship. Afterwards, Kat broke up with Jay because once she had slept with him her feelings of insecurity increased and her fear of losing him intensified. She wanted to leave him before he left her. After Kat slept with Jay she also felt guilty and ashamed—like she had done something wrong and dirty. She didn't enjoy the sex at all and she felt as though she had given an important part of herself away. She felt worthless—cheap. Now she understood why people used that word.

Why did Kat try to hurt herself?

It is likely that Kat has a history of suppressing her feelings—especially anger. Instead of being outraged and confronting the situation, Kat became enraged—she turned her anger inward and expressed the feelings of betrayal and rage toward herself. When Kat pretended to forgive Jaz, she cut herself off from her true feelings. At a time when she most needed a friend, her best friend had betrayed her. Kat then betrayed herself by sleeping with Jay when she wasn't ready, and afterwards she became depressed and even more anxious. She then isolated herself even more by breaking up with Jay. Finally, unable to cope with all the feelings locked up inside her, she tried to cut herself off from herself—she tried to stop having the feelings by attempting suicide.

What could Kat have done differently?

Kat did not know that there was a way to say how she felt without losing everything. If she had realized that she could express her anger in an assertive way, without losing her temper, she may have been able to get all her feelings out on the table. She could have looked Jasmine in the eye and told her in a strong but calm voice, "I care about your drinking problem but I'm really angry and I feel betrayed." Then Kat could have expressed a clear boundary by taking a time-out from their relationship with the condition that her friend get help with her drinking problem. Once her friend was in treatment she might have chosen to work on rebuilding trust. A long-term friendship like that may be worth fighting for, but only if both people are working on it.

How would handling the situation assertively have affected Kat?

If Kat could have dealt with her friend in an up-front way, her self-esteem would have been more intact. First, she would have felt better about herself for standing up to her friend, and she would have felt less of a loss if there was still some hope for their friendship. With more of her focus on herself and her long-term relationship with her best friend, Kat would feel less fear of losing her boyfriend. From this stronger place, she may have had the courage to tell him how angry she was at him. She could have seen that her boyfriend wasn't trust-worthy and broken up with him before she slept with him.

What assertive message would Kat be communicating if she handled the situation in this new way?

By being assertive with her friend and her boyfriend, Kat would be expressing her anger. She would be expressing a healthy outrage at what was an outrageous betrayal. In doing this, she would be saying to Jaz and Jay—and most important, to herself—"I have value, I am worth standing up for, I don't deserve to be treated this way." With her friend, she would have asserted a healthy boundary by saying, "I care about you but I'm not responsible for your problems."

Feeling Outraged

When girls' and women's self-esteem is eroded by demeaning and objectifying remarks we have the right to feel outraged. When our bodies are violated by rape or assault we need to have permission, without hesitation or qualification, without justification or explana-tion, to feel outraged. Women desperately need to find and reclaim the voice that says "How dare you!"

Unfortunately, little girls are shamed for expressing and in fact even feeling anger. The message to little girls is that there is something wrong with them deep inside—"rotten to the core"—if they feel anger. They are taught at a very early age to repress their angry feelings and to transmute anger into emotions that they are permitted to have, such as sadness and fear. Teen girls and adult women are often confused and humiliated when they try to stand up for themselves. To their horror they may find themselves standing before a co-worker or a boss crying and blubbering instead of speaking up in defence of themselves. The inability to connect with anger can be an enormous personal and professional handicap, and a potentially life-threatening one.

If we do not know when we are being violated, we will not know when to defend ourselves.

Feeling Enraged

Anger is a powerful life force; suppressing it takes an incredible amount of energy. When a female suppresses her anger it is usually because she is afraid. She is afraid of not being liked and not being wanted, and she is afraid of being killed. She is also afraid of losing control and hurting others, and then she fears the resulting guilt and remorse. So females become very adept at suppressing anger. But when we sit on our anger we often find that all our feelings get squashed down at the same time. After years of ignoring, pushing away, covering up and denying angry feelings, it is a common female experience for an overall deadness or flatness of body and spirit to occur. Everything that is passionate is suppressed along with the anger: sexuality, desire, enthusiasm, physical energy and joy.

The irony is that even when feelings are repressed so successfully that the person genuinely does not experience them, they do not actually go away. Repressed anger can turn into a volcanic disaster waiting to erupt or a seething undercurrent of festering resentment that poisons us and all our relationships.

"Most women have not even begun to touch this anger except to drive it inward like a rusted nail."

—Adrienne Rich

Clean Anger and Old Anger

Learning to determine the difference between clean anger and old anger is enormously important. When we find ourselves sobbing at a corny old movie we can easily determine that there is probably something in the movie that is triggering a deeper and more real pain or loss in our life. In the same way, we can learn that any situation that has the key elements can trigger a past violation and engender a huge amount of anger. In those moments we can learn to hold our reaction until we get clarity and take the time to separate what is appropriate to the current situation from what happened in the past. Holding a reaction or taking a time-out does not mean that we repress the anger.

In order to experience the anger rather than repress it, we first have to validate our right to feel it. In order to release the anger so that it does not turn inward and join the thousands of other unexpressed angers that many of us store over the years, an action is usually required to right the wrong. When anger is fresh and clean, meaning when it is related to the present violation and not attached to a whole lifetime of wrongs left unconfronted, it is not necessarily a negative or unpleasant experience.

Clean anger can feel simple and quite matter-of-fact. A powerful message delivered with equanimity: Strong words, calmly spoken.

Part II: **MIND**

The SafeTeen violence prevention work is framed by an intricate understanding of gender and power dynamics. How we are conditioned as females and males affects our relationship to ourselves and to each other, and it profoundly affects our relationship to violence. In order for a shift to occur in the deeply entrenched patterns of gender-based behaviours, we have to unravel the complex weavings of gender conditioning and examine with a clear and thoughtful mind the ways in which it impacts how we engage with power.

In Part II: MIND, we will explore the sensitive and volatile topics of power, gender, sexuality, relationships and intimacy, self-esteem, emotions, sexual harassment and sexual assault. I see these issues as profoundly multi-layered and I will attempt to dig underneath the surface in hopes of shedding light on the root causes of destructive patterns between females and males. I believe that in understanding lies the possibility for change.

Chapter 5

Gender and Power

I N THIS CHAPTER, we will look at gender issues and offer positive ways of redefining masculinity and femininity. Most important of all, we will explore ways in which both males and females can be empowered. When young women and men feel strong and secure in their respective identities, they can relate to each other in meaningful ways without the threat of violence

Falling and Flying: A Gender Progress Report

Males today sometimes say that they feel attacked for being men. They express confusion about gender relations in their personal and professional lives. They say they have become afraid to crack a joke, give a compliment or attempt to initiate a friendship with someone of the opposite sex. As a result, they sometimes feel angry, awkward and even paralyzed in their personal and professional relationships with the opposite sex.

Males are being pushed out of their comfortable positions of privilege and power. In essence, the rug is being pulled out from under them. Many intelligent and compassionate men understand that it is fair to equally share the power. Nevertheless, to be in the position of having to give up the power that you have been taught is your birthright is still a loss. Boys who were raised to believe that they would someday rule the world have grown up to live in a world that demands that they abdicate the throne that they have become accustomed to.

As males descend from power, they are feeling uncertain about everything. One young man asked in frustration, "Am I supposed to cry or break things? Will someone please just give me a clue?" The paradox is that they are being told they have all the power but they don't feel powerful at all. As they are being forced off their pedestals, the male experience is often one of feeling powerless and out of control, as though they are falling.

Females today are reaching for their full power in the world. They are breaking free from years of oppression in both their personal and professional lives. As females stride out into the larger world, they are energized and excited but they are also afraid. One young woman worried, "If I am too strong, men will feel threatened and I will never get a boyfriend." Many adult women confess that they are afraid that if they claim their full power within a relationship, they will lose their mates. In a workshop for nurses, one woman said, "If I say no to sex, my husband might go somewhere else to get it."

As well, females today know that to choose empowerment means taking full responsibility for their economic lives. The generations of gender conditioning that taught women to rely on men makes it more psychologically difficult for females to succeed financially. As well, glass ceilings are very real and hitting their heads up against these professional limits can be painful and exhausting. It's as though females are running in the same race as males with none of the preparation or conditioning—and with twice the hurdles in front of them.

Females today are also confused. For instance, girls and women are often simultaneously offended by and complimented by sexual harassment. Years of being addicted to the male gaze for affirmation of their attractiveness (and therefore their value) doesn't disappear overnight. And females are tired. They are keeping up with males in the academic and corporate worlds while still carrying the majority of the responsibility for child rearing, care giving and domestic work.

Regardless of their fears and confusion, females are moving forward and upward toward empowerment. They are taking enormous risks and discovering new strengths. However little "outer world" power girls and women actually have, their experience is often one of exhilaration because they are ascending.

Power and Empowerment

The concept of power is often thought of in a negative light and is generally associated with "power over." However, being powerful is not the same as abusing power. Traditional ideals of masculinity and femininity have provided a warped view of power. When we think of empowerment, we often think of it as something that females need more of. The truth is that empowerment for males is as important as empowerment for females. But the kinds of power that each gender needs more of is different.

Outer World Power
Traditional masculinity teaches males they must have the power to fight, to win, to be in control. This power is about money and mate-

rial possessions and status and the physical body. Because the male gender has more of these power symbols and because this type of power is so visible and absolutely controls the world, both males and females tend to consider it the most important power to have. This type of power wins and dominates. That is why I refer to it as "power over." In essence, the male world defines what is powerful and what is not.

> Males take up 70 percent of the speaking time in western culture. Even in elementary schools, when the girls get up to 40 percent, the boys get upset and say the girls are talking too much (Dale Spender). Adolescent and adult males have louder, deeper voices that carry further and can easily drown out female voices in a debate. Boy children are less inhibited about calling out and being loud. Males interrupt more often, go on send, listen less, compete and try to win in discussions, and respond more quickly because they don't tend to process emotionally first.

Inner World Power

Females traditionally have the power to intuit, to surrender and to feel. This power is about people and relationships and healing the heart and nurturing the spirit. It is power that communicates and shares. A power that rests in a belief that all people are powerful and all people deserve to be treated equally. That is why I refer to it as "power with." Because this power is invisible, not concrete, and is traditionally female, it is devalued and sometimes not even considered "real." When girls and women throw a ball, run a race (physical or political) and do business in their own way, they are told they are doing these things "like a girl." A grave insult. The realm that females occupy is diminished in the shadow of "real" power in the "real" world of men.

Males as a gender have little or no access to the inner world and avoid it at all cost because they have no idea how to navigate in that world. When forced to confront the inner world, they feel inadequate and afraid—and yes, lost. These feelings are intolerable to them so they negate the female world as much as possible. When males busy themselves obsessively in outer world activities such as work, acquiring material gain and sexual conquest, they abandon their own humanity. They cut themselves off from their own inner worlds and they are at risk of becoming profoundly lonely. Because outer world power is inherently unsatisfying and leaves the human spirit hungry, these males are also at risk of becoming abusive.

If males are to be whole and healthy human beings capable of intimacy, they desperately need to open and explore their inner worlds. They need to learn how to feel and communicate all their feelings— especially their fear and their grief, not just their anger.

Males perpetrate 89 percent of the violent crimes on this planet. There is little hope for the world if men don't heal their hearts and nurture their spirits.

Females can be afraid of embracing their full power in the world because it means taking full responsibility for themselves. Not only have females been conditioned to believe that they aren't capable of taking control of their lives, they have been taught that they aren't worthy of the status that the outer world has to offer. Many women who become successful suffer from the imposter syndrome—a pervasive fear that at any moment someone will find out that they are not worthy of their status and they will be exposed as frauds. Outer world power also represents a value system that is contrary to what females have been conditioned to believe is right and good. For example, a woman may feel guilty about making a lot of money when she is aware that other people have so little. It can be difficult to be motivated to achieve something that she has been taught to believe is "the root of all evil."

If women do not claim their right to equal material power and therefore equal power to contribute to the governing, law-making and running of the world, they will never be in control of their own lives.

Without financial independence, women cannot truly be free. For example, if a woman cannot leave a relationship because she cannot support herself and her children, then she is trapped. In order to survive she must prostitute herself either within the relationship or outside the relationship as a way of supporting herself.

If men were to embrace inner world power and women were to embrace outer world power, then both genders could begin to nurture their daughters and sons without gender stereotypes. Both mothers and fathers could show youth how to be whole human beings. Both females and males could model success and skill in the material world. Our children could have the choice to express their full potential in both worlds.

Girl Power

The phrase "Girl Power" was made popular by the singing group The Spice Girls when they were a hit in 1997. Although many parents felt threatened by the short skirts, platform shoes and especially the sexual image of the group, their enormous popularity among pre-teen girls was a force to be reckoned with. Something about these five women spoke to nine- to thirteen-year-old females, and the concept of Girl Power was a key piece of the attraction. However ambiguous the message was—and the ambiguity wasn't lost on most of their fans—The Spice Girls provided a perfect vehicle for girls all over the world to have a valuable discussion on the true meaning of Girl Power.

Asked what they think
Girl Power is, some
Grade 7 girls said:

having fun
strength
believing in yourself
confidence
girls in control
working together
girls can do anything
being equal to guys
girls being leaders

As parents and educators we need to hear what these young women were saying to us when they responded so ravenously to the concept of Girl Power. We need to respond to our daughters' hunger for affirmations of their power—not just as individuals but as girls. And I think we need to acknowledge the ways in which they are disempowered as girls.

In a society that is run by men and shines a bright light on the achievements of men, it is important to look at what females do better than males. This is not a way of putting men down but a way of focusing on the gifts that girls and women have and perhaps questioning why males in our society hold the majority of the power. It is important for females to be able to tell the truth about their experience without feeling they are putting men down.

Our society puts females down in our language, humour, attitudes, employment practices and popular media. At the same time, anything that is pro-female is assumed to be anti-male. Consider the following quote: "Feminism encourages women to leave their husbands, kill their children, practise witchcraft, destroy capitalism and become lesbian." (Pat Robertson, U.S. politician, 1992, from CATH TATE CARDS, London, U.K.). The word "feminism" is often considered to be synonymous with male bashing; in fact, it simply means "a doctrine or movement that advocates equal rights for women" *(Collins Dictionary).*

The truth is females are wired by hormones and brain patterns to be better than males at certain things. Of course there are always exceptions to every rule, but it is generally true that females:

• read body language and emotion better;

• begin speaking earlier, are better readers, understand what's said better, learn foreign languages more easily and are better communicators (doesn't it make you think we should be world leaders?);

• are better drivers;

• have greater stamina and energy, live longer, are less likely to get major diseases and are more likely to recover if we do;

• see more of the world in one glance because we have wider peripheral vision.

We do see the world differently than men do. In SafeTeen workshops we encourage girls to trust their own vision/version of the world.

Did You Know?
To be a girl and live in a world where the majority of the world leaders are male, most books are written by males, most heroes in movies and in history are males and even God is portrayed as a male can have a profound effect on female self-esteem. The history books we read in school (his-story) tell us far more about male achievements and experiences than female. It is important for us as parents and educators to balance that out a little bit by making a point of telling our girls some of the things the female gender is famous for. Here are some examples of female prowess.

Did you know women invented: the bullet proof vest, the fire escape, the navy signal flare, the circular saw, solar heating, invisible glass, computer programming, email, bridges and canals, pneumatic tires, the white line that divides the road, ice cream cones, pottery and weaving, how to keep foods by freezing?

Did you know that a woman wrote the first novel? *The Tale of Genji,* was written by Lady Murasaki Shikibu in eleventh-century Japan.

Did you know a woman was responsible for ending child labour?

Abraham Lincoln won the right to vote for one million American people (African American men). Did you know that Susan B. Anthony won the right to vote for 26 million American women?

("Did You Know" items from *Why It's Great to be a Girl* by Jacqueline Shannon, Warner Books, 1994.)

We have to ask why women haven't been acknowledged for their achievements and what effect this has on female self-concept. In a list of Nobel Prize statistics we can clearly see how females have been left out. The first Nobel Prize was given out in 1901. And the winners are:

Physics: 2 women / 157 men; Chemistry: 3 women / 129 men; Economics: 0 women have ever won; Peace: 10 women / 77 men; Literature: 9 women / 87 men;
("NoBelles" from *MS Magazine,* October/November 2000 volume 10, number 6)

If someone accuses you of doing something "like a girl," learn to say thank you and honour the inherent value in the way females tend to do things.

How Gender Stereotypes Affect Our Relationships

Even today, outdated notions about gender can still strongly influence our thinking and behaviour. We must challenge ourselves to go beyond the stereotypes about masculinity and femininity. Stereotypes keep males from being nurturing or leading emotionally fulfilling lives (valuing and communicating their feelings, paying attention to others' feelings) and keep females from expressing their desires and abilities (because they are too concerned about taking care of other people's feelings). In this next section, we'll examine how sex-role stereotypes affect teenagers as well as society at large.

What Does It Mean to "Stereotype"?

Stereotypes are generalized beliefs about people based on limited information or experiences. Because the limited information and experiences are commonly believed to be true, they are projected onto all people of specific types. The types are categorized by things such as race, culture, religion and gender.

There is no such thing as a positive stereotype. When we stereotype, we erase the uniqueness of each individual. All stereotypes are limiting. People just want to be seen and valued for who they are.

People come in all shapes and sizes and colours. This is not just true of our physical appearance; we come in all shapes and sizes and colours on the inside as well. When we stereotype people, we are creating boxes with labels on them and stuffing all the wonderful, unique individuals of all shapes and sizes into the very limited, very square little boxes.

For example, some common stereotypes are that black people are good dancers, Asian people are smart, male athletes are dumb, red-haired people have bad tempers, women are bad drivers. These people have all been placed in boxes and other people will tend to relate to them according to the labels on the boxes. Unwittingly, some people who are labeled in this way will even begin to believe these things about themselves and act accordingly, thereby reinforcing the stereotype.

Why Is Stereotyping People According to Gender a Problem?

Traditional stereotypes of masculinity and femininity are almost complete opposites. For example,

- a man is strong / a woman is weak:
- a man is aggressive / a woman is passive;
- a man is in control of his feelings / a woman is overly emotional;
- a man is a leader / a woman is a follower.

Notice that the female stereotype often has a more negative slant. If we impose limits on males and females in our language and in our expectations we contribute toward conditioning our girl and boy children toward those limited standards. Boys will not be encouraged to explore their full range of feelings and girls will not stretch themselves to achieve as much as they are capable of.

Polarizing the genders makes it very difficult for males and females to communicate with each other. The female/male stereotypes have the two genders so far apart it's like we are two different species from two different planets. That's a lot of distance to cover in order to connect! The most serious problem with stereotyping by gender is that it sets up a dynamic where females are likely to be victims and males are likely to be victimizers/aggressors. Let's examine how this works for both females and males.

Females As Targets of Violence

When females are perceived as vulnerable, they are more often targeted as victims. There are many subtle and not so subtle ways that female social conditioning teaches girls and women to give up their power. Some of these ways are:

- being reactive instead of pro-active (only speaking up if asked a question; moving away instead of saying "Stop")
- asking permission to speak ("May I ask a question?")
- being modest (not claiming credit when credit is due)

- ending with a questioning tone sentences that are statements
- approval-seeking behaviours (punctuating their dialogue with "You know?")
- not finishing sentences ...
- referring to others' previous points ("As you said earlier ...")
- overapologizing (especially when it's not their fault)
- allowing men to fill in names, figures, dates
- allowing interruptions
- crying when angry
- not speaking up
- using a too quiet or childlike voice
- smiling when making strong statements
- avoiding confrontation by conceding
- not making eye contact
- fidgeting and other childlike body language
- not defending their boundaries (not saying "No")

Although they are not in any way at fault for being victimized, these subtle and unconscious ways of giving up power make females easy targets. To make even seemingly small changes in these patterns of behaviour, for instance, saying "sorry" less often, can have a profound effect on a female's sense of self and how she is perceived in the world.

Snipping Your "Sorries"
Most people know someone, usually a female, who says "sorry" too often. Females tend to be more self-effacing and self-blaming than males and are generally more guilty of overusing the word "sorry." It has been discovered that people who overapologize get respected less. They also are more likely to be harassed, bullied and even assaulted. In the business world it has been discovered that employees who are able to field complaints from unhappy clients without using the word "sorry" are better able to defuse the complaint without escalation. Of course there will always be a place for the word "sorry." It is not our aim to eradicate it from the language altogether. It is the unnecessary and especially the inappropriate "sorries" that we are on the lookout for. For example, if someone isn't watching where they are going and

bumps into you, it would be extremely common—but unnecessary—for the person who was not at fault to say "sorry." If someone is pushing to the front of the line while boarding a bus and rudely pushes past you, it would be inappropriate for you to apologize. These are obvious examples and good ones to work with.

The more difficult situations are the ones that are more subtle. For instance, if you need to ask someone for assistance it is not necessary to begin your request with "Sorry, but could you help me ..." If you feel you may be imposing, it would be more assertive to say something like "I need some assistance, would this be a good time?" Another example would be the very common telephone response, "No, I'm sorry, my mom's not home." Is it your fault? There is no reason to apologize in this instance. It would be equally polite to say, "My mom's not home right now, can I take a message please?" There are many ways of being respectful without saying sorry.

Many girls and women who work on getting rid of the inappropriate "sorries" from their vocabulary find that over time a profound change occurs, resulting in a shift in "emotional posture." The effect of this shift is a deepening of the sense of "I have a right to be here." If we can claim our right to exist, we are more able to feel we have the right to defend our personal space, our beliefs and our bodies.

Self-esteem is based on self-acceptance. That means acceptance of all our thoughts and feelings. Girls aren't supposed to have angry or sexual or selfish thoughts and feelings; in order to be "feminine" they are forced to deny self. If self does not exist, one cannot defend it.

For an exercise on "Snipping Your Sorries," see page 275.

Males As Aggressors

The common social conditioning for boys and men is to deny their vulnerability and act out aggression. Because of this some men abuse their power. Unfortunately, male violence is accepted as "normal" in our culture. Male conditioning instructs boys and men to dominate in other, more subtle ways as well.

Males abuse their power by:

- using a loud voice
- taking up the majority of talking time
- standing too close
- interrupting
- delivering monologues (instead of having conversations)
- never admitting uncertainty (can't ask for directions when lost)
- never saying "I don't know"
- sexual harassment (objectifying females as a way of asserting dominance)
- inappropriate touching (to assert dominance)
- abusing power (using status, physical size or finances to dominate)
- making demeaning or trivializing comments
- physically threatening gestures (making a fist)
- demonstrations of anger (hitting or throwing objects, swearing and yelling)

It is important for young men, especially in their developmental stages, to receive support and a strong affirmation for being the kind, sensitive beings that they are. And it is important for young women to receive support and affirmation for being the powerful, pro-active beings that they are.

Stereotypes at Work in Dating and Interpersonal Relationships

Stereotypical male gender role rules include:
1. The guy has to ask the girl out.
2. The guy has to drive.
3. The guy has to decide where they are going.
4. The guy has to pay.
5. The guy has to initiate intimacy.
6. The guy has to be successful sexually (using whatever means it takes to wear down her resistance and score: liquor, declarations of love, persistent manoeuvres or even force).

Stereotypical female gender role rules include:
1. The girl has to look and act sexy.
2. The girl has to wait by the phone.
3. The girl has to let the guy choose the activities.
4. The girl has to let the guy drive (even if it's her car).
5. The girl has to take care of the guy's feelings (laugh at his jokes and listen with interest to his stories).
6. The girl has to meet the guy's sexual needs (or get out of it somehow without hurting his feelings).

You may be thinking, "Aren't these rules really outdated? Haven't times changed?" Our conversations with males and females of all ages indicate that people continue to act in gender-stereotyped ways. The good thing is that today's teens know the rules aren't healthy. They are actively struggling with gender roles and are making some changes. Teenage females insist on paying their own way much more often than they used to, and teen guys are letting them. Guys admit that it feels like too much pressure to have to come up with all the money and make all the decisions. Teen guys are also expressing an assertive desire for females to take more risks in initiating relationships, and more young women are claiming their right to ask guys out. However, these are small steps and a minority of teens are making them. The gender roles are very deeply rooted.

What Changes Do Guys Have to Make?

Many adult men who are in their forties and fifties today, when asked to reflect on their youth, have to admit having done things during their dating years that today would legally be considered sexual assault. And surveys show that a majority of younger males still believe that it is all right to force a woman to have sex under certain conditions, such as "if she is leading a man on" or "if they have had sex before." Some males feel the girl owes the guy sex if he paid for the date. The strength of this opinion increases with the amount of money spent.

Because all males grow up in a society that continues to reinforce stereotypical masculinity, most guys need to learn about the dynamics of acquaintance rape. In particular, males need to learn to pay more respectful attention to any signs of unease that females on dates may be feeling. If a guy is picking up mixed messages from his girlfriend, he shouldn't take advantage of her uncertainty or lack of assertiveness. It is not solely the girl's responsibility to say "No" clearly. It is up to the guy to make sure that he's not doing something she doesn't want to do. He can ask for clarification. If the girl is acting afraid or confused he could say, "Hey what's up? I'm picking up mixed messages. You know, if you're not sure you want to, then that's OK."

To explore what constitutes consent, see exercise on page 297.

The average age for men who "date" rape is 18 ½ years.

When guys free themselves from the rigid sex-role stereotypes, it opens the door to the possibility of equal and healthy relationships and closes the door to acquaintance rape.

Guys can have their own boundaries. Given the opportunity to be honest, most males admit that they don't want to have sex all the time and that there are people that they wouldn't want to have sex with. If a young man is in love with someone else, it may not matter how attractive the girl he is with in the moment is, he may not want to have sex with her. If a girl is too drunk, he may feel repulsed and not want to have sex with her. If the girl is anxious or afraid or confused, he may not want to have sex with her. If the guy is clear that he doesn't want to have sex with a girl who is hesitating, he can set his own boundary about this. He could say, "If you're not sure, then I don't want to go any further. I don't want to have sex with someone who isn't sure she wants to." This would take a lot of maturity and it would mean that the guy would have to become more aware and appreciative of both his own and others' feelings. Males conditioned to ignore their own feelings will not likely pay attention to female hesitations or fears.

Males need to get rid of any belief they may hold that it is ever all right to force a woman to have sex. They need to fully accept that even when a girl has said "yes," she still has the right to change her mind. And finally, males need to examine the conditioning they have received that compels them to dominate women and to "score."

Don't Girls Have to Make Changes Too?
Traditional female conditioning teaches passivity and indirectness. Girls are famous for giving mixed messages. Having poor boundaries and limited skills to defend them means girls often don't know how to

say "no" or they say "no" too late. Being overly concerned with guys' needs and feelings causes young women to give up their most basic rights. Surveys show that young women often believe that they deserve to be assaulted, that they ask for it by the way they dress or behave, that if they get a guy turned on they have to finish what they started, that if they have had sex with anyone in the past, they don't have a right to say "no" in the present. Females also tend to believe that all males want to have sex at all times and males who don't want to have sex are weird or gay.

It is very common for girls to feel they owe the guy some sexual activity if a guy pays for the date. Girls need to take responsibility for themselves financially, which will enable them to feel more powerful and in control. When she has her own spending money and her own car or cab fare, a teen woman is not dependent on the guy for gifts, treats or necessities like a ride home. As well, a girl who has her financial independence usually has better self-esteem. She is less likely to put up with abusive behaviours and more likely to assert boundaries.

Girls will be safer if they have better boundaries, better self-esteem and more financial independence. They will also be safer if they make wiser choices such as not using alcohol or drugs. One of the most important things a female can do to keep herself safe is to listen to her intuition. If the person she is with or the situation she is in feels wrong, she needs to do something to make herself safe. She can say "No" strongly, resist strongly, push the guy away, get out of the car, make noise, yell for a friend, leave the party, call a cab, call her parents, ask for help, run.

Remember: If it feels wrong, get away!

Chapter 6

rocking the gender-power boat and making waves...

Boundaries and Relationships

L EARNING TO IDENTIFY and in some cases reconstruct boundaries is the first step in learning to be assertive. If we do not know where our boundaries are, we will not know when to defend ourselves, either verbally or physically. Without good boundaries, we can't have healthy relationships. If we understand where our boundaries are, we can build relationships based on trust and equality — relationships in which each partner respects and supports the other.

What Is a Boundary?

Remember the image of the hard house to break into? A boundary is a "force field" or invisible fence that surrounds us and has an alarm system to alert us when our emotional or physical space is being invaded. If our boundaries were repeatedly invaded when we were children, our fences have probably been damaged. This damage can occur in many ways. For example, calling a child "bad" or "stupid" or "lazy" can damage emotional boundaries and lower self-esteem to the point where the child no longer feels s/he has a right to be treated well. Being aggressively affectionate (smothering children with hugs and kisses when they are not in the mood) communicates to them that they are not in control of how and by whom they are touched. This can put them at higher risk for inappropriate touching.

Physical discipline of any kind undermines a child's boundaries. Even unwanted verbal affection can make a child's boundaries unclear. More overt abuse such as beating or sexually abusing a child results in severe boundary damage. By the time the child whose boundaries have been consistently violated reaches adolescence, s/he has usually survived this damage in one of two ways:

1. S/he has no boundaries at all and does not experience an "alarm" until it is too late. This person does not know how to say "No" and gets taken advantage of repeatedly. This person may even violate her/his own boundaries by not having a sense of who is safe to share themselves with verbally or physically. For example, have you ever told someone something personal and then had that information used against you later? That is a good example of a situation in which you might want to examine your boundaries around who is safe to confide in.

2. S/he has constructed a brick wall around her/himself so that no one can get in. The problem with this is that it is very isolating and the person who "walls themselves in" also can't get out. If we are trapped, we are no longer in a fortress, we are in a prison.

Example: Do you ever feel isolated and lonely because you don't trust your real feelings with anyone? That is an example of someone who has walled themselves in. If you feel that way, you may want to examine the possibility of opening up your boundaries a little — if you feel safe enough to do so. Healthy boundaries are strong but flexible. They can change depending on the situation and how we are feeling in any given moment. Remember that you are the only judge of your own boundaries.

As you read the following story, see if you can identify points in the story where having good boundaries would have been useful for Jill.

Jack and Jill: Going All the Way

Jack and Jill have been going out for three months. Jack is a very popular guy in school and Jill feels she is lucky to have him as her boyfriend. Jack has been pressuring Jill to go all the way since their first time alone together, two and a half months ago. Every time they're alone, he tries to get her to have sex with him. So far, they have done everything but actually have intercourse. Jill feels like she loves Jack but she doesn't feel good about how far they've gone and doesn't want to go any further. She has a really hard time saying "no" to Jack though and feels trapped and anxious every time they start making out. Jack gets really turned on as soon as they start kissing and she feels like it's her fault and that she has to do something about it. He tells her she has to finish what she started.

One evening Jill's parents are out of town and Jack is over watching movies. Jill is anxious all evening because she knows Jack will try something. He already made a joke before he came over about " bringing his pj's." Jill can't think of a good excuse for why he can't spend the night. Part of her wants him to stay with her because she doesn't like being alone in the house at night. But she knows he'll want to do it and she knows she doesn't want that.

After the first movie, Jack starts telling her he loves her and then he suggests they go to the bedroom. He pulls a package of condoms out of his pocket and tries to pull her up off the couch. When she resists, he gets quiet and turns away from her. He says it means she doesn't love him. He says if she loved him she'd want to as much as he does. Jill tells him she does love him and that she does want to. When he asks what the problem is, in a pissed off way, she doesn't know what to say. He tells her he knows she's not a virgin, that her old boyfriend told everyone all about how hot she was. He says this as though it's a compliment but Jill feels sick inside. She feels like crying and she just wants him to hold her. She senses that if she says "no" this time, he'll leave. Jack gets up and leads her to the bedroom and she goes with him.

Let's take a look at what was going on for Jill. See if you can add any of your own thoughts to the questions posed.

Why does Jill feel like it's her fault when Jack gets turned on?

Like many girls, Jill feels that the way she dresses and behaves gets guys turned on. She is instructed by magazines and movies to look and act as sexually attractive as she can. Secretly, she likes it when Jack finds her attractive and she wants him to want her. Then he does want her and when things get out of control she feels guilty, as though she is responsible for pushing him too far. She believes that he can't stop once he gets to a certain point in his arousal. Jill feels that she has "started something" and that she has to "finish it."

Does she have to "finish what she started"?

What Jill doesn't understand is that Jack's desire belongs to him and is entirely his responsibility. Regardless of how strong Jack's desire is, he is capable of stopping his sexual activity if he chooses to. Jack doesn't have the right under any circumstances to coerce Jill into finishing anything. If his arousal level is uncomfortable for him, he is perfectly capable of finishing it himself.

Jill told Jack that she wanted to have sex, when she knew she wasn't ready to start a sexual relationship with him. Isn't that giving him mixed messages?

Sometimes girls give mixed messages. They do this usually because they have mixed feelings. When Jill is aroused, she may feel like she does want to have sex, but when she's feeling anxious about being pressured, she isn't in touch with her desire and she only feels confused and anxious. She may feel too shy to talk to Jack so openly about her desire and how it comes and goes. His desire seems to be there all the time and he wields it as proof of his love. She fears that maybe there's something wrong with her, that maybe she's frigid. She fears that maybe Jack is right and this means she doesn't love him. Her body and her rhythms of desire are all new to her and she's confused. It's difficult to communicate clearly when we are confused. Jill says "yes" when she means "No" because she is afraid to tell the truth about how she feels.

Why does Jill give in so easily and follow Jack into the bedroom?

By the time Jill finally has sex with Jack that night, she had been resisting his persistent advances for almost three months. She has run out of excuses and delay tactics. She senses that he won't wait any longer without getting angry. Jill feels lucky to have Jack as a boyfriend, which is a sign that she has low self-esteem. She may not feel she could easily get another boyfriend. She may have been dumped by her last boyfriend and was left feeling insecure. Jill's self-esteem is so low at this point that she feels any boyfriend is better than no boyfriend at all. Jill's fear of being left is compounded by the fact that she is afraid to be in the house all night by herself. She doesn't want Jack to get angry and leave. If Jack leaves feeling sexually frustrated, he might go get it somewhere else. Even if he hasn't actually said this to her, Jill fears it as a possibility.

What could Jill have done differently?

Jill could have been assertive with Jack. When he pulled out the condoms and started pressuring her to go to the bedroom, she could have put her hand up in a "stop" gesture, made good eye contact and said, "Jack, I'm not ready for this." If he continued to pressure her, she could have repeated her message three times, just like a broken record. No matter what he said after that, Jill could have backed up her message by just giving him strong, consistent eye contact. Doing that while holding your silence says "I meant what I said." When Jack started pulling her up off the couch, Jill could have stood up and walked toward the door, saying, "I don't feel comfortable with how things are going. If you're going to keep pressuring me, I want you to leave." She has the option of repeating this message three times if necessary.

Isn't asking him to leave a little extreme? Her boyfriend wouldn't hurt her, would he?

Jill needs to give very strong messages in this situation. She is in a very vulnerable position. Most sexual assaults happen in the woman's own home. The vast majority of them by someone the woman knows. Jill being home alone makes her a very easy target.

Is there anything Jill could have done to stop things from getting to this point?

Jill had a previous experience of being sexually active. After that relationship ended Jill could have done some serious thinking about the wisdom of being sexually active with someone she doesn't know very well and hasn't had time to build trust with. If she had spent some time thinking about what she wanted and needed from a relationship, maybe Jill could have told Jack where she was at when they were first getting to know each other. Jill could have been assertive. As soon as she realized that he wanted to go faster than she was willing to go, Jill could have looked Jack in the eye and told him that she wasn't planning on having a sexually active relationship at this time in her life. She could have told him she was wanting to work on trust and companionship first.

It is a good idea for us to prepare ourselves in advance for the possibility of having to assert a boundary. It is hard to be thinking clearly in the middle of making out with someone. Their desire, your desire, all the various pressures and fears can get in the way of clear thinking. If you have decided ahead of time what you want and don't want and rehearsed exactly how you want to say it, being clear will be much easier. Also, it's important to communicate early in the relationship what your needs and limits are.

Jill needed to be up-front with Jack, the very first time they were together, that she didn't want sex.

If Jill told Jack she didn't want sex, wouldn't he just dump her?

If Jill had been true to her feelings early on she would have found out a lot sooner what kind of guy Jack was. If he chose to leave her then, at least she would have had less at stake. Her emotional investment at two weeks would be a lot less than at three months — especially if she hadn't slept with him yet.

What if Jill is assertive but when Jack gets turned on he pressures her anyway?

Jill could have reminded Jack each time they were alone and before they started kissing that things were not going any further. In the moment when the guy is aroused is not always the best time to tell him you don't want to go any further. If he has not received any previous message from you to slow down, he will not have put any restraint on his desire and it is more likely that he will feel frustrated and pressure you to continue.

There are obvious and more subtle ways for people to pressure you. Jack turned away from Jill when she resisted him. This body language communication is a subtle threat. When a guy withdraws in that way, it is an indirect way of saying he will leave if you don't comply with his wishes. This is a form of emotional blackmail and it's an unfair play of power. It would have been assertive of Jill to tell him right then that she didn't like it when he did that. She could have told him how it made her feel and that she didn't think it was fair. Each and every time Jack pressured her in any way Jill would have been in her right to tell him she was feeling pressured and that she didn't like it.

Jack is so pushy. What if Jill just can't stop him?

The most effective action that Jill could have taken to avoid what happened that night would have been to avoid being in the situation at all. Jill could have predicted that Jack would try something that night and made a choice not to have him over. With a pushy guy like Jack, it would have been a wiser choice not to let him know her parents were away. If she was afraid to be on her own she could have set it up ahead of time to have a girlfriend over or to stay over at a friend's or relative's for the weekend. Jill also had the option of being assertive with her parents and telling them she didn't feel safe being alone.

Some attacks are not avoidable. If Jack starts to force Jill to have sex with him, she has the right to fight back. Taking a self-defence course is a really good idea. All women have the right to know how to defend themselves. In a self-defence course Jill would learn where to hit him and what with. She would learn all his vulnerable points. Even if she doesn't know any fancy moves, strong physical resistance is often enough to let a guy know you mean it and are willing to fight. Women who resist strongly, especially at the beginning of an attack, and yell as loud as they can and then run as soon as they can, get away most often.

If Jill does get raped, isn't it sort of her fault for inviting Jack over when no one was home?

Jill has made an unwise choice. It is never the woman's fault if she is raped. Jill is having some serious problems with her boundaries. If she doesn't know where her boundaries are, she won't know when to start defending them.

The Stolen Word

When someone's boundaries are damaged, it can feel impossible to say "No". This is very common for girls and women because female children receive such consistent and pervasive messages to be good and obedient and not make a fuss. To disagree, resist or confront can produce extreme anxiety for girls and women. Even in the face of physical danger or loss of self, they may feel incapable of saying "No". In a sense, female upbringing robs us of the ability to say "No"— and we end up doing things we don't want to do. Few adult women can say they actively chose and felt in control of their first sexual experience. Many women will identify their first sexual experience in much the same way as a nurse did in a 1999 assertiveness workshop: "I had sex with the first boy who tried. It wasn't that I wanted to and it wasn't that he forced me — I just didn't say "No."

Most teenage girls will identify with the experience of feeling compelled to do what is expected of them—get in the car, go to the party—even though a voice in their head is clearly saying, "Bad idea, very bad idea!" In this next scenario, Anna is a sixteen-year-old girl who is on a first date with an older guy.

Anna and Rick: The First Date

(excerpted from *The Last Chance Café* by Anita Roberts, Polestar)

Before Anna had a chance to ask where they were going, Rick turned into a parking lot. Sans Souci Motel, the sign said. Anna's worry about not being mature enough turned from a nibbling into a gnawing. She looked up at him. He was looking at her and smiling. It was a hungry smile.

"Now you just wait right here, sweetheart, and I'll be right back," he said. He was in charge. He knew what he was doing. Anna felt as though an ancient signal in her body had begun to change her from skin and bone to a more malleable substance. Something soft and fluffy and timid. She felt it first in her face as she returned his smile. Her cheeks plumped out like bread dough. The skin around her eyes followed the upward curve of her putty lips with acquiescent crinkles.

"OK," she said. Her eyes dropped to the pattern on her skirt. She traced each fat teardrop shape carefully with her finger. The late October sun shone coolly on her lap, making the colours bright.

While Rick was gone, Anna felt an overwhelming desire to run. Her legs twitched and her breath came in shallow gasps, but a voice deep inside whispered, "Don't move, little rabbit." Anna shivered and the hair on the back of her neck prickled. The paisleys blurred. Rick came back to the car.

"So, we're all set ... Mrs. Smith!" His grin was sharp. Anna could see his teeth gleaming at her wetly. Somehow she got her body out of the car. She caught the glint of metal in his hand as they approached the motel room door. She was mesmerized by the key fumbling briefly at the hole and then sliding smoothly in with a quick twist. She felt it, that twist, in the bottom of her womb like a sharp pinched NO! The door swung wide and she felt as though she were falling. His hand was at her back, just at that vulnerable place below the ribcage, where there is no resistance.

He guided her gently toward the bed. If he had touched her roughly, she would have fought him off. "Wait a minute! You can't make me do this!" she would have said. If he had touched her on her shoulder, she would have shrugged him off. On her bum, and she would have said, "Hold it right there, buddy. No one treats me like that!" But that in-between place on her back was open and full of fear. His sweaty hand was where she had no defence. He pushed her effortlessly, as a strong wind would bend a small tree to the ground.

Is it hard for you to understand how Anna could "let" this happen to her?

If you find yourself thinking, "No way! I would never put up with that!" this is a sign you have good healthy boundaries. If you find yourself judging Anna and thinking she is pathetic for "allowing" this to happen to her, this indicates that you may not fully understand what it is like to have had your boundaries damaged. It is natural to lack empathy when we haven't had a personal experience of something to identify with. It may also be difficult for us to admit that we could be that vulnerable. Our aversion to this vulnerability may cause us to judge someone in Anna's situation as stupid or weak. It's important to have compassion for Anna in this story because what happened is not her fault. Anna, like so many girls and women, has had her "No" stolen. Just being female in a society which expects girls and women to always consider others' feeling before their own puts us at risk of being taken advantage of—both in small and profoundly damaging ways.

Boundaries within Relationships

When we are in intimate relationships—whether they are with family, friends or romantic partners—it can become difficult to find and assert our boundaries. Our own needs can get lost in the intensity of the other person's needs and our fear of losing connection can inhibit us from being as firm as we need to be. As well, our genuine caring and desire to please or protect someone we love can cause us to put our own needs aside. When we do this often enough, it can become difficult to find our own needs at all. Asserting a boundary with a stranger or someone we don't know well or care deeply about can be uncomfortable and even scary but at least the boundary is clear. With loved ones the place where the other person ends and we begin can be fuzzy.

Here are some things to remember about boundaries:
1. Your information belongs to you. You can choose what to share with your partner. Keeping something sacred by keeping it private is not the same thing as keeping secrets. In a situation where you have been clear about what your boundaries are and what you have shared with your partner is later used against you in a moment of anger or shared without your permission with someone else, this is an indication that your boundaries are not being respected by your partner.

2. It is important to go slowly. Sometimes it is not easy to know for sure whether or not it is safe to expose your innermost secrets with someone—especially if you have not known them for very long.

3. If you're not sure, ask your body. Your body will instinctively react when your boundaries are being crossed. Signs of fear and anxiety are tightness in the solar plexus; held breath or shallow breathing; sweaty palms; nails digging into palms. Anger can be identified by tight jaw, tense stomach, clenched fists, held or shallow breathing. You may shrink away, cringe or step back without deciding to. You may feel trapped or cornered.

Trust your body reactions. The body doesn't lie.

4. Communicate your boundaries. People aren't mind readers. It is unlikely that your partner will know where your boundaries are so it is important to be clear about them beforehand. It is also important to think about them beforehand and make some decisions about what your limits are so you are prepared.

Reconstructing Personal Boundaries

If our personal boundaries have been damaged, we need to rebuild them. In order to rebuild boundaries we need to learn assertive ways of defending our boundaries appropriately and effectively when they are threatened. Then we need to practise defending these boundaries in a safe and controlled atmosphere.

Boundary exercises can teach us how to identify where our boundaries are now, how to adjust them according to the situation, and how to "re-wire" and then tune in to the alarms so that the boundaries can be defended. The result is a feeling of empowerment and a sense of control over who we allow into our space, when it is safe to let them in and how close (physically or emotionally) we want them to get. By learning about personal boundaries, we come to understand that we have a choice about how we interact with other people. When we learn how to exercise that choice, we reclaim the stolen "No."

The exercises on boundaries outlined in Part IV help us to identify what it feels like to be in control of our boundaries. It's important not just to have a mental picture of what our boundaries feel like but to experience it in our bodies. When we know what it feels like to be safe, we can more easily identify when we are feeling unsafe.

For exercises about boundaries, see page 276.

What Does a Healthy Relationship Look Like?

As we learned in the last section, we cannot have a healthy relationship without healthy boundaries. In this section we will take a look at some of the other qualities of a healthy relationship: Respect, Acceptance, Trust, Equality, Conflict and Safety.

Respect
In healthy relationships there is mutual respect:
1. both partners respect each other's decisions and choices;

2. both partners really listen to each other;

3. both partners take responsibility for meeting their own needs;

4. both partners accept the limits asserted by their partner.

With mutual respect, there's no room for name-calling, put-downs, sarcasm, denigrating jokes or gestures. People who do these things are abusive. The longer you stay in a relationship with an abusive person, the harder it is to leave. When we don't have self-respect, we will likely be drawn to people who will be disrespectful of us. Disrespect is very common in relationships and is a clear sign of an unhealthy relationship. Lack of respect for self and others is a result of low self-esteem. If you find yourself constantly putting your partner down it is a clear sign that your own self-esteem is low.

Respect yourself and your right to a healthy relationship.

Acceptance

In a healthy relationship, you both recognize that you can't change the other person. It is possible to learn respectful and supportive ways of letting your partner know that you need their behaviour to change. There is a difference between feeling critical of your partner's behaviour and feeling critical of who your partner is. Two key things to watch out for in your partner and in yourself:

1. The Controller: The only person you can change is yourself. You can't force another person to be who you want them to be. If one partner changes their behaviour because of being controlled, manipulated, coerced or threatened, they have not really changed. If the changes don't come from an internal motivation to change, the change is neither permanent nor trustworthy.

2. The Chameleon: Sometimes people try to become who they perceive the other person wants them to be. People learn this approval-seeking behaviour in order to survive as children. They can be very skilled at pretending they are everything you ever dreamed of. The person who has fallen into this pattern is not being their authentic self. They have become a chameleon, and like the chameleon, they will continue to change colours in order to gain their partner's approval. In the end, they gain nothing that is real and lasting and what they lose is their own identity.

When there is acceptance in a relationship, you have a strong belief in yourself and your own values and you are not compelled to change in order to please or appease your partner. In other words, you accept yourself. As well, you are not obsessed with changing your partner to be someone they're not. In other words, you accept your partner.

In a healthy relationship, differences are seen as interesting and sometimes challenging: they are opportunities to learn about yourself and each other.

Trust

Without trust there is no relationship. Three basic trust issues are jealousy, freedom and loyalty.

1. Jealousy: This is one of the most powerful human emotions. What jealousy actually is, is deep fear of loss. Because we all experience moments of insecurity, it is normal to feel jealousy sometimes.

In a healthy relationship, jealousy might feel like a rush of anxiety accompanied by insecure thoughts. You can tell your partner you feel jealous and ask for reassurance. Jealousy can be easily comforted by a hug and some words of reassurance. In a healthy relationship you can have close relationships with other people of both sexes. Flirting is playful and both people are allowed to play. When you trust each other, playful flirting doesn't feel like a threat.

In an unhealthy relationship, jealousy will feel like an all-consuming obsession, accompanied by thoughts of self-hatred and violent images. You keep your jealousy a secret and feed on it. You constantly ask for reassurance and it's never enough. You feel paranoid and don't trust your partner out of your sight.

Other signs of jealousy in an unhealthy relationship are: you use jealousy to control and demand that your partner restrict their freedom to be who they are; you use jealousy to isolate and don't allow any friendships outside your relationship; you use your partner's jealousy to manipulate by flirting when you know it will make them insecure.

2. Freedom: This is one of the most basic human rights. Not just freedom to come and go and make our own choices, but freedom to be ourselves. We all deserve the freedom to choose who our friends are (and have both male and female friends); choose our activities, sports, jobs and studies based on our own needs; be social and playful and take pleasure in other people's company; feel attractions for other people and not act on them; choose our image (how we dress, wear our hair, etc.); spend time outside our relationship with other people; spend time alone; keep some personal things sacred and private and not be unfairly questioned about any or all of the above.

3. Loyalty: When you entrust a person with your heart and your body and perhaps your deepest secrets, you have the right to expect their loyalty. If there is loyalty in a relationship you will have a partner who stands by you when you need physical, material or emotional support; comes to your defence if people say hurtful things about you when you are not there; doesn't talk about you behind your back; takes your side when you are under public attack, even if s/he doesn't agree with your position at the time; honours your boundaries and limits; keeps your secrets sacred and honours your right to privacy; is truthful with you at all times and is sexually and emotionally committed to you for the duration of the relationship.

Trust is something that grows based on your experiences together. If it becomes clear that the person you're with doesn't trust you or isn't trustworthy, remember: *Without trust, there is no relationship.* People who have deeply rooted abandonment issues or very low self-esteem may be too fearful and insecure to be trusting or trustworthy.

Equality

It is important to have equal power in a relationship so one person's needs aren't getting met at the expense of the other. It is important to have some clear boundaries around whose needs are whose and who is responsible for meeting them. In a healthy relationship you genuinely care about the other person's feelings. You are invested in both of you getting your needs met. You are willing to negotiate around whose needs are going to be met when there is a conflict.

Here are some basic guidelines around meeting needs and establishing equality in a relationship:

1. It is not your job to meet your partner's needs. Choosing to meet someone's needs and feeling you have to are different. Each person is ultimately responsible for their own satisfaction, happiness and fulfillment in every area of their lives.

2. Not all your needs will be met by your partner. One person cannot possibly be everything you need. It is not realistic or even healthy to

expect you can be everything to someone or that you will get all your needs met by one person. In order to have all your needs met, you will have to look to friends, family and most of all yourself. Intimacy through sex is one need that can only be met by your partner (and of course yourself) without causing a breakdown of trust and safety in a relationship.

3. Sometimes it is OK to put your own needs aside. Some give and take in a relationship is a sign of unselfishness and genuine caring. This is true for things such as who will rub whose back, which movies you will see, how much time you will spend together and apart, spending time with your partner's family or friends when you don't feel like it or perhaps spending the evening watching TV with your partner instead of going to a party because s/he isn't feeling well.

4. Some needs are not negotiable. Our body is our most sacred place. If we do not want to be touched, we have the right to defend that need at all times. If we do not want to engage in sexual activity, no matter how desperately our partner wants it, we have a right to assert our need for space. If we permit sexual contact when we don't want it, we have to disassociate from our bodies and this abandonment of self should never be expected or required of us. We should never be coerced or manipulated into crossing this sacred boundary and we should never be emotionally or physically punished for defending it.

Signs of an Equal Relationship:

- *you make decisions regarding your sexual (and other) activities together;*
- *you ask each other for clarification if you are getting mixed messages;*
- *you respect each other's limits;*
- *you value each other and enjoy each other regardless of how much sexual activity you are engaging in;*
- *you know that the amount of sexual activity is not an indication of commitment or love.*

Conflict

When we have conflict in a healthy relationship, we can feel free to express our opinions, disagree and communicate our anger because we don't feel afraid of the other person's anger. It is normal for two people to disagree with each other sometimes. In fact, it may mean that they have reached a point with each other where they feel safe enough to disagree. It is also normal to feel frustrated and even very angry in relationships.

Disagreeing or feeling angry isn't the problem. How we express our anger can be. Angry feelings that get out of control can turn into abuse. It is smart to create a list of rules that you agree in advance are your relationship laws. You and your partner could agree that to break these rules is against the law in your relationship.

The following four laws are essential in a healthy relationship:

Relationship Law #1: No yelling, name-calling or violent threats.

Whoever wrote "Sticks and stones will break my bones, but names will never hurt me" lied. Verbal abuse can really hurt. It can be like having someone beat you up on the inside.

Using a loud, threatening voice is unfair because it can make your partner feel afraid of you. Violent threats or violent gestures like making a fist at someone is the same as actually hitting in that it is controlling your partner through fear. To pick up a weapon—even if you don't intend to use it—is a form of emotional terrorism.

Relationship Law #2: No throwing things or hitting things.

People who throw or hit things—including dolls or teddy bears or pets that you love—when they're angry don't usually stop there. That is a sign that they are out of control. You could be the next thing they throw or hit.

Relationship Law #3: No touching in anger.

Obvious examples of angry touching include hitting, shoving, grabbing, slapping and kicking. There are also lots of subtle ways of being touched in anger. A person could jab their finger into your chest, grab your clothing, hold on to your wrist to stop you from leaving, hold you down on a bed and even have sex with you in a way that is insensitive or too rough. The no touching rule can be very important. If a partner knows they are not even supposed to touch you when they are angry, it's going to be much harder for them to cross that clear, strong boundary into abuse.

Relationship Law #4: No emotional blackmail.

To threaten to commit suicide is the worst kind of emotional blackmail. It is also emotional blackmail to threaten to leave or to threaten to have sex with other people in order to punish, control or get what you want in a relationship. Not only is it unfair to try to control someone with these kinds of threats, it doesn't work. The person may stay for the moment but it is sure death for the relationship eventually.

Ask yourself: If it's against the law for a stranger to do these things to me, why should it be "legal" in a loving relationship?

For an exercise on healthy ways to express disagreement, see page 278. To learn about unfair fighting and fair fighting, see exercises on page 279.

Other behaviour boundaries that you may want to establish for your relationship include:

1. No "character assassinations." Criticizing behaviour is OK, criticizing who your partner is, is not. If you stick with commenting on behaviours, you can express your frustrations and still be fighting fair.

2. No "digging up the graveyard." If your partner keeps bringing up an old issue over and over every time you get into an argument, it can feel that they are using it as a weapon. It probably means the issue was never properly buried. When our issues aren't resolved and properly laid to rest, they become ghosts, and like ghosts they keep coming back to haunt us. If this is happening, your partner needs to tell you that the old issue isn't dead, that there is still a ghost that s/he can't seem to get rid of. Then you can work on it together or you can get help through counselling. Once you agree that it's buried, it should be left alone. Everyone has the right to make mistakes and everyone has the right to be forgiven.

3. No "walking out." If you have agreed to a "No Walking Out" rule, this doesn't mean that neither of you can ever leave for any reason during a conflict. It just means that you both agree that you do not

just walk out in the middle of an argument. If things are getting too intense and you need to leave in order to cool out or process your feelings alone for a while, say so. Time-outs are OK and can be very useful when feelings get out of control. You might also agree that the time-out never goes longer than an hour (or whatever time restriction you both agree is reasonable) without some form of contact.

4. No "nuclear weapons." There are certain things that you get to know about each other in an intimate relationship. You may know what each other's most vulnerable secrets are. It is unfair to use things against each other that put either of you at extreme emotional or physical risk. Tell your partner which things put you at emotional risk and make a "sacred rule" that s/he is not allowed to do/say that particular thing no matter how mad s/he is. Make an agreement with yourself and your partner that you are allowed to leave if s/he breaks a "sacred rule." When you have the power to threaten your partner's safety or well-being, these areas should be identified as potential nuclear weapons or just going too far.

> *Everyone has the right to make mistakes and everyone has the right to be forgiven ... but some behaviours indicate that you are not with a safe person. It is important to know which behaviours are just going too far.*

To learn more about behaviours that are "going too far," see exercise on page 280.

Safety

We often hear the term "abusive relationship," as though the relationship itself is an entity that is being abusive. It is the person who is being abusive and it is their behaviour that is the problem. If you must make a choice to stay or leave, do not base your decision on what your partner says but on their behaviour. This is important because sometimes a person knows intellectually that a change is necessary but is emotionally incapable of making that change. Or sometimes a person will promise to make changes to manipulate a partner into staying in an unsafe relationship.

How do we know when we are safe? If your body is calm and you are feeling relaxed, your palms aren't sweaty and your breathing is normal, you can usually feel certain that you are safe. Sometimes the messages in your head can be confusing and it can be helpful to check in with your body instead.

There are many reasons for wanting to be in an intimate relationship: to have someone to share things with and someone to hang out with. Someone to talk with and laugh with and cry with. Someone special who thinks you're special. Someone to be affectionate and physical with. Someone safe.

For an exercise about safe and unsafe relationships, see page 281.

Sex, Desire and Intimacy

Sex, desire and intimacy involve the heart, mind, body and spirit. These concepts, although separate in meaning, interface in many ways and are intricately interwoven into our experience as human beings striving for connection.

Sex

Sex is a very complex physical act that can trigger enormous emotion, vulnerability and power. Many adults find it difficult to contain the intense feelings that can be awakened by sexual activity with another person. When two people with limited life experience, questionable self-awareness and fragile self-esteem expose their naked bodies to each other it can trigger shame, insecurity, inadequacy, revulsion and fear—as well as positive feelings such as pride, freedom, awe and, of course, desire. Sex for adolescents is rarely what they expect it to be. To have sex for the first time is a huge step. It has the potential to take a human being to a whole other level of being. And it can take the relationship between the two people to a more intense and complex level as well. Not very many teens have the emotional maturity to handle all these new feelings. Our society barely prepares young people for the physical safety of the experience, let alone the emotional and spiritual enormity of baring their bodies and souls.

We have been educating our youth about protected sex for many years. In more recent years, we have been educating our youth about "Safe Sex." We can tell teens that using condoms is a non-negotiable issue. We can tell them to abstain from sex. We can also tell them how to engage in limited and safe sexual activity. Whatever we, as educators and parents, choose to tell our kids, in the end it is the young people themselves who will choose what they do or do not do. It is empowering for teens to make decisions about their own bodies and lives. We need to tell our teens that it is up to them to decide how far they will go and that it is up to them to communicate that to their partner. They need to learn how to have the conversations about sex, and some of those conversations need to be about what they want— not just about what they don't want. For example:

"Yes, I want to hold hands; no, I don't want to kiss."
"Yes, I want to kiss—but not with tongues."
"Yes, I like what we were doing before—but I'm not comfortable with that."

Asking for what we want is the flip side of saying "no."

For exercises on assessing sexual attraction, see page 284.

Desire and Intimacy
Desire is a yearning for, a moving toward, a hunger, a wanting. Originally, desire was the necessary motivator to get humans to procreate, but now what is the role of desire? What is this urgent need that feels like a deep hunger? Hunger for what? Sexual pleasure? Orgasm? We can have these through masturbation. Desire may be partly about sexual satisfaction but clearly it is about connection.

When we speak to each other, we are striving for connection so we can feel less alone. In a way, sex is an act of communication, a joining. A profound sharing through body language. A telling of the story of yourself and a listening to the story of another with our bodies.

When two people first get to know each other, it is common to have many intimate conversations where we tell each other our personal herstories/histories. We tell our stories in long roundabout ways, in exquisite detail, in small bits and long-into-the-night chapters. We tell ourselves to each other over time. Not all at once, and not an abridged version. With sex, it can be the same way. There are so many different ways of playing sexually, most of them more pleasurable than just "doing it." We can use our creativity, our imagination. Sexual play can make sex more interesting, more orgasmic (particularly for females), more emotionally and physically safe. When we engage in sexual play we can let each other in slowly, over time. There can be more intimacy because there is more safety. Sex can become something you do "with" your partner rather than "to" your partner.

When you start a sexual relationship—especially the very first time, but even if you've been in one before—the emotional dynamics can get really intense. It can seem as though the love is stronger but the fear can be stronger too. There is more emotional risk involved so both people feel more vulnerable. There is likely to be more jealousy and less autonomy. It can feel as though now you "belong" to your partner. Everything can seem heavier and more serious. The other thing that can happen is that sex becomes the whole focus of the relationship. Before engaging in sex, the time spent together was more about enjoying all aspects of being together and doing a variety of activities. After sex, the focus can be just where and when to have sex. Even sex can get boring. Especially if it's "bad" sex.

Good Sex

Teens get ideas about sex from Hollywood and television, which rarely represent the reality of the sexual experiences they themselves are having or will have at some point in their lives. Regardless of when this activity takes place, it is important for young people to know ahead of time what the elements of a positive, pleasurable and healthy sexual relationship are. Although technique and practice are elements that make any physical activity better, these are not necessarily the key elements to "good" sex.

Sex between two people is a kind of communication and like all good communication it needs to go both ways. Have you ever had a conversation with someone who is "on send"? They don't ask any questions about you or your life and when you try to participate in the conversation they just talk over you and at you. The person just talks and talks and you get the feeling that you may as well not even be there. There is only one other thing that is more unsatisfying or boring than that experience: sex without intimacy with a partner who is on "sexual send."

Sex doesn't have to be wild and passionate or dreamy and romantic like in the movies. It can be playful or tearful, or deep and quiet. The experience will be as individual and unique as the people themselves and whether it will be good or bad will depend on what each person brings to it. As long as both people have chosen to be there and want to be there, and there is an equal and caring connection between them, a positive and healthy sexual experience is possible.

In the following story, we will look at some of the issues we have been reading about in this chapter. A female's right to stop, mixed messages, sex, desire and intimacy are all explored in this story. Through the eyes of Nina, we will gain an inside view of a young woman's first experience of her own desire, the power of those feelings, her confusion and her inner conflict.

Nina: A Hunger of Her Own

Nina didn't plan to go all the way. She really liked this guy and she had decided to wait until she was very sure about the relationship. She was determined that she would stop him no matter how turned on he got or how much he pressured her.

When they parked the car and started kissing, Nina was waiting for him to start groping her, the way other boys always had. But things didn't happen that way. He just kept kissing her—slow, sweet kisses with his hands cupping her face like she was something delicate and precious. Then his arms folded around her and lifted her up onto his lap and it made her feel so small and safe to be held like that. Then he was kissing her more urgently and the heat of him and the tension in his body excited her. He kissed her hair and her face and her neck and it felt so good. Goosebumps shivered down her arms and raced up and down her spine. She liked the hunger she could feel from him. It made her feel wanted.

And then Nina felt a hunger of her own beginning to burn low in her belly. The skin on her breasts became tight and they felt full. Her nipples strained against the fabric of her T-shirt, the movement of the soft cotton causing them to burn with a sensation so intense it was almost pain. She felt her body begin to move against him all on its own and shoots of pleasure flashed down between her legs and took her breath away. Nina had never felt this way before. As though an animal self was taking over. A part of her that was wild, with an ache so deep inside her it was as though her bones were hungry. She felt a desperate need to have him closer, she couldn't get him close enough. She was starving for him.

Nina had never felt these feelings in her body before. Especially this yearning feeling, as though something deep inside her was calling urgently. Wanting something, yes, like hunger, but she didn't know for what and she felt as though she was turning inside out and she felt suddenly too raw, too hungry. She was beginning to feel anxious, as though she were lost inside an unfamiliar self, like she didn't know who she was. And then there was a sudden awareness of him and a sense that she didn't really know who he was and then she felt deeply afraid.

He didn't appear to notice that her feelings had changed and in fact it seemed that he wasn't really aware of her at all. It was as though she, Nina, wasn't there but her body was. He was breathing hard and making wet sucking noises in her ear and biting on her neck and she suddenly had the terrifying sensation that his hunger was real and that he was feeding on her. That's when his hand moved down her arm and onto her breasts, and he grabbed first one and then the other, his huge hand swallowing them and squeezing each one hard. It hurt so bad her eyes filled with tears and a sharp sound came out of her throat. He must have thought the sound meant she liked what he was doing because his hands started moving all over. He grabbed her roughly between the legs and before she could react to that his hands were back on her breasts and then back between her legs and then around behind her grabbing at her bum.

And that's when she started laughing. Not that it was funny. Not really laughing, just nervous small laughs. And she pulled his hands away, but he put them right back. Then he pushed her down on the seat and she tried to push him off but he just kept leaning his weight onto her and then he was on top of her. He thrust up against her over and over. She could feel the pressure of him pushing between her legs and his collarbone pressing against her cheek hurt. Nina's breath came in short shallow gasps. She felt trapped and panicky. She bent one knee and tried to push him off by thrusting her hips forward. At first she thought he was getting the message because he started to move off her. He shifted his lower body to the side but the weight of his chest was still pinning her down and his one hand clawed into the back of her neck and the other was undoing his pants and then scrabbling up and down her body like a hungry, blind rodent biting and pinching her flesh. It felt like things were speeding out of control, like she was in a runaway car with no brakes, going straight downhill.

That's when Nina said, "No." Not loud. Not angry. Just a little whiney "No." It was so hard to get it out somehow. Like it was stuck in her throat. She was afraid he'd get mad. Afraid he'd break up with her. But she was even more afraid that if she did let him do it, he'd break up with her anyway. She didn't want to be used and then thrown out. So she made herself say it. She thought it would be enough, that little "No". It never occurred to her that he wouldn't stop. And then she said "Please stop" in the same small voice. That's when he said something about her not being a virgin and when she didn't say anything back he just kept right on going.

Why do you think Nina felt so out of control?

Can you see how unfamiliar and overwhelming Nina's feelings of desire were to her? It would have been enormously helpful to Nina to have known ahead of time about the power of her own desire and how difficult it could be for her to deal with.

Why did Nina have such difficulty saying "No"?

Once again, Nina, like many young women, was afraid to assert her boundaries in case she was punished in some way. Nina was afraid of making the guy mad and she was afraid of being abandoned.

It never occurred to Nina that saying "No" wouldn't be enough. Why do you think just saying "No" wasn't enough to stop the guy?

The guy Nina was with made a mistake many young men make. He felt he had the right to continue after Nina told him to stop. He may have believed that girls don't really mean "No" when they say "No"— or he may be the kind of guy who just didn't care about what she wanted. Either way, what he did was rape.

Do you think the guy who raped Nina would identify what he did as rape?

Many young men who commit rape don't think of it that way. Typically these young men would call what they did "scoring."

Dynamics of Violence in Teen Relationships

Sexual assault and rape are just one form of violence in teen relationships. Violence can take many forms: verbal, physical, sexual and emotional. And violence can take place between same gender or opposite gender intimate partners or peers. In the following segment we will look at the dynamics of violence within a variety of teen relationships.

He Hits/She Hits
The majority of physical violence in intimate teenage relationships is perpetrated by males against females. However, it is not uncommon for a young woman to hit her boyfriend. When this happens, the girl often feels that she deserves what she gets back. "But I hit him first!" she will say as a way of justifying his violent behaviour. It is not justifiable for anyone to hit. If the young woman initiates the violence, she

needs to take responsibility for her actions and may need to learn to express her feelings in non-violent ways. If the guy has been hit and he is angry, he also has the right to express his anger but in a non-violent way.

Even if she hits first, the woman is still not responsible for what the guy does in reaction to her violence. He is, without exception, responsible for the way he chooses to act out his anger. There is a fundamental difference operating here. When a female hits a male, he is rarely actually afraid. If he responds by hitting her back, she inevitably feels fear and is far more likely to be seriously injured.

Remember: Males are generally physically stronger than females. When the girl hits her boyfriend, the guy gets mad. When the guy hits back, the girl gets hurt.

Remember: The thing males are most afraid of from females is being laughed at. The thing females are most afraid of from males is being killed.

Female Friendship and Betrayal

When we ask girls why they fight other girls, nine times out of ten they tell us it's over a guy. In this segment we will look at the complex underlying factors being played out in this dynamic.

Young women can be very physical in their relationships with their girl friends. They style each other's hair, hug, cry together, dance together and hold hands. They drape themselves over each other in dramatic poses and lie with their heads in each other's laps stroking each other's brows, very much like lovers. They also support each other emotionally through traumas big and small, holding each other and listening to each other's stories of the heart.

These girl/girl relationships are very intimate and deeply sustaining but extremely fragile. Female friendships have no support in the larger heterosexual culture and there is almost no expectation that they will honoured in the face of a potential male attachment. The mainstream culture encourages women to compete aggressively with each other for male attention. Truthfully, the battles between young female adolescents over boys are as much about the betrayal and loss of each other as "significant other" as they are about who "gets the guy." When one girl leaves her girlfriend and goes after a boy, especially if it is a boy that they have both identified as attractive, she is saying that she cares more about having a boyfriend than she does about her friendship. Immediately upon forming the new alliance, it is common for girls to cut off all contact with their girlfriends and focus their full energy and time on the boyfriend. The abandoned girlfriend is left with an enormous loss and no way to justify her feelings.

Given the conditioning of males to be divorced from their nurturing feelings, the girl can expect to get very little by way of emotional sustenance from the guy, yet she chooses to be disloyal to her friend. The betrayed girl rarely expresses the hurt she feels toward her disloyal friend for abandoning their friendship. Instead the betrayed girl expresses anger at her friend for stealing "her" boyfriend. Her anger is not directed toward the boy for "taking her friend away." In this way, females are continuously in a competitive relationship with each other. The question of why one relationship has to be sacrificed for the other rarely comes up. It is as though the deep and profoundly intimate relationships between girls and women mean nothing in the face of the opportunity to get a boyfriend. This phenomenon speaks directly to the desperation females feel to be validated by males. Spinsterhood, the greatly feared state for women in past ages—the state of being passed over, unchosen—still lives in the hearts of young women today. An unfortunate result of this fear is an ongoing and increasingly dangerous acting out of physical violence amongst girls—an unwelcome addition to the vicious verbal violence that females are famous for.

Words As Weapons

If you were told that there are students in a school who are carrying a very dangerous weapon with them to school every day and that this weapon could permanently wound and even cause death, this would clearly be a matter for serious concern. If you were told that the students carrying this weapon are primarily girls, would you be surprised?

In grade 7 to 10 classrooms—in small towns and in big cities, in inner city schools and private girls' schools—we asked girls, "What are some of the words girls in this school use against other girls?"

The lists they generated consistently included these words:

bitch	dyke
slut	lesbo
whore	fat
ho	ugly
cunt	skank

While boys tend to use physical violence more often, girls are more likely to use words as weapons. Females can be highly skilled and brutal wielders of cruel words. The seriousness of the damage done through the use of hurtful words is vastly underrated. Words cut deep and they can make us want to die. Suicide attempts by teens are frequently due to persistent name-calling and teasing and verbal harassment. Name-calling is a form of hatred. Hatred is a form of violence.

To develop skills for dealing with verbal violence, see exercises on Wise Woman/Solid Guy on page 258 and assertiveness role-plays on page 261.

Striving for Stud Status

In the male world being sexually active is a status symbol, and it is especially a boost to a guy's ego to "deflower" as many females as possible. When a man "scores" in this way he will gain a highly coveted reputation as a stud or a player. However, the stud dynamic has a hidden danger for young men. It sets a standard for all young men to aspire toward and dictates that achieving that standard precludes any feelings of desire for emotional connection that a young man may have. The pressure to score can potentially provoke males to engage in sexual activity when they may not feel ready to or don't genuinely want to. In this mind set, males will also be more likely to exclude the feelings and needs and boundaries of the young women they are engaging with.

When males are cut off from their own feelings and not considering the feelings of the female, they are more likely to use coercion, force and violence to achieve their goal. It is obvious that this puts females at risk. What is less obvious is that young males who are engaging in this type of coercion are also at risk. *They are at high risk of committing a crime.* More and more young men who thought they were just being "normal boys" are finding their lives turned upside down when they are expelled from schools and universities and left with criminal records.

Our boys need to be informed that the comments they make daily toward girls in the halls at school will get them fired at work under the sexual harassment laws. Our boys need to know that when they are pressuring a young woman sexually, they could be breaking the law. They need to know that when their anger is feeling out of control and they feel like hitting their girlfriend, beating up another guy or driving their cars too fast, these are signs that they are in trouble. These are signs that they need help. Of course a "Real Man" would never ask for help. This is a very real trap for young males. As well, young men who buy into this version of being a real man will be likely to engage in unsafe sexual activity. "Real Men" don't wear condoms because "Real Men" are invincible.

For an exercise about guys in trouble, see page 285.

In 1998 there were 22,145 youths (mostly male) charged with violent criminal code offences in Canada. This is a 93 percent increase from ten years ago.

Each year in Canada, 1 in 10 women are hit, kicked, punched or threatened by their husbands or boyfriends.

Striving for stud status increases the incidents of male/male violence as well because the male world dictates that young men prove their manhood via their sexual conquests and compete with each other while doing so. It used to be that a guy punched another guy in the nose for making out with his girlfriend; young males today are more likely to cause serious physical harm, and the use of weapons is increasingly a risk.

For an exercise to challenge "stud status," see page 286.

For an exercise on redefining masculinity, see page 287.

What Does an Unhealthy Relationship Look Like?

No one plans to end up in an unhealthy relationship. It is something that happens organically. One thing just leads to another and then you wake up one day and there you are in an unhealthy relationship. Once you're in it's hard to get out. Looking for warning signs of unhealthy relationships can help you to avoid getting into one.

Controlling Behaviours

One of the warning signs to look for in a relationship is controlling behaviours. When your partner starts giving you advice about what to wear, how to act, what to say or not to say, these are warning signs. If your partner seems to feel threatened by your friends and puts them down constantly, and pouts when you're involved in projects at school and criticizes your interests—these are warning signs. A partner who manipulates you into doing things you don't want to do with either charm or coercion or threats to leave you—this is a warning sign. If your partner asks a lot of questions about your activities, whom you talk to, where you were, at first you may think s/he is interested in your life and you may feel complimented. After a while you realize it's an inquisition. You may find yourself being careful about what you say because you don't want to trigger one of his/her "moods." This is a warning sign.

Abusive Behaviours

Another warning sign is abusive behaviours. If your partner puts you down or makes jokes at your expense, flies off the handle over little things and apologizes after s/he blows up but doesn't change the behaviour, these are warning signs. If a partner makes threatening gestures or verbal threats or touches you in anger—even grabbing clothing or pushing—these are loud and clear warning signs.

Signs That You Are in an Unhealthy Relationship
You find yourself "walking on eggs" around your partner and trying too hard to please her/him. When you do get approval, you are elated and try even harder. You get so that you are grateful for crumbs. After a few months, your partner has so much power in your life that you feel you can't live without her/him. You've stopped seeing your friends and are no longer involved in school, sports or work the way you used to be before you met your partner. If your partner doesn't call or see you on weekends you are devastated. Family and friends tell you that you've changed. They tell you that they don't like how you are being treated. Even though you know it's true, you defend your partner. You think you have the power to change her/him.

Even though you're not happy in the relationship you would rather be in it than alone. It feels as though you don't exist unless your partner is there, looking at you. When your partner calls you ugly and stupid, you feel ugly and stupid. You've come to believe that the way s/he sees you is the real picture. What started out as true love has turned into a nightmare you can't wake up from.

Unhealthy relationships can happen to anyone—in male/female relationships and same-sex relationships. When a male is trapped in an abusive relationship with a female, the dynamics are very similar with the exception that serious injury is less likely and he rarely fears for his life. A female being abused in a relationship with a male is by far the most common scenario. There are many compelling reasons that people stay in abusive relationships. In the following segment we are going to look at females in abusive relationships and why they stay.

Why Does She Stay?
Conditioning: Even though his behaviour is violent and abusive, the abused woman feels that deep down he is really a good person. It's as though she sees this little light in all that darkness and she feels

compelled to nurture that part of him. She sees the broken little person on the inside and she thinks, "I can fix him."

Survival: An adult woman or a parenting teen has children to feed and often has no other means of support and nowhere to go.

Isolation: His controlling behaviours have created a situation where she has been cut off from friends and family. She feels completely alone and unable to ask for help.

Shame: The emotional and psychological abuse that often come with the physical abuse have damaged her self-esteem to the point where she feels she deserves to be treated badly. She is full of self-hatred and feels the abuse is her fault. She doesn't want anyone to know.

Compassion: When he loses his temper and hurts her, sometimes he breaks down and cries. He apologizes and begs her to forgive him. He promises that he'll never do it again.

Guilt: When he's remorseful and upset he begs her not to leave him. He tells her he can't live without her and that he'll kill himself if she leaves him.

Fear: When he's angry he tells her that if she leaves him he'll kill her. She believes him.

That's why she stays.

Seventy-five percent of women who are killed by their husbands or boyfriends were trying to leave when they died.

Opening the Door to Healthy Relationships

We can't change him but we can change ourselves. In order to open the door to being in healthy relationships, we need to take a close look at the kinds of guys we are attracted to. By examining the types of people we are attracted to and why we seem to keep repeating the same patterns of attraction, we can begin to unlearn old patterns.

We are usually in relationships with people who are at the same level of emotional damage as we are. If we have poor self-esteem we may feel we don't deserve to be treated well. We may find ourselves thinking, "If he likes me that much there must be something wrong with him." We will lose respect for anyone who tries to give us genuine caring because deep down we find it impossible to believe that a truly valuable person could love us. If this is the case, we need to work on our self-esteem.

For exercises that develop self-esteem for girls and redefine "good girls," see pages 291-296.

Why Do Nice Guys Seem Boring?

The nice guys are the ones that we feel safe with. The guys we hang out with who are kind of like our girlfriends in that we can tell them our deepest secrets and they listen and support us without judging us. They're the guys that we keep wishing we could feel attracted to but we just don't.

Why aren't we attracted to the nice guys? If we had to work really hard to get our parents' love and approval, we can grow up thinking it's normal to have to win someone's love. If you had this childhood experience, nice guys can seem too easy. You may find yourself thinking, "He's boring, there's just no challenge."

If we were put down and emotionally abused as children, it can feel acutely uncomfortable for someone to treat us with respect and consideration. When we are with nice guys, we may feel as though something is missing. We don't realize that what we are missing is the intensity that comes with the threat of violence. This is the familiar feeling of being on the edge, all senses alert, which we learned from past experience goes hand-in-hand with love. If you had this experience as a child, nice guys will seem "too nice" and you may find yourself thinking, "He's boring, he's just too nice."

Remember: When you're with a guy and you feel your heart pounding and your hands sweating, and there's a knot in your stomach and you can't think of a thing to say, these are intense feelings. You may think you're in love. That's not love, that's fear.

When we are abused within our families, we can grow up confusing love and fear. Being with a potentially abusive boyfriend will feel very familiar (of family) and in fact comfortable. When we are with nice guys who treat us well, it can feel unfamiliar (not of family) and therefore uncomfortable. But as your self-esteem increases, you will naturally find yourself attracted to healthier guys.

Why Are You Attracted to the "Bad Boy"?

If you're with a really screwed up guy, you may find yourself working hard on his problems. You may begin to notice that you are always complaining to your friends and family about him and his problems. You may feel like the strong one in the relationship. You might want to ask yourself, "If the guy's such a loser, what am I doing with him?" If you get professional help and work on yourself, you have a chance to get healthy and strong enough to move on and meet someone who is also working on himself—someone you don't need to save.

You need help to learn why you're attracted to this type of guy and how to change that. You learned how to be the way you are a long time ago; getting counselling and working on your self-esteem can help you to see through these guys and be less drawn to them. You can learn to understand why you find the "bad guys" sexy and the "nice guys" boring. If you are committed to making this change in your life it can be done.

Here are some rules to remember about the "Bad Boy":

1. If he acts like a jerk, he's a jerk. (That's how you tell.)
2. You can't fix him, save him or change him. Period.
3. He needs help. He needs professional help in order to change his attitude toward women. He learned this behaviour a long time ago as well and it will take a long time to change it. The more you try, the less responsibility he has to take. He is the only one who can fix himself.

Perhaps you are saying: "I'd rather go out with a guy who's sexy and exciting—there's no way I'm gonna end up with some geek." There is nothing more sexy and exciting than power. Truly powerful guys are guys who have good self-esteem and don't feel like they have to prove themselves all the time. Guys who feel good about themselves are more likely to be successful, interesting, adventurous, healthy, fun and loving. Guys who care about themselves are more likely to care about their partners. They are more likely to be good communicators and considerate lovers.

Most importantly, guys who are in touch with their true power won't feel threatened by your power. They won't need to put you down to make themselves feel big. In this kind of relationship both people can grow.

To explore what females and males want from intimate relationships, see exercise on page 289.

rocking the gender-power boat and making waves...

Sexual Harassment and Sexual Assault

IN THIS CHAPTER we will examine the dynamics of sexual harassment and sexual assault. We will take an intricate look at the legal and personal impact of these two issues and the complex gender factors involved. Although both females and males are affected by sexual harassment and assault, there is an enormous difference in female and male experience both in regards to frequency and impact.

Let's begin by considering the legal definitions of harassment:

1. Harassment: Physical, verbal, psychological threats. Examples: verbal or physical threat to your person, being followed or stared at threateningly, raising of fist or hand as though to strike.

2. Gender Harassment: Physical, verbal, psychological threats that are linked to gender. Examples: "Women drivers"; "If you weren't a woman I'd ..."; "Women are too emotional"; "All men want is sex." Homophobic comments (gay bashing) are also examples of gender harassment.

3. Sexual Harassment: Physical, verbal, psychological threats, but with

a sexual connotation. Sexual harassment involves a wide range of behaviours ranging from unwelcome sexual references and sexist comments to unwelcome sexual advances.

According to the Canadian Human Rights Commission (1991) and the United States Civil Rights Act of 1964, there are two broad categories of sexual harassment:

1. "Quid pro quo" harassment: sexually coercive behaviour, with its threatened consequences for a person's employment or academic status.

2. "Hostile environment": any verbal or physical behaviour that creates an intimidating, hostile, or offensive environment, thus interfering with a student's ability to learn.

In this next section we will look specifically at sexual harassment with the focus on females as the primary targets of this most common of crimes of violence against girls and women.

The constant glances, stares, comments, insinuations and jokes that every female experiences as a "normal" part of her life has an insidious and damaging impact that urgently needs to be exposed.

Sexual harassment objectifies. It is a systemic and persistent erosion of a female person's self-esteem. It erases her humanity and overexposes her physical body. It usurps her power, each and every time it happens, by identifying her in that moment as object of the male gaze.

A female is conditioned to feel she should feel complimented by this type of male attention and when she feels offended and attempts to protest she is told she is man-hating, uptight and can't take a joke. Sexual harassment is not funny. It's against the law. Most offenders will deny that they "intended " to offend. That is why, under the law, "intent" is irrelevant.

The fear of accusing an innocent man stops girls and women from defending their boundaries. Because our society raises males to believe that they have the right to do the things they do, males who sexually harass females may genuinely feel they are giving them a compliment. It may not be in their frame of reference that their positive appraisal might be an invasion or an insult. They really believe that an "8" is a pretty good score on a scale of 1 to 10. It is not our job, as females, to be concerned with where they are coming from. It is not even our job to educate them, although we hope that will be the end result if we are assertive. Our job is only to find our personal boundary, acknowledge our unconditional right to it (even if we can't explain in any rational terms why we feel that way) and then to defend that boundary assertively.

Some examples of sexual harassment are:

- Verbal threats to violate another person sexually; unwelcome "compliments" or sexual remarks; verbal "assessments" of a person's body or sexual performance; jokes, innuendoes or taunting about a person's clothing, body or sexual activities.
- Staring at breasts/body or "scanning" a body.
- Pressure for sexual "favours."
- Displaying of pornographic pictures.
- Leering, ogling, making obscene gestures.
- Subtle or overt abuse of power, such as demanding sexual favours accompanied by implied or overt threats concerning one's job/education.
- Spreading sexual rumours.
- Pulling someone's clothes off, flipping up skirts, pulling at bra straps.
- Touching, pinching, grabbing, hugging with a sexual tone (it could be touching someone's hand or hair or face in a sexual way—it doesn't have to be specifically a sexual area of the body). When physical contact is involved it may cross over into the legal definition of sexual assault.

Sexual harassment can take place in person, via note, letter or email or on the telephone. It is considered to be discrimination on the basis of sex, and it is illegal.

Sexual Harassment in the Schools

Sexual harassment crosses all marital, race, class, gender and sexual orientation boundaries. For teens, most harassment comes from their peers. The highest risk group for sexual harassment are adolescent females between the ages of fourteen and eighteen. While both females and males harass, males do most of the harassing.

According to the "Hostile Hallways" study (American Association of University Women Educational Foundation, 1993) of 1,600 students from grades 8 to 11

- 85 percent of the girls reported being victimized by sexual harassment;
- 65 percent of the girls reported being touched, grabbed or pinched in a sexual way;
- 13 percent had been forced to do something sexual other than kissing;
- 86 percent of the female victims reported being sexually harassed by their peers;
- 25 percent reported being sexually harassed by school staff.

They reported experiencing harassment in the hallway (73 percent), in the classroom (65 percent), on the school grounds (48 percent) and in the cafeteria (34 percent).

Dr. Aaron White, the psychologist who contributed to the development of the SafeTeen Boys' Program, has been going into Canadian schools on a regular basis for many years to present the program to boys and to do research on sexual harassment and adolescent males. Here are some of his observations:

"I asked many teachers and counsellors throughout British Columbia and the Northwest Territories how much sexual harassment was going on in their schools. I was frequently disappointed when their estimates of what was going were so at odds with what the kids reported. Many staff claimed there wasn't much of a problem at all.

"Harassment in North American schools is so normalized that staff don't even seem to see or hear it. I remember being appalled a few times when a staff member was leading me down a hall and he ignored the verbal harassment going on around him (put-downs, leers and catcalls). I saw instances of gender harassment among the boys at every school I visited. A small amount of it seemed to be relatively good-natured joking among boys who genuinely liked one another, but most of it was quite vicious stuff aimed at verbally wounding the targets for not being manly enough. I even witnessed some male teachers taking part at times.

"And of course all of those incidences of males putting down other males are an outgrowth of patriarchal beliefs that females are not as good as males (most put-downs of other males are negative slang names for females: bitch, pussy, sissy). Homophobic comments abound in every school. The kids in the AAUW (1993) study rated being called gay or lesbian as the worst form of harassment—even worse than being physically harassed! If homophobic put-downs are that aversive for straight kids, imagine how awful it is for gay and lesbian students!"

Bullying happens once every 7 minutes on the playground and once every 25 minutes in class. The vast majority of youth violence goes unreported.

For an exercise on examining gender-specific harassment, see page 290.

The Effects of Sexual Harassment

In her article "Peer Sexual Harassment: A Barrier to the Health of Adolescent Females?" Dr. Susan Dahinten, assistant professor at the University of New Brunswick, states that lots of boys report being harassed at some point in their lives. She reminds us, however, that girls are harassed many more times during their lives than boys are. Boys are also far more likely to experience same-sex harassment. Most importantly, boys experience sexual harassment differently. For instance, in the Hostile Hallways study, a much lower percentage of boys who were harassed reported changing their behaviour or wanting to stay home from school because of it. Fifty-two percent of the girls but only 19 percent of the boys said they were upset by the experience.

In the AAUW study, 43 percent of the girls who had experienced harassment reported feeling less confident about themselves, 39 percent reported feeling afraid or scared, and 25 percent reported that the harassment left them feeling confused about who they were. One young woman described her response as, "I feel bad about my body and I wish that I was a boy."

- *A Canadian university study found that 1 in 6 female graduate students had altered study plans (avoided taking a class from someone or restricted their choices of thesis supervisors) to avoid sexual harassment.*

- *One in 12 male students surveyed had committed acts that met the legal definition of rape or attempted rape.*

- *Ninety percent of working women report receiving unwanted sexual attention on the job.*

The effects of sexual harassment can pose a significant threat to women's health and well-being both physically and emotionally. Some reported effects are:

Physical effects:
headaches
fatigue
sleep disturbances
weight fluctuations
gastrointestinal disorders
back pain
jaw tightness
respiratory infections
urinary tract infections

Emotional effects:
anger
anxiety
depression
increased fear of rape
decreased self-esteem
decreased self-confidence

As well, studies of sexual harassment among adolescents provide compelling evidence of serious educational consequences, including attention difficulties, decreased class participation, and absenteeism (AAUW, 1993).

One of the most devastating effects of peer sexual harassment among adolescents is the possibility that it may contribute to sexual and physical violence in future intimate relationships. Because high schools play such an enormous role in gender socialization, it can be argued that if sexual harassment is left unchecked, the schools may function as training grounds for violence. Places where girls are "trained to accept battering and assault" and boys "receive permission, even training, to become batterers." (M. Stein, in Dahinten, 1999).

Sexual harassment is so common that often the behaviours will be defined by the perpetrator and sometimes by the victim as harmless flirting or "just a joke." Under the law, it is the impact of the behaviour, not the intent, that is relevant in determining if sexual harassment has occurred.

To explore issues relating to self-esteem and media images of females, see exercises on pages 293-296.

Sexual Harassment: Myths and Truth

The following are myths:
1. Women invite sexual harassment by their behaviour and/or dress.
2. Women often make false claims.
3. Women who object to sexual harassment have no sense of humour.
4. Sexual harassment is normal and harmless male behaviour.

The truth about sexual harassment:

1. Standard female fashion is designed to be provocative. A woman who wears what is currently in fashion is not inviting harassment or assault. When a woman flirts she is inviting sexual attention, not violation.
2. There are no more false claims of sexual harassment than there are false claims of any other crime.
3. Sexual harassment is against the law.
4. According to the law, intent and motivation are irrelevant. Ignorance or insensitivity are not defences.

Sexual Harassment: The Dynamics of Dominance

Males sometimes feel compelled to assert their position of dominance by establishing their right to assess a female's appearance. When compliments are given at inappropriate times and in inappropriate places, they are sometimes insults masquerading as compliments. They may be objectifying (turning you into a sexual object), infantilizing (referring to you as childlike) or condescending (not giving you the respect you are due). The purpose of these types of remarks is not to enhance self-esteem but to assert status. When males do this they are reminding you (and themselves) that you are female and they are male and therefore of higher status. Insecure males tend to make these comments particularly when they feel threatened or challenged in some way by a female. It is possible, however, that an inappropriate comment made by a male does not have this intention. He may have a cultural belief in his right to comment on female appearance or genuinely believe he is giving a compliment—or making a harmless joke. It is important for females to remember that the intention of the other person does not determine whether or not we have been complimented. What matters is how we feel. Any discomfort or confusion at all and the comment should be suspect. A true compliment isn't confusing. It just feels good.

An "essence" compliment is a comment that speaks to who a person is as opposed to what they look like. Although an essence compliment doesn't focus on physical appearance as it pertains to stereotypical attractiveness, it could include a physical feature. For instance, to say a person has beautiful hair is focusing on the physical attribute. To say you admire the way a person does their hair is a comment about an internal quality. It is actually praising their creativity.

For exercises on how to identify the difference between a compliment and an insult and how to give essence compliments, see pages 295-296.

For an exercise on powerplays, see page 296.

What Can You Do about Sexual Harassment?

A person who is being sexually harassed has a number of options. You can:
1. Confront the harasser assertively (if you feel safe/strong enough).
2. Confront the harasser with the support of co-workers, family or friends.
3. Document incidents of harassment.
4. Talk to others whom you trust; find out if anyone else has experienced harassment from the same person.
5. Report to your teacher, guidance counsellor or employer (your employer is legally responsible for harassment that takes place on the job by co-workers/clients.
6. Report to the police.
7. Call for advice or to make a complaint to an organization such as the B.C. Human Rights Coalition or the Canadian Human Rights Commission.
8. Get legal counsel.
9. Call a local Rape Crisis Centre for counselling/guidance.

Eighty-five percent of assaults are committed by someone who is known to the victim.

Six out of 10 assaults are by an acquaintance or friend.

In Canada, two women every day are killed by their husbands or boyfriends.

Seventy-five percent of these women were trying to leave when they died.

Sexual Assault: A Clear Picture of Blame and Accountability

Gender-based beliefs about female sexual power and male enslavement to their own sexual urges run through the very core of our culture. These beliefs inform our value systems and our social and legal systems on a very profound level. Deeply imbedded in our thinking on the issue of sexual assault, a stubborn and persistent cultural voice says "It's the woman's fault." A blaming finger points at the female— at the way she behaved and the way she dressed. The slanted view on this issue is evident in the attitudes of many men, women and teens. In sexual assault court cases, judges have been known to blame females—even when the females are small children. The following items of judicial wisdom, all listed in a recent newspaper article, illuminate this problem further:

British Columbia:
A Vancouver county court judge described a three-year-old female sexual assault victim as sexually aggressive and handed down a suspended sentence to her assailant. When the Crown appealed the sentence, calling it grossly inadequate, the B.C. Court of Appeal stood by its man and dismissed the Crown's appeal. The Appeal Court judge declared that the conduct of the child had to be considered in assessing the punishment to be imposed on the accused.

Ontario:
A man convicted of raping and beating a woman was sentenced to 90 days to be served on weekends. The judge said at sentencing that the man came from a good family. He went on to explain that the victim was drunk at the time of the assault, and he pointed out that her assailant had since developed an ulcer, which proved he was remorseful. He concluded with his opinion that the assault upon the woman was very traumatic but of short duration.

Florida:
A jury acquitted a man accused of raping a woman at knife-point. The jury foreman told reporters that jurors felt the woman asked for it by the way she was dressed.

British Columbia:
A judge sentenced a former teacher to 45 days for repeatedly sexually assaulting a thirteen-year-old female student. The defendant also admitted to sexual assaults on other female students for which he wasn't charged. The judge said he was reluctant to jail a teacher with such a fine teaching record, and he described the assailant as "Order of Canada" material.

British Columbia:
A jury acquitted a man charged with repeatedly sexually assaulting his adopted daughter after the judge reminded the jury that an accusation of sexual misconduct was easy to make but very difficult to disprove. The judge warned the jurors that sexual neurosis, fantasy or spite can prompt such an allegation.

British Columbia:
A judge declared the victim of an attack was at fault to some degree for walking alone at midnight through a park. The woman had been walking home when the assailant, who had a previous conviction for forcing a woman to undress at knife-point, confronted her, stuck a knife to her ribs and forced her into the cemetery.

British Columbia:
In 1987 a provincial court judge dished out a suspended sentence to a man who pleaded guilty to sexually assaulting a thirteen-year-old girl. The judge noted the assailant was an exemplary employee whose co-workers said the assault was out of character. The judge announced that he felt incarceration would serve no purpose other than revenge for the victim and her family.

The same judge decided a man's drunken assault against his common-law wife, whom he was prohibited from seeing, warranted five days in the lockup.

Part I. Carmen and Jack: "I know you're not a virgin."

In the following scenario, ask yourself if you can hear the "blame the female" voice in your own mind.

Carmen has the hots for Jack. He's a few years older than she is and she doesn't know him very well but he hangs out with her brother sometimes. When he was over the other day, he asked if she wanted to go to a party. That was a definite yes! Carmen knows she'll probably have to put out a little because he'll think she's a baby if she doesn't. Carmen has already gone all the way. She lost her virginity with her last boyfriend. It wasn't what she'd expected and he'd dumped her after so she has no intention of doing it again until it's with the right guy. But she doesn't mind fooling around a little. She wears her sexiest bra with a see-through lace shirt and her little stretchy black skirt that hugs her bum like a second skin. Carmen knows she looks hot. Her older brother's friends always call her a "babe." She tells them to f_ off but secretly she likes it.

Jack picks Carmen up and takes her to the party. When they get there she is shocked to see people doing drugs—not just smoking pot but in the kitchen shooting up with needles. She doesn't know anyone and feels really uncomfortable so she asks if they can leave. He seems pissed off and when they leave he doesn't talk to her. Soon she realizes that he's not taking her straight home. Jack takes her to the parking lot near the beach. He starts kissing her and she lets him touch her up top. She lets him keep kissing her and groping her and she makes all the right noises like she's really into it. But Carmen isn't really into it. She feels anxious and confused because she can feel that Jack is angry. Then he starts pulling roughly at her clothes. Carmen pulls away but Jack won't stop. She tries to get out of the car but he pushes her down on the seat. "I know you're not a virgin," he says. Then he tells her she has to finish what she started and forces her to have sex with him.

> *Fact: Sexual assault is not a crime of desire. It is a crime of power. The oldest rape victim on record is a woman in her nineties. The youngest is an infant.*

Fact: Most females who are sexually assaulted are wearing blue jeans.

Fact: Only 27 percent of women whose sexual assaults met the legal definition of rape thought of themselves as rape victims.

Now let's look at a similar scenario but we'll switch the gender of our main character so that Carmen is now a young guy named Devin.

Part II. Jenna and Devin: "I know you want it."

Devin is going out with Jenna. He's really excited because he's had a thing for her for months. Jenna's a bit older than he is and he never thought she'd go out with him. He didn't have the nerve to ask her and then she just came up to him and asked him if he wanted to take her to a party on the weekend. Devin was glad he'd been working out. He felt pretty good about his body. He'd grown three inches since grade 9 and he could tell the girls at school thought he was hot. They teased him sometimes— called him a "babe" and once he heard some girls say "Nice butt" as he walked by. It embarrassed him but he liked it too.

He decided that he could use all the help that he could get on this date so he wore his muscle shirt, the short one that wouldn't stay tucked in, and his low-slung loose-fitting jeans with the band of his underwear showing. He knew his well-defined stomach muscles were a big turn-on for girls. Before Devin left, he grabbed a couple of condoms from his desk drawer and stuffed them in his jacket pocket. You never know, he thought, I might get lucky.

Jenna picked him up. He felt kind of dumb about not having his licence yet. She didn't seem to mind though. She kissed him right on the lips when she said hello! But when they got to the party, Jenna totally ignored him. She was hanging out with some older guys that Devin didn't know. They kept looking over at him and laughing. He didn't know anyone else and he felt really awkward. Finally, he asked if she wanted to go. Jenna didn't say anything. She just grabbed his hand and led him into one of the bedrooms. She pushed him back on the bed and started kissing him and moving on top of him. Devin wasn't into it. He was hurt and angry about how the evening had gone and just wanted to leave. He tried to push her off but she started pulling at his jeans and saying, "C'mon baby, I know you want it." Devin pushed her off him and sat up. He decided he would just find his own way home.

Suddenly the three older guys that Jenna had been hanging with earlier came into the room. They locked the door behind them and pushed Devin down on the bed, pinning him down while Jenna did what she wanted. Devin couldn't move. His body responded but he hated what was happening. He closed his eyes and all he could remember on the cab ride home was all of them laughing and laughing.

Was it his fault?

Where Devin was clearly not at fault, we may have felt Carmen "asked for it." Although it is extremely common to hear comments about what the female was wearing and how she behaved when a sexual assault occurs, it is interesting to note that it is very rare to blame the victim in any other crime. For example, if a young man washed and polished his car and drove it around showing it off and then later it was stolen, no one would say, "Well, he asked for it!" If he left his car running while he ran back into the house to get something, and it was stolen, perhaps this would be considered an unwise choice but it would be clear that the person who stole the car was a thief and entirely to blame.

When we look at the issue of fault and blame from different angles—and look at the same events from both a female and male perspective—the ways in which our thought patterns may be biased become evident.

In the following two scenarios we can take a look at the same issue but from a slightly different angle. We will see the difference between making unwise choices and asking to be violated.

Maria Takes It Off

VERSION 1

Maria wasn't allowed to go to the party. She was angry at her parents and when an older guy asked her to go she said yes. She told her parents she was sleeping over at a friend's. The guy picked her up at the 7-Eleven. He gave her some hard liquor to drink. Then he gave her a drug he said would make her really happy. She took that too. It did make her feel good. By the time they got to the party she was really high. Maria felt wild and crazy and free, and although she would normally never do such a thing, she got up on a coffee table and danced. The guys sitting around started cheering her on and she started stripping. It was as though she didn't have any inhibitions and she loved all the attention she was getting. Maria ended up taking off all her clothes and dancing naked on the table.

Maria didn't remember much of what happened. One moment she was dancing on the table having the time of her life and the next thing she knew she was in a bedroom and guys were coming in and taking turns with her. When she woke up the next day, she knew she had been gang raped but she didn't tell anyone because she knew it was her own fault.

Let's look at the exact same scenario—same girl, same party—but with a very different ending:

VERSION 2

... The next thing she knew, Maria was down off the table and a guy was putting a jacket around her shoulders. He was asking what her name was. She tried to kiss him but he pushed her away and asked her again what her name was. He gathered up her clothes and sent her to the bathroom to get dressed. When Maria came out of the bathroom he was still there and he put her in his car and drove her home. He walked her right to the door and told her parents that someone had spiked her drink and that nothing bad had happened.

In version 1 and version 2, Maria's behaviour was the same. What was different was the response of the guys at the party. In the first example, the guys who took advantage of Maria were rapists. In the second, the guy was a decent and caring human being. Many of us can think of guys we know who would fit both these scenarios.

There is a difference between being accountable for our own choices and being responsible for the choices of others. Maria's choice to lie to her parents and go to a party she wasn't allowed to go to may have been unwise. Her choice to have too much to drink and to do drugs was very unwise—especially given the reality of the violent world we live in. A person who gets so high on drugs and alcohol that they don't know what they are doing may behave in sexually inappropriate ways. A person who is lacking in healthy boundaries, suffering low self-esteem or who has been previously abused could also behave in this way. People who behave like this may be asking for attention, or they may be asking for help with a substance abuse problem. They may be guilty of being naive and they are guilty of making unwise choices. They are not asking to be violated.

Developmentally, adolescence is a phase in the journey toward becoming an adult. Adolescence is about making our own choices and learning from our mistakes. Teenagers are adults-in-process. It seems highly unfair to accuse young women of asking to be hurt when they are doing precisely what they are meant to be doing at the developmental stage they are in. There is a deep injustice in this socially accepted blame-the-victim attitude.

Acquaintance Rape: A Soul Wound

In many young women's minds, rape is something that happens to "bad" girls (who have somehow brought it on themselves) and is perpetrated by strange and creepy men. Rape is pictured as a sudden and violent attack by a depraved psycho. The rapist is imagined as an evil, almost cartoon-like monster with excessive body hair and fangs. Like the bogeyman, he lurks behind bushes or in dark alleys. It does not occur to many girls that a seemingly nice and normal guy, someone they know and think is good-looking, could be a rapist.

It is very common for a young woman who is raped by someone she knows not to identify what happened as rape. When she thinks about what happened, she may feel stupid. She may tell herself she should have known what the guy was after from the beginning and she may feel she should have been able to prevent it. She may also feel guilty if she dressed in sexy clothes or flirted or wanted him to find her attractive. If all these things happened, the young women probably feels she just got what she asked for. If this is how she feels, she won't be likely to tell anyone, believing that friends or family will just confirm that it was her fault.

To be raped is one of the deepest ways a woman can be hurt. When the rapist is someone a woman knows and trusts there is a profound and devastating element of betrayal involved. To be raped by someone we know can be more painful and damaging than a physical beating because to be raped is to be hurt on the inside. Rape is a violation of our whole selves. It is a soul wound.

When I met Tim, a pleasant-looking, middle-class sixteen-year-old, in one of the SafeTeen Boys' Program workshops at his school, he admitted that he had already raped one young woman. Of course he didn't call his behaviour "rape," but in listening to Tim tell his story it was apparent to me that he had committed date rape on a young woman he met at a party. Lacking in empathy and ignorant about the laws on sexual assault, Tim was well on the way to committing more serious aggression against women.

In our workshop, Tim was amazed when he found out that almost none of the other boys considered sex to be the main thing to look for in a relationship. He was dumbfounded when the other boys in his small discussion group argued with him about what constituted "consent" in a dating situation. Tim listened silently as I related to the young men what women have told me about how they feel when they are sexually harassed, and I assumed he was feeling defensive and defiant inside. It was my turn to be amazed when I read Tim's evaluation of the workshop. "I didn't know how it makes women feel," he wrote. "I didn't know that I had hurt girls."

—Dr. Aaron White

The Right to Stop

When a young woman chooses to kiss the boy she is with, she has agreed to kiss him. She has the right to kiss him for as long as she likes without going any further. If she agrees to go part way and then feels uncomfortable, she has the right to stop. If she has agreed to have sex but finds herself feeling unsure—even if it's in the middle of making love—she has the right to stop. That is not an example of a woman leading a guy on or asking to be raped. That is an example of a person who is exploring her boundaries, being honest about her feelings and changing her mind. It is developmentally appropriate for young women to be confused and ambivalent about sexual activity.

By beginning the process of exploring her desire, she has not agreed to go all the way. Regardless of the wisdom of her choices, given the expectations and conditioning of males, a young woman should have the right to begin sexual activity and then stop. She should have the right to change her mind—a right that a young man takes for granted.

When a young woman is exploring her sexuality and experiencing strong feelings of desire that are new and overwhelming and confusing, it is very unfair that she is expected to be responsible not only for saying "No" to her own desire, but for saying "No" to his. It is doubly unfair that when she communicates either verbally or with body language that she is unwilling to proceed, or that she's confused and unsure about proceeding, she should be made to feel guilty, or be threatened, coerced, manipulated or pressured in any way. It is unthinkable that she would be forced into sexual activity and a gross violation that she would be blamed after the fact for not giving clear enough messages.

Mixed Feelings = Mixed Messages

When females are accused of giving mixed messages, it is as though the assumption is that this behaviour is a premeditated and pernicious conspiracy to frustrate and confuse males. The puzzle is not so much why females engage in this yes/no behaviour but why males find it so baffling to deal with. It seems perfectly obvious that a person who is giving mixed messages probably has mixed feelings.

A teenage girl may not be sure how she feels about the male or the relationship or her own readiness to engage in sexual activity. She may feel physically ready to engage and her own powerful sexual feelings are urging her forward while her fears about the consequences for herself and the relationship hold her back. Even when she is clear that she does not wish to engage, either because she does not feel the desire or because she doesn't feel it is a wise choice at that time, she is socialized very strongly to care more about her partner's feelings than her own. Feeling responsible for meeting his needs, coupled with being afraid that he will leave her if she doesn't, can be why she gives mixed messages. If we are able to see the mixed messages as a clear communication that a female has mixed feelings, we may be able to see that she is in fact saying both "Yes" and "No."

Females need to have permission to have mixed feelings without being accused of being screwed-up, immature "cock teases" who are playing mind games. If we didn't fear these judgements, we would be better able to interpret our own inner turmoil as a clear sign that we are not ready to engage, and we would be better able to say "No" more clearly. We would also be able to say "Yes" more clearly to activities that we do choose to engage in.

To learn how to articulate yes/no feelings clearly, see exercise on page 298.

It would serve guys well to consider a mixed message a clear "No" for the time being. Silence could also be considered a "No." In fact, it would be safe to say that if a guy has not heard "Yes, I definitely want and choose and desire to have sex with you right now" (and this from a female who is sober and coherent), he should consider it a "No."

Mixed messages are exactly what they appear to be: an honest and very human response to a very complex set of emotions and circumstances that could have enormous impact on a woman's life. The young woman often has more to risk because it is she who may have to bear a child or suffer an abortion. As well, she has her reputation to think of. To be labelled slut, "skank" or "ho" (whore) could be personally and socially devastating.

Disclosing Abuse

It is difficult to get accurate statistics on sexual abuse simply by documenting disclosures and legally reported incidents. We must take into consideration the percentage of incidents that occur but are not reported. There are many reasons why a person may not formally report—or even tell someone they know—about an incident of abuse. Self-blame, shame, fear, protecting the abuser, denial—all of these things may come into play. A very common reason why teens don't report when they are harassed or assaulted is a lack of a safe person to tell. They either fear exposure and punishment, have heard of a friend who has had her anonymity betrayed or been blamed, or they have direct experience of this themselves.

Schools and families rarely have secure, safe harassment and disclosure policies and systems in place. Many parents and educators are not trained to handle disclosures in a way that protects the victim of the abuse. We keep telling our kids to "tell," but personal and societal judgements, legal red tape and lack of skill often result in the child or teen feeling violated, retraumatized or simply unheard and unprotected. In the SafeTeen program evaluation process we have learned that approximately one out of four teens in B.C. schools are "keeping secrets" and a vast majority do not feel they have "a safe person to tell."

Even the child or student of a highly skilled parent or educator may not choose to report. Recently, a school counsellor who was known for her skill in this area was horrified to learn that her own teenage daughter had been brutally raped. She didn't discover this until her daughter attempted suicide—almost a year after the incident occurred.

We must not underestimate the power of shame to silence our children and we must all learn how to hear our children when they do decide to speak out.

When you are approached by someone who wants to make a disclosure of sexual abuse, remember that this may be the first time the person has ever told anyone. However it seems at the time, know that it is a tremendous act of courage on their part. How you respond can make an enormous impact on their recovery.

Disclosure Outline

Five things to say when you receive a disclosure of sexual assault:*
1. "I believe you."
2. "I'm sorry that happened to you."
3. "I'm glad you told me."
4. "It's not your fault."
5. "I'll help you to get help."

If the person disclosing is of legal age (nineteen years) you are not legally bound to report unless a younger person is still at risk (i.e., an under-age sibling still living at home with an abusive parent).

If the person disclosing is of legal age it is imperative that they make their own decisions.

(*Reprinted from B.C. Ministry of Social Services and Housing pamphlet.)

Points to Remember about Disclosure
1. Before the person makes the disclosure, tell them that you are legally bound to report it if they are under the legal age. If this stops them it may mean that they are not ready to take it that far and you can give them some time to prepare. You can also encourage them to report in the third person and write it down. If they are not currently at risk (and no other member of the family who is a minor is at risk) you can give them more time to prepare for the " fallout" of a report. If they are at risk and you make the choice to report them against their will, tell them and remind them: "This information belongs to you. You can deny it or choose not to talk about it once I have made the report."

Reinforce how important for their healing process getting help is.

2. Ask "Do you want some help?" You may be legally bound to report the disclosure and it is far better if the person has agreed or given you permission.

3. Be honest about what will happen once you report (that is, other people such as parents, police and social workers will get involved and ask a lot of questions).

4. Respect the person's boundaries. Don't touch him/her without permission.

5. Don't try to "fix it." What the person needs is to be heard, believed and offered options to begin recovery. Don't say, "Everything will be all right," or "Don't worry, I'll handle it."

6. Use a strong and compassionate tone. Do not use a "mothering" tone of voice as it may entrench them in a "child posture," which is disempowering (unless you are prepared to take them through a longer term therapeutic process).

7. To make statements about feelings is OK and can be helpful. For example, "It is not OK for someone to treat you like that," or "I feel so angry that he did that to you." However, do not display your own emotional reactions (anger/despair/shock/fear). These are your feelings and are often more about you than the person you are helping. The last thing a person in crisis needs to deal with is someone else's feelings. They will be reassured by a clear, sincere but calm response.

8. If the person displays strong emotions during a disclosure, do not say, "Calm down." It is more helpful to assert clear boundaries about behaviours (e.g., "This is not a safe place for you to be this upset," or "It is not OK with me for you to yell/break things)." Remind the person to take a deep breath, hand them a tissue and mirror what you see that they are feeling. This will help them to regain control much more effectively.

9. If someone begins to show very strong emotions which seem inappropriate to the incident which they are disclosing, it may be that the smaller incident is triggering a more traumatic incident which they may or may not consciously remember. Do not minimize the experience (don't say, "God, Jane, he just touched your knee…"; instead say, "He touched your knee and I can see how upset you are. You have the right to be upset. He had no right to touch you like that."

10. Validate the person's right to feel what they're feeling by "mirroring without entrenching." For example, if the person says, "I want to kill myself," an entrenching response would be: "You want to kill yourself." A validating response is: "You are so upset right now that you are talking about suicide. You must be very, very upset."

11. Never reinforce the person's belief that the incident was their fault in any way, even if you have personal judgements about the incident and how it occurred. For example, don't say, "You're right, you shouldn't have had so much to drink / worn that outfit / gone so far." Instead, you can affirm: "It's harder to be clear about your boundaries when you have had a lot to drink—and what happened still wasn't your fault."

12. In a group situation when a person seems emotionally "out of control," do not ask/tell him/her to leave. Ask, "Is this a safe place for you to be feeling like this? Would you like to find a quiet place to be for a while?" Accompany them to a safe place, stay with them or provide a safe person to stay with them and invite them to rejoin the group later. Ask them if they would rather be alone and respect their choice. Tell them, "You know what's right for you." Do not leave them without a contact or access to follow-up.

13. Try to end the session with an affirmation: "You did the right thing by telling me" and a comment that affirms their self-esteem and strength. For example, "It took courage for you to tell me this," or "I admire your ability to express your feelings—that takes strength."

14. It can be helpful to tell the person who has just disclosed that they are not alone, many people have these experiences and the fact that they have taken this first step indicates that they have the strength to get through it. Reassure them that healing is possible and that when we get through to the other side we are stronger, more compassionate people.

15. If a friend discloses "for a friend," keep in mind this could be a disclosure done in the second person. Watch for signs of intense emotion and connectedness to the story. Use the same five point response in third person. Tell her/him that secrets hurt, even when they are not your own, and that s/he has been a good friend but carrying her/his friend's secret is hurting her/him. Offer to help her/him find help.

For an exercise on how to handle disclosures, see page 299.

Part III: **SPIRIT**

The spirit of SafeTeen is the passion that drives the work. It is the part of the work that is bigger than just the physical body of work. It is deeper than the intellectual theory behind the work and it is more than the skills that make up the heart of the work. The spirit of this work was born out of my desire to heal myself and to contribute to the safety and empowerment of girls and women. The sustained passion I have for this work comes from a lifetime of focusing almost exclusively on healing the great ugly wound in the world that is violence. In the spirit of SafeTeen, I hold my hope for a more peaceful world.

In Part III: SPIRIT we are going deeply into the core of the issues, into the guts of them, exposing the bone. I have always felt compelled to push the edges of what is usually written or said out loud. I feel compelled to do this the way one might feel an urge to release a bird from a cage — even knowing it may not survive out in the world.

Chapter 8

The Spirit of Girls and Women

A S MUCH AS there are infinite differences in experience and ways of being, I also believe that there is a common thread woven into the intricate tapestry of each individual woman that binds us together. In this section I am writing the female body of experience.

Virginity: Reclaiming a Spiritual Barrier

The concept of virginity is one that belongs in the Middle Ages, a time when women were chattels to be bargained off in marriage. A time when a woman's worth was completely dependent on her chastity. A woman who was not a virgin was thought of as used goods. In ancient times, a woman who lost her virginity was considered absolutely worthless *regardless of the circumstances*. Even in the case of rape, it was common for a woman to be severely penalized. She may have been shunned, forced to marry her rapist or even stoned to death. These practices still hold true today in some cultures.

Virginity has more to do with males protecting their "property" rights than it has to do with women. By definition, a virgin is a woman who has not been penetrated (or "taken") by a man. The old belief that non-virginal women were without virtue and of no moral worth meant that they were unmarriageable. Being unable to marry meant having no means of financial support, which in turn meant being a burden on their families and often being relegated to a life of prostitution. In current times, in some cultures, the groom and his family still require medical proof of virginity before the bride is approved. In these cultures, a young female may be forced to have her virginity verified just because she has been seen alone with someone of the opposite sex. Another carry-over to current times is that non-virginal females are often stigmatized as sluts and "easy." A female who has been labelled in this way is perceived as available for casual sexual activity and is more vulnerable to sexual pressure and acquaintance rape.

The physical state of virginity is not functionally relevant to a woman's life and yet the keeping and losing of her virginity can have a profound effect on a woman's destiny. In modern North American and European cultures, once a woman has lost her virginity she can feel as though someone has removed a physical and psychological barrier. She can feel that she no longer has any control and cannot defend her right to not engage in sexual intercourse.

The concept of virginity specifically refers to the hymen, a thin membrane that partially covers the vaginal opening. The physiological definition of "being a virgin" is to have the hymen intact. To lose one's virginity is to have the hymen ruptured. The possibilities for how this could happen are numerous: childhood sexual abuse, self-exploration, sexual assault or even using a tampon could all potentially rupture a hymen. The physical barrier, however small and inconsequential in terms of actual protection from forced entry, can be representative of a woman's psychological and emotional boundaries. The loss of a female's virginity can have an enormous impact on her sense of self and on her ability to assert herself.

*"Women are the guardians of the doorway of life. We must decide
who comes in and who goes out."*
—MARGE PIERCEY

In order to regain control, women need to redefine the concept of
virginity as a spiritual barrier that they are in absolute control of and
that has nothing to do with past experiences or physical realities. This
barrier can be seen as the gateway to her body/temple. When a woman
does this, she can reclaim her virginity over and over again as simply
the state of not choosing to welcome anyone into her most sacred place.

Testimonial: One Young Woman "Reclaims Her Virginity"

A couple of years ago after I had presented the SafeTeen program to a
group of grade 9 girls several of the participants approached me after
the workshop, as they often do, to thank me. I noticed one young
woman hanging back at the edge of the group. She waited until all the
other girls had left. This was a common enough experience and I had
learned over the years that a disclosure was usually about to take place
when this happened. But this girl merely wanted to thank me and tell
me a specific story. "Tasha" told me that she had attended my presen-
tation the year before and that she wanted me to know how it had
affected her life. She went on to explain that at that time (when she
was in grade 8) she had found herself in a relationship with an older
guy. Studying her feet the whole time, she told me she had been having sex with him and that she hated it. She said she felt that once she
had let him the first time, she didn't feel she could stop it. Then she
looked up at me and I saw her eyes were shining with tears. "What I
wanted to say," she said, "well, after I heard you tell the group last year
that you can start a sexual relationship, realize you aren't ready and
change your mind—I went that day and told my boyfriend I didn't
want to have sex anymore." She said he broke up with her but she was

so glad she didn't have to do it anymore she didn't care. She went on to say she had "reclaimed her virginity—just like you said I could" and that she was still choosing not to be sexually active. "I just wanted to thank you," she said.

I was very deeply moved by this girl's story. It was so validating to hear that my words had impacted a young woman's life in such a concrete way. It affirmed for me that we, as adults, have the ability to give our daughters "permission" to be assertive—simply by telling them their bodies belong to them.

Female Desire: The Invisible Body of Writing

It is commonplace to hear discussion about boys and men and their all-consuming interest in sex. The presence of and power of male desire is seen, spoken and written about. We don't often hear, see or read about female desire.

The awakening of desire in the female body can be very powerful, and the feelings of wanting to move toward completion of the sexual activity can be overwhelmingly strong. The raw physical desire and the desire to be connected emotionally can become fused and this fusion can intensify a female's desire and create enormous conflict between body and heart.

Young Women's Emerging Sexuality

Young women in their early teens are in the process of individuating. They are pushing themselves away from their parents. They are defining their own opinions, tastes, style and values. This separation process often includes resisting physical contact with parents. Even though this is usually a healthy and natural expression of autonomy, it can be a lonely time for an adolescent and a time of strong yearning for touch.

For young women who have been neglected or abandoned, physical desire is often confused with intense emotional need. What a teenage girl can feel alongside physical desire is a deep loneliness and fear of being alone, a desire to be a part of someone else, to be absolutely connected and especially to be wanted. A desire to have someone's arms open to her and enfold her, making her feel small and protected the way she needed to be when she was little. To feel so profoundly welcomed into the sphere of another human being's body and energy when she is feeling alone and unloved can be as intoxicating and as addictive as any drug. Like most addictions, it is rooted in the desire to fill an inner emptiness.

"Boy crazy" girls who are obsessive about boys and behave inappropriately in order to get the attention of males are often acting out of this inner emptiness. For these young women the sensations that are awakening in their bodies often have less to do with orgasm and more to do with emotional hunger. Just this emotional craving by itself, without the element of sexual stimulation, can be a force to be reckoned with and can be experienced as irresistible desire. In the event that the woman is also stimulated skillfully enough to begin the journey toward orgasm, the task of saying "No" becomes monumental.

Young women need to feel it is their own choice whether or not they will be sexually active. When we are choosing, we are empowered. When we are informed we are empowered.

An empowered teen will be more likely to choose to abstain or take responsibility if she pro-actively chooses to be sexually active. She will be more emotionally prepared, more likely to use protection and more discerning about who she chooses to engage with. When we look at teen pregnancy rates and sexually transmitted disease statistics we know that no amount of external guidance or threats of dire consequences will ensure our youth will abstain from sexual activity.

When a young woman feels empowered, choosing *not* to be sexually active can become a goal—something to work toward, plan for and fight for. When a young woman decides she does not want to be sexually active, it is imperative that she be clear about this goal before putting herself in potentially intimate situations. In order to stay in control, she must have an awareness of her sexual body and the rhythms of her own desire. She must feel absolutely that she has the right to stop at any time. She also needs the assertiveness skills to communicate clear messages at a time when the other person may not be very invested in listening.

The silence surrounding female sexuality participates in keeping young women from being in synergy with the rhythms of their desire and therefore their destinies.

Rhythms of Female Desire

Female desire can move in cycles and range from one extreme to another. At times in a woman's cycle she may feel revulsion (she feels completely disinterested in and even repulsed by the idea of sex and cannot imagine why anyone would engage in such a smelly, sweaty activity). At times she may feel indifference (she is in a neutral place where, given a charming and artful enough approach she can be convinced to engage). And at times she may feel consumed by indiscriminate lust; times when the corners of tables become unexpectedly interesting and she has urges to proposition strangers in the street.

Males are strongly conditioned to believe they have the right to insinuate their needs and desires on females, and in fact are taught that to pursue females aggressively and to be successful in this pursuit is the ideal expression of masculinity. A women often finds herself so involved in asserting her right to say "No" to sexual activity and defending her right to her boundaries that she loses touch with whether she does or does not actually feel desire. The struggle becomes more about whether or not she has a choice. When extricating herself from situations where she feels pressured to have sex becomes the focus, not wanting to have sex becomes the most familiar emotional posture. All the passionate energy is directed into regaining control of her body on a very basic level.

When we do not have the space to feel the rhythms of our own desire and the freedom to stop and start sexual activity as we feel the need in our own bodies, a sexual deadness can occur. It is as though in order to protect our space, we shut it *all* down. When we shut down our desire in order to feel a sense of control over our bodies, we often feel bad about ourselves because we cannot meet the consistent sexual demands of our partners.

Until females can feel absolutely in control of their physical space and their right to want sex or not want sex, they will not become familiar with their own personal ebb and flow of desire. Until women can feel their absolute right to assert their desire and their boundaries, they will not feel safe enough to open to their desire. Many women are afraid to express any physical affection in their relationships with men because they fear it will be interpreted as starting something that they will then be powerless to stop. If a woman feels she must always finish what she starts, she will start something less often. It is difficult for a woman to be in touch with wanting something that is constantly expected from her and that she has no control over once it has begun.

A woman who is caught in this dynamic can feel tired and genuinely lacking in passion. She is often accused of being frigid and cold, which supports her own belief that she is inadequate. The irony is that since it is still not fully acceptable for a woman to express her desire without being labelled a slut, she risks being shamed if she freely initiates sex when she *does* feel desire.

The dynamics of desire are complex and full of contradictions for women. If the woman says "No," she risks being punished. She could be verbally abused, made to feel guilty, shut out, temporarily abandoned, cheated on or permanently replaced. If she says "Yes" and expresses strong desire, she risks being shamed. If the woman does engage in sexual activity but doesn't express strong desire, it may be interpreted as an insult to the man's masculinity. Women are very strongly conditioned to boost the male ego. Many women know from experience that a fragile male ego can be synonymous with a violent man. In order to assure that the man continues to feel good about himself (thereby keeping the peace and keeping herself safe), a woman may pretend to feel desire. When she does this, she enters into a dishonest relationship with her partner and with herself.

To pretend desire is to accept the myth that desire does not exist within one's own body. To pretend desire is to give up hope of connecting with the genuine desire that lives within us. In order to pretend desire, a woman must disassociate from her body and her heart, in effect leaving herself and acting out a role. To not allow one's genuine self to be exactly what it is in any given moment is a betrayal of self and an abandonment of self. In her desperation to avoid abandonment (motivated by her fear of being alone) she has become more truly alone than she would ever have been if her partner had left her.

Our bodies are our most sacred places. We have the right to live in our bodies and be true to whatever feelings we have or do not have in any given moment.

Our bodies are our most sacred places. Our hearts and minds and spirits live in our bodies. We have the right to live in our bodies and be true to whatever feelings we have or do not have in any given moment. If it doesn't feel right, stop doing it. If it feels good and right, move toward that feeling with your whole self. We need to reclaim our bodies as clean and beautiful and especially as ours. We need to keep them safe and well and strong. We need to feel in control of our bodies and we need to feel free to take the space to learn what our bodies do and do not want to do.

Revealing the Female Body

Sex education curricula used in schools today commonly define female sexual organs as the vagina. Likewise, progressive parents tell their daughters they have vaginas. As well-intentioned as parents and educators may be, it is as physiologically inaccurate to refer to female genitalia as solely the vagina as it would be to refer to the mouth just in terms of the throat without mentioning the lips, teeth and tongue. And just as absurd.

The vagina is the part of the female anatomy that our culture is most comfortable with because it is the birth canal. It is related to procreation and reproduction and is therefore less threatening because we can talk about it without any alluding to female desire. The vagina is also the focus of male sexual pleasure, which is more acceptable to talk about than female sexual pleasure. Female genitalia are most commonly referred to in the context of sexist comments and misogynist humour, and usually only in reference to male desire. To quote a common joke: "What is the definition of a woman? A life-support system for a vagina."

The part of the female body that is visible and easily touchable is the vulva. The vulva includes the labia majora (outer lips), the labia minora (inner lips), and most importantly, the clitoris. The clitoris, as natural a part of our bodies as our arms and legs or the nose on our face, has only one function: female sexual pleasure. The blatant omission and covert cover-up of this psychologically and functionally important part of the female body is extremely revealing.

Erasing Female Desire

In many Middle Eastern and African cultures it is still common practice to subject female children to genital mutilation, otherwise known as clitoridectomies (the surgical removal of the clitoris) or infibulation (removal of the clitoris, scraping of the labia to remove sensitivity, and sewing up of the vagina). These procedures, which are often done without anaesthetic or sterile equipment and at great risk of infection and even death, are performed to ensure the chastity and future fidelity of the females.

In 1985 I attended an international forum on women's issues in Nairobi, Kenya. I listened to women of all ages talk about their personal experiences with this practice. One old woman spoke of the women who had died from infections or in childbirth due to difficulties stemming from the procedure. She went on to explain that there was no hope of having the practice banned. The most the African women at the forum felt they could hope for was to have the procedure performed in clinics and hospitals with anaesthetic and lower risk of infection. When asked about women's right to sexual pleasure, she laughed and told us that they could never even bring this issue up as a reason to stop the practice. She explained the complexity of the issue within her culture. Females who did not undergo the surgery were seen as deviant and were not marriageable. The girls are told that a clitoris grows into a penis and that no man would marry a woman with a penis. A female who could not marry was a burden to her family. For these women, accepting genital mutilation is an economic survival matter as well as an issue of belonging to a culture and a community.

The history of clitoridectomies has solid roots in European and North American culture as well. Physicians recommended the surgical removal of the clitoris as a cure for female masturbation (thought to be the cause of insanity, hysteria, epilepsy, nymphomania and spinal irritation, among other things) as early as in the tenth century. As late as 1937, a respected American medical school text, *Holt's Diseases of Infancy and Childhood*, stated that the author was not averse to "circumcision in girls or cauterization of the clitoris."

I believe that it is important for us to courageously look at the female body and insist on seeing what has been silenced, erased and literally removed. I believe that girls need to see, touch and speak about their bodies without shame and without fear. To become familiar with our bodies will give us the language and the voice to be seen and to be heard and ultimately to be in our full power.

Filling in the Blanks

In 1989 I visited a place in Norway where hundreds of sculptures of the naked human form are displayed in all shapes and sizes. The sculptor, Gustaf Vigeland, began work on these sculptures in the 1940s and made it his life's work to sculpt, in the most exquisite detail, every aspect of the human body. Seen up close, one can see the fine veins on the backs of hands, intricate lines around the eyes, dimpled babies' bottoms. The life-size nude male forms are complete with veins on the penises and wrinkled scrotums surrounded by delicate curls of pubic hair.

Every female form that I saw there had a blank Barbie-doll V in the place of genitalia. It was a deeply disturbing and powerful testament to the fear of female sexuality and the need to silence it.

We have lawn ornaments of little boys peeing. Can you imagine a lawn ornament of a little girl squatting with a fountain of water streaking down between her legs? Female genitalia are invisible in language as well. When pressed by children's curiosity and persistent questions, parents commonly tell their girl children, "You don't have a penis; only boys have penises." The unspoken message in this statement is that girls don't have anything. A girl child playing with her baby doll or Barbie doll could easily believe this message. And yet the male doll, Ken, displays an unmistakable bulge. If Ken can have a bulge, why can't Barbie have a crack?

Expressing Female Desire

A female who embraces her sexuality and expresses her desire in flirtatious mannerisms and body language, even if she is not fully sexually active, is commonly called a "slut" or "ho." If a young woman has been sexually active, even if it was only with one boy, she will most likely inherit the much dreaded reputation of "slut" when she and her boyfriend break up. The boy, on the other hand, will be able to add a notch to his belt and proudly brag to his buddies about his success. The double standard and unfairness inherent in this dynamic is strongly felt by young women. Being labelled a "slut" can damage self-esteem and break down a young woman's boundaries, making it more difficult for her to say "No" to sexual activity when she doesn't want it. Often women labelled "slut" are cut off from other females and are targeted as easy prey by males who are looking for sexual conquests.

The word "slut" is a weapon used to divide females from each other. Young women spit the word at each other as though it represents the most vile and filthy thing imaginable.

The male/female social/sexual world is set up in such a way as to pit females against each other in order to vie for male attention. Young women frequently betray their close female friends in order to "get" a boyfriend. It is as though there is an unstated belief that all females

have "slut" potential—the potential to be overtaken by their desperation for a boyfriend. "Sluts" will do anything in order to get a guy.

Young women don't seem to have any awareness of the ways in
which they are being set up by this patriarchal divide-and-conquer
game. When they lose a desired male's attention to another female,
they direct all their feelings of rage and betrayal toward each other.
The faithless boyfriend is off the hook and remains the object of
desire. A key factor in understanding the subversive forces at work
here is the way in which females are conditioned to need the validation of male attention at all costs. The "slut" dynamic serves to usurp
female power on the playing field of sex and relationships.

What Are Girls and Women So Afraid Of?
In some parts of the world, a woman's sexual desirability is literally a
life-or-death question. If she is not desirable then she is not marriageable and because her parents cannot afford to feed her she could die.
This concrete life and death threat does not apply to most contemporary North American women; however, the desperation to be desirable has persisted across the ages, continents and cultures. North
American women starve themselves to death and surgically alter their
bodies in order to be desirable. This behaviour begs the question,
What are they so afraid of?

There is a cruel game that adults sometimes play on small children.
When a group of adults is sitting around a room and a small child of
three or four years old is present, one adult will begin by saying,
"Where's Tommy?" The child will usually respond by announcing,
"I'm right here." The game continues with all the adults looking
around and in fact right through the child, repeating the question,
"Where's Tommy? Has anyone seen him?" At first the child asserts
his presence with confidence, based on the assumption that he exists
and will be seen. After a very short time, this confidence begins to
crumble and he begins to display more and more anxiety, until finally
he loses all ability to believe that he does, in fact, exist. At this point he
is consumed with terror and cries his heart out. Then the adults laugh
and reassure him. Aside from the fact that this game amounts to nothing less than emotional terrorism and psychic child abuse, it points to

the inability of a child at a certain developmental phase to confirm his own existence.

I believe this same phenomenon comes into play for teenage girls and plays itself out in their desperation to be seen by boys. In a world that undervalues females, in a patriarchal culture that relentlessly and systematically erodes the female ego by rendering the female presence virtually invisible throughout history, it is as though women—like small children—are not able to confirm their own existence. A woman's very sense of herself as existing can be so fragile that she is dependent on being seen by a man. This is why young women slander and even physically fight each other to compete for visibility.

Ultimately what they are afraid of is being erased. A young woman can feel extreme anxiety and even existential terror if she feels invisible in this way. Teen girls are obsessed with boys and the teen suicide rate is higher than ever. At a time when they should be focusing their energies on their developing selves, heterosexual teen girls do nothing but think and talk and write in their journals about boys. Unlike teen boys, their focus isn't on sex but on being noticed by boys. *He looked at me, winked at me, smiled at me, talked to me, asked me out: He saw me, therefore I exist.*

If the only way that a young woman can count on being seen by guys is by being sexually desirable and available, she will go that route. Not even the death threat of AIDS will keep her from her quest to be seen.

If a woman walks into a room but there is no man present to see her, does she still exist?

Teenage girls have told me that they feel any boyfriend is better than no boyfriend at all. To be part of a couple is a prerequisite to successful social functioning in our society. There is a tremendous stigma attached to being single, and the pressure to hook up with a mate starts when we're very young.

In one Canadian school, grade 9 girls are signing each other's year books "H.A.G.S. and F.A.G.S." ("Have A Good Summer" and "Find A Guy Soon"). In another, the announcement of a Valentine's Day dance in a grade 4 class created a flurry of who was asking whom to the dance, creating extreme anxiety for the unpopular girls. It was evident that popularity was determined primarily by appearance, with thinness and light-coloured skin being the most desirable qualities. These children were nine and ten years old. Research on eating disorders tells us that girls begin dieting in grade 4. The quest for the male gaze and the struggle to compete for it begins at a very young age.

Invisible Girls: Objectification and Sexual Harassment

Most women can remember back to a time when they were just a kid. When I take a moment to remember, I see a snow-suited body that is spread-eagled on the snow making angels. I see a supple body hanging upside down from a monkey bar with her dress fallen over her face, arms swinging wildly. I see a little girl skipping along the side-walk in time to a song she is singing out loud. There is energy and openness in this female body. She is unafraid and unselfconscious. Like a gymnast dismounting, arms outflung, the girl child embodies a feeling of "Ta-da!"

Most women can remember the moment when they were looked at "in that way" for the first time. In that instant we are no longer human. We have become objects. This is a transformational moment for us. It is the ritual which, in the patriarchy, welcomes us to womanhood. It is the moment when we lose not only our childhood, but our personhood.

The little girl notices someone is looking at her "funny." It could be a relative, a family friend, a teacher, a strange man on the street. At first she is confused. Then she feels a self-consciousness she has never experienced before. She sees herself through his eyes. Her cheeks flush red and she looks down at her feet. She feels the male gaze and her skin contracts as though the gaze is a physical touch from which she is pulling away. Her arms fold over her chest, protecting the little bumps there, not wanting them looked at, somehow knowing they are what he's looking at. Denied this territory, his gaze scans down her body. Immediately her hands drop down and clasp awkwardly in front of her pubic area. Then her shoulders curl inward so that her upper arms partially cover her breasts. But it is hopeless, she can't completely cover her female body and she feels exposed. Then he tells her she's pretty. Standing there, pinned like a butterfly by his gaze, she says, "Um, thanks." She knows somehow that she is supposed to want this attention, that she is supposed to feel complimented by it, but deep inside she hates it.

Her body has been acknowledged but without her in it. Instinctively she hates the feeling of separation from self. She senses that who she is has been left out. She sees that her obvious discomfort and embarrassment are ignored. She doesn't want to be rude. She squirms under his gaze until he releases her and then she runs, the wind in her face cleansing away the shame. Until the next time.

Sexual harassment objectifies. It is a systemic, persistent erosion of a female person's self-esteem. It erases her humanity and overexposes her physical body. By identifying her in that moment as object of the male gaze, it usurps the woman's power each and every time it happens.

Over time the little girl learns that if she does not attract the male gaze, she will begin to disappear—that not to be seen by a man means that she does not exist. She will begin to crave the feeling of being seen. She will feel that she cannot live without it. She will develop an obsession with looking at herself in the mirror. She will begin to paint her face, decorate her body with jewellery, expose parts of her body and move in ways that attract the gaze. She will starve her body and mutilate her body and cripple her body in order to feel noticed. No matter what she does or what standard of beauty she achieves, she will despise her body and see it as ugly and imperfect. If she attracts too much of the male gaze, she will be called slut. If she is raped she will be told she asked for it. If she doesn't attract the gaze, if she is not white enough or pretty enough or thin enough, she will be called "unattractive." If she behaves as though she doesn't want the gaze, she will be called "lesbian."

As she gets older she will become progressively less visible. But she will spend the rest of her life detoxing from the addiction to the gaze and struggling to make herself visible to herself. Finally when she is an old woman, she will be free from the gaze once more. But now she is like a wild thing that has been long in captivity and will not leave its cage although the door has been opened. She will not swing her arms akimbo and sing out loud to herself—not at first.

The Quest for the Princess Poison Antidote

Once upon a time there was a beautiful Princess. She sat around all day waiting for her Prince to come and rescue her, as princesses are supposed to do. She had heard about the kissing of the toad thing, so she checked out every toad she saw and even kissed a few. They remained toads so she just went back to waiting. Waiting was hard. It was boring and the Princess was looking forward to "Happily Ever After." Finally, her Prince arrived. He swept her off her feet (a rather frightening and unexpectedly off-balance experience) and carried her off to his castle. When they got there, he locked her in a high tower. The Princess was shocked. It turned out that being rescued felt a lot like being captured. And, she had the toad thing all wrong. It turned out that it was the Prince kept turning into an ugly toad—not the other way around—and the only way to turn the toad back into a Prince was to kiss it. If she refused, her Prince would remain a toad, his constant croaking making her life miserable. And she was afraid he'd hop away, leaving her stranded in the tower. When she kissed the toad, he remained a Prince for the rest of the day. She learned quickly that it was easier to just kiss the toad whether she felt like it or not. The trouble was that each and every morning the toad was there again, demanding another kiss. With great disappointment the Princess realized that her story didn't have a happy ending after all. She realized that being a Princess meant it was her job to keep her Prince "Happily Ever After."

The End

Women who have oversubscribed to traditional femininity have what I call a lethal dose of "Princess Poison." Princess Poison is lethal because it means a death of self. The girl who sits around waiting to be rescued from her own life *will* in fact be "rescued" from her own life. She will be imprisoned in someone else's life. She will never be "self-realized," will never fulfill her potential and she will be a slave to her Prince. The Princess will never be free. She will stay locked up in her tower with a good view of a world that she can never participate in. The longer she stays in there, the more trapped she will become. Her fear of leaving the safety of the castle will stop her from venturing out.

The Princess knows that she must behave and do everything that is asked of her with a pretty smile on her face. Even if she does everything right, she has a terrible fear that when her beauty fades she will be abandoned by her Prince. If this happens, she will be tossed out into the wild world with no skills to survive and accustomed to a standard of living that she could never recreate herself. The Princess lives in terror of this and spends hours in front of her mirror, mirror on the wall …

The Princess must banish herself from her own tower, cut off her hair, shatter the mirrors. She must hunt down the dragons, tame them and ride them. She must go on a quest for the Princess Poison Antidote. The antidote is in the Land of Economic Independence. The Princess will never be free unless she gets there.

"We feel a peculiar tenderness for the young women on whose shoulders we are about to leave our burdens. The younger women are starting with great advantages over us. They have the results of our experience; they will find a more enlightened public sentiment for discussion; they will have more courage to take the rights which belong to them.

"Thus far, women have been mere echoes of men. Our laws and constitutions, our creeds and codes, and the customs of social life are all of masculine origin. The true woman is yet a dream of the future."

—Elizabeth Cady Stanton,
speech to the International Council of Women, 1888

Chapter 9

The Spirit of Boys and Men

THERE ARE MANY deeply loving and good men in the world. Given the fact that social conditioning for males encourages men to be incapable of intimacy, emotionally inarticulate and potentially violent, I have always wanted to know how the little boys who grew up to be wonderful fathers and sensitive partners got that way. If we can determine how good men overcame their traditional upbringings and the powerful influences on them to be precisely the opposite, we can begin to map out a new path for our boys to follow toward manhood.

Bridging Female and Male Experiences

There is an enormous chasm between female and male experience and very few bridges. It may be difficult for a young man to understand what a young woman feels—for instance, why she would agree to begin sexual activity and then stop and then start and then change her mind and want to stop. There are few situations in a young male's life where he could identify with the desire and the fear and indecision a female may feel in sexually charged situations. The following story segment may help young men make that jump into empathy.

Devin: Taking a Dive

Devin has just been asked if he wants to go skydiving. The guy who asked him is an older friend—a guy Devin thinks is really cool and wishes to impress. Without thinking, Devin says "Yes" right away. It makes him feel special to be asked and he is thrilled at the idea but deep down he feels a little scared. He has always been afraid of heights and once when he was on an airplane as a kid he got really sick and threw up. The more he thinks about it the more anxious he becomes. The next day he asks his friend how much it costs to go. It turns out it's really expensive and Devin feels relieved because this gives him an excuse to get out of it. He tells his friend that he just can't afford it. His friend asks if he really wants to go and Devin assures him that he'd love to but repeats that he doesn't have that kind of money. The friend offers to pay. Devin tells him he couldn't accept, that he could never pay him back, but his friend insists on paying. Devin doesn't feel comfortable with his friend paying for him to go. It's way too much money and Devin knows he'll feel like he owes him. But his friend is persistent and he feels like he can't say "No" and he can't get out of it. The one thing he knows for sure is he can't tell his friend he's scared.

Over the next week, Devin's friend takes him out a few times to a practice field. He shows him all the equipment and they practise jumping from a ledge, learning how to land and roll. This part seems pretty easy and Devin has almost convinced himself that maybe it'll be fun.

On the day of the event, Devin acts all excited and puts on a big show of looking like he knows what he's doing. A bunch of his pals from school have come out to watch and he knows they all envy him. He tells himself it's OK, that he can do it. He tells himself not to be such a wuss. But when his friend goes over the equipment with him for the last time Devin can't concentrate. His mind goes blank. As they walk toward the small plane he feels sick. They get in the plane and when they take off Devin breaks out in a sweat. His friend punches him in the arm and asks if he's OK. He pretends everything is cool. Inside he is panicking.

Then the moment comes. Devin is standing by the open door with a freezing cold wind blowing in his face. His friend is shouting in his ear but the engine is thrumming and the wind is screaming and he can't hear a word. He looks down and in that moment he knows that he can't do it. He looks at his friend desperately, his face begging him to understand. He feels tears spring to his eyes and is grateful for the wind that blows them dry. His friend screams at him, "GO! NOW!" Devin backs away from the open door and shakes his head, "No." His friend laughs and grabs him by the shoulders and shakes him roughly and tells him, "You can do it. Don't be a 'girl.'"

Devin wants more than anything to please his friend. He feels terrible because of all the money his friend spent for the jump. He feels like he has to do it. He goes to the door again. He is gripping either side of the door so hard his hands ache. When Devin looks down this time he is filled with such terror that he is paralyzed. He wants to turn to his friend to tell him "No," that he's changed his mind. He doesn't care anymore about being laughed at or disappointing his friend but he can't move. He squeezes his eyes shut, fighting the nausea rising in waves, and tries to force himself to step back from the doorway.

Devin doesn't get a chance to back away and tell his friend that he's changed his mind. He feels two strong hands on his back and a scream rises in his throat as his body falls.

Do you see the parallels between Devin's experience in this story and what a young woman could be feeling when she is being pressured for sex?

Like Devin, the girl may have mixed feelings. She may think it's a good idea and then the reality of the situation could scare the heck out of her. She may feel a strong desire to please and even impress her boyfriend. And she could also feel peer pressure at a time and in a society where being a virgin is synonymous with being immature and uncool. And, like Devin, she could be forced to do something she really doesn't feel ready for.

Understanding Consent: It Doesn't Take a Rocket Scientist

Over the years there has been much debate about what constitutes consent. Most of the debate has centred around whether or not the woman has said "No." This topic is debated as though males are truly not capable of determining whether or not females want to participate in sexual activity.

Males complain that females give mixed messages. When we focus on mixed messages as the problem, once again the onus is on the woman. The more serious problem is the ways in which males are socialized to prove their manhood by successfully talking as many females as possible into having sex with them whether or not the females actually want to. Rather than asking why women give mixed messages, a more pertinent question might be, Why would a man want to have sex with someone who is unsure, afraid or even unconscious? Why is it that we applaud the males in our society as brilliant in academic and scientific and literary fields yet accept that they are incapable of determining the willingness of a sexual partner? How is it that we are expected to believe that people who can send rockets into outer space and write Nobel Prize-winning novels can't understand the most basic of human interactions? It doesn't take a rocket scientist to determine when someone doesn't want to have sex.

Why don't men stop and ask for clarification when they get mixed messages? Is it so much to ask for a man to stop and ask, "What's going on for you? I'm picking up mixed messages, don't you want to do this?" Should we not expect them to say, "Actually, I don't want to do this unless you are sure you want to. I only want to have sex with someone who is sure they want to have sex with me."

Interpreting the discomfort and fear displayed with body language and facial expression is not so difficult. Why is the actual word "No" necessary to stop someone from hurting us, especially if that person says he cares about us? Why is it not sufficient to communicate with our whole body? And why is it that when women do say "No," we are not believed?

Male Desire: A Separate Matter

We often hear about how driven men are by their desire, as though it were an entity unto itself and their bodies just the vehicle. An out-of-control vehicle without brakes. We hear about how they can't stop. We hear about how they can't help themselves—as though they are not accountable for what their bodies do once they are turned on.

The language commonly used to express male desire reflects this attitude of the transference of accountability. As a way of expressing strong desire, men will sometimes say "You're driving me crazy" or "You drive me out of my mind" or "You turn me on." These expressions all have the metaphor of the male as the vehicle with the female in the driver's seat. It is interesting to examine the power dynamic inherent in this relationship. "You turn me on" most clearly illuminates the paradoxical yet pervasive belief that females literally turn males on—as though there's a mysterious hidden switch that women flip to the "on" position and then the man's ready to go and there's nothing to be done. She's started something that she now has to finish. The image of the female as the one in control is deceptive.

It is a myth that women are responsible for male desire. Boys in puberty sometimes have wet dreams, often wake up in the morning with an erection and get spontaneous erections throughout the day. When a young man displays his erect penis and says to a young woman, "Look at what you've done to me. You have to finish what you've started," it would be useful for young woman to remember: his penis, his problem. His state of arousal is about his body and is entirely his responsibility. He can finish it himself; he knows how.

It would also be useful for young women to know that it is a myth that men can't stop. Consider this: a young man is in his bedroom masturbating and his mother walks in. Is there any question as to whether or not he can stop? If a young man was making out with his girlfriend in the back seat of a car and the young woman's father suddenly appeared, the boy wouldn't say, "We'll be right out, I just have to finish."

Traditional male socialization teaches a separation of the mind from the body and doesn't include the heart at all. This thinking supports the belief that men are not responsible for what their bodies do. It extends to an attitude that the penis has a mind of its own, as though it were a separate person. When we examine how common it is for males to ascribe names, personalities and even voices to their penises, we see clear evidence of treating the penis as a "third party." Males dialogue with them, create scripts for them and refer to them as though they were separate entities. As light-hearted and humorous as this play-acting may seem, it underscores the separation of men from their bodies and absolves males of responsibility for their violent behaviour.

It is as if we are asked to believe that male sexual desire is so powerful that the man's penis can be overtaken by an irresistible urge to be inside a woman's vagina. We are further asked to believe that in this state of arousal the penis has the ability to lead an otherwise stable and socially functional man into the act of forcing a woman into gratifying that urge. We are asked to believe that this violent act is committed somehow against the man's better judgement and in fact against his will, as though he is not in full control of his body at this time. To add insult to injury, we are then told that he is in no way accountable for his actions because what he did was triggered by the behaviour, the clothing or even just the sight of a female.

The irony is that females are taught that having this effect on males is a good thing. Fashion magazines model sexual poses and clothing for attaining the optimum desirability. Women compete for, strive toward and hunger for the male gaze. To be so desirable as to ignite an out-of-control reaction in a man is the highest standard of female attractiveness that a woman can achieve. To follow this logic is to believe that to cause a man to commit rape is a testament to a woman's desirability.

A male is *not* a machine that a female turns on and then cannot find the "off" switch to. The penis as tool or weapon is a clear reflection of the separation of body and heart in male socialization. It is an enormous insult to men's humanity to support the image of males as robotic monsters with pre-programmed search-and-destroy chips embedded in their genitals. And it is dangerous to children and women to collaborate in this version of men.

The World of Boys

Every day we send our boys out into the world of other boys. A world where they have to constantly be on their guard against potential humiliation and physical aggression. If our boys relax their guard for even a moment—if they display a moment of fear or confusion or sadness—or even a moment of compassion or empathy—they are at risk of being attacked. They risk being called "gay" or "faggot" or "wuss." In other words, they are at risk of being called "girl." Being a girl in this context means not being a man. Any male who is identified as unmanly is in grave danger from other males. He is in danger of being publicly ridiculed, tripped, pushed into lockers, spat on, urinated on, stolen from, hit, beaten, raped and even killed.

In Part I of the following true story we will meet Billy, a "normal" boy from a rural town who went to high school in the mid-1960s. Billy will tell us the story of how, along with a group of friends, he mercilessly bullied another boy. In Part II Billy will tell us what it was like for him growing up in his family. By looking at the life of a bully through the eyes of a bully, we can better understand some possible root causes of the devastating and life-altering act of bullying.

Bullying is a social disease of epidemic proportions among children and adolescents. In the same way that we need to examine physical diseases under a microscope, we need to deconstruct the dynamics of bullying so that we can better understand how to combat it.

Exposing the Bully

Part I

I'm not sure how it started. We were in grade six and the kid had red hair and freckles and glasses. And he was fat. It was like he was just walking around with a "Victim" sign stamped on his forehead. Anyway, I started calling him "carrot-head" and "four-eyes," really clever things like that.

Some of the other kids would laugh when I did this and that really got me going. This kid, he would never stand up for himself. He would just ignore me and then pretty soon a couple of the other kids started in on him too. After a while it became the focus of our school day. Before school, on the bus, during recess, lunch hour and after school. Every day. We just got meaner and meaner and the kids who were into it with me, we became this kind of gang. Nothing like the gangs you see nowadays, no weapons or anything like that. We did throw stuff at him, small rocks and snowballs and dried up horse "apples." One time we got him with a hose before school. He was soaked and he had to go home. One time I put a large thumbtack on his seat and he sat on it. I never heard anyone yell so loud in school. He had to go to the hospital in an ambulance. The teacher told us later that the tack had punctured his testicle. That was one I felt bad about. It's not so much that I felt bad for him, the person ... just a kind of male empathy for how much it must have hurt.

You know, what was weird was how he would kind of suck up to me and my pals. Like he would give us chocolate bars or even money if he had some. It was like he wanted to be our friend and we were just awful to him. He was a geek and it was as though just the sight of him reminded me of my own geek potential. I felt disgusted by him. The more disgusted I felt the meaner I got. In the beginning it was just a matter of taking opportunities that presented themselves. After a while, I would look for opportunities to get him.

Donny Farquar, that was the kid's name. We called him Bonnie Fart Queer. Getting Donny became elevated to the level of a sport. At first it was solely a team sport. It was strange but if I ran into him when I was alone, say walking past him in the hall or coming out of the can at school, I just ignored him. As long as there were other kids around to help me get him or other kids around to laugh, it went on. Getting Donny went on all the way through grades 6 and 7.

I remember this one time, at the end of grade 7, on the last day of school, we were all hanging around waiting for the bus. Everyone had armloads of stuff, books and projects they had made that we were bringing home. I saw Donny standing over by the school doors. He had the kite he had made for this science project we'd just finished. It was such a good kite. His dad had helped him with it and the teacher had made a big deal of showing the whole class how beautifully designed it was and how much time Donny had put into it. He reminded us that it was fine for our parents to help us as long as we were in charge of the project. Donny's dad had come to the school to watch Donny fly the kite for the class. Later we called him "Daddy's little boy" and laughed at his kite, but I was just eaten up inside. It wasn't that I wanted the kite, or that I wished I had made it. It was that his dad would come to school just to watch him fly it.

When I saw that kite perched carefully on top of his binder that day, I felt enraged. All I could think of on the way home on the bus was punching Donny's face over and over. When I got off the bus, I waited beside the door and stuck my foot out at the exact moment when Donny stepped down. He went flying. His binder and books scattered and his kite skidded across the grass. I didn't think about it at all. I went over and stomped on it with both feet. I just kept jumping on that kite until it was a mess of splinters and shreds of rice paper. When there was nothing left to stomp and I finally looked up, my group of friends seemed kind of horrified.

Then the unthinkable happened. Donny, his face furious red and his fists balled by his sides, ran at me. I noticed right then that he had grown the last year. He was actually taller than I was and what used to be baby fat had kind of spread out and turned him into a fairly chunky kid. I felt fear but I knew I couldn't show it. I stood my ground. As a matter of fact, I remember I had this half smile on my face, my hands folded across my chest. When he got right up to me, I could see he was kind of fizzling out. It was as though I had some kind of power over him that had been built up over years of bullying him. But he didn't turn away. He hauled off and he kicked me in the shin. He was wearing these big brown oxfords (my pals and me, we all wore high-cut canvas All-star sneakers and had spent a fair amount of time laughing at those sturdy brown "geek shoes").

The pain that shot through my leg was agonizing but somehow I managed to just stand there. He must have thought I was Superman. I barely flinched and kept smiling, just as if I *were* Superman. His anger turned to tears of rage and frustration. Blubbering, he picked up his kite fragments and turned and ran home crying like a baby. The crowd of kids that had gathered quickly dispersed and after my friends all left I limped home. I still have a scar where Donny kicked me. I know the scars he has today from the years I tormented him are much worse.

I didn't see Donny much that summer but my friends and I did catch him once and push his face down into a pile of cow manure. It was odd that his kicking me hadn't had the effect of stopping us. It was almost like after that we had to reassert our power over him.

When school opened the next fall, I had grown and I was a full head taller than anyone else in my grade. I was on the basketball team and pretty popular with the girls. Even though I had other things to think about—like girls—and even though I didn't even feel the scorn I was displaying anymore, "Getting Donny" pretty much picked up where we'd left off. It was almost like a habit that I couldn't break—as though I was addicted to the feeling it gave me. And now it seemed I didn't need my gang of friends around to get me going.

I had learned this clever way of sticking my foot out as I came alongside someone, which, while not sending them flying, would cause them to lurch forward and look stupid. My older brother had used it on me enough so I knew how stupid it made you feel. I used that one on Donny a lot. I would come up behind him in the hall at school. It worked every time. If I saw him coming toward me down the hall, I would suddenly veer in his direction and throw my shoulder into him, banging him up against the lockers.

One day our class was in the library. We were supposed to be doing research for an oral report assignment (which I really hated doing and in fact was pretty bad at). Anyway, I was in one of the aisles looking for a topic to write this essay on, which I felt really anxious about, when I noticed Donny was standing just a few feet away, his face buried in a book. The minute I saw Donny I felt better. It's hard to explain. One minute I felt stupid and like a loser and the next minute I felt like a king. I pulled out a book and, looking out of the corner of my eye, I casually side-stepped a little closer to him. He stepped away. I stepped closer. He stepped away. Each time he stepped away, I remember feeling a pleasant sensation surge through my body. It was as though I was sucking the power from him through an invisible straw and ballooning up with it. I had felt this feeling before while picking on Donny. It was as though I was satisfying a kind of hunger, but I only felt satisfied while I was doing it. I always felt empty again immediately afterward.

Anyway, this particular time as I moved yet again closer, I could see that we were getting to the end of the book aisle. I felt a snicker forming low in my throat as I imagined casually following him around the library for the whole hour. Then something absolutely unexpected happened. Donny didn't move away. I slid a half step closer and still he didn't move. Now we were standing shoulder to shoulder. I was still looking down at my book but I could see in my peripheral vision that Donny had lowered his book and was looking directly at me. I felt suddenly awkward. Then he turned his body and faced me directly. I looked up from my book, prepared to sneer something brilliant like, "What're you looking at, moron?" but before I could say anything, Donny, his eyes looking firmly and directly into mine, said, "Billy, why are you doing this? Why do you always do this?" His voice was dead calm and he just stood there not looking away. It was really weird, like all the power I had been sucking from him suddenly oozed out of me and into him. I had been all puffed up and so sure of my power and now I felt empty, like a deflated balloon. It seemed as though he could see right through me. I was just standing there looking stupid and I remember feeling, like ... how do I get out of this? Really uncomfortable. I couldn't think of one cool thing to say so I said something like, "Whatever, loser," and turned and walked away.

Something changed after that. I started avoiding Donny and when the gang went after him I always found an excuse to disappear. It's not that I cared. I don't know what it was. I just didn't have the urge to go after him anymore. There were a couple of other kids that I harassed from time to time but for the rest of our high school years I never bothered Donny again.

Part II

When I was growing up, dinnertimes were so stressful that to this day, my own kids and I eat in front of the TV. As a kid, every evening my two younger sisters and I got ourselves washed up and made sure we were sitting at the dinner table before six o'clock. At 5:59 my father would come in, usually from his workshop in the basement, and sit down at the head of the table. At six o'clock on the dot he would clear his throat. This meant my mother should say grace. When she was done, he tapped his fork on his dinner plate a couple of times. This meant that we could start.

My mother always served him first and throughout the meal she kept an eye on his plate to offer him seconds. If she missed the moment when my father wanted to be served a second helping, he would clear his throat, and if that didn't produce immediate results he would tap his plate with his fork, a rapid ting-ting-ting-ting until my mother passed the potatoes. If he spoke at all it was usually to make a pronouncement about some item that was in the news or more often to offer an opinion, always negative, about some "G.D. hotshot" politician or another. The only other thing I ever remember my father talking about was sports, the news or the weather. Morning and night he delivered an ongoing commentary about the local weather and sometimes we would get bits and pieces on what the weather was doing in other parts of the country. Out of the blue he would say, "Snow in Winnipeg, last night. Eight inches."

There were only certain things the rest of us were allowed to talk about at dinner. School was usually an OK topic. Or sports. As long as it was good news—but at the same time we had to be careful not to brag about our achievements. My mother sometimes talked about illnesses or misfortunes in the lives of friends or neighbours—he tolerated listening to that. When my father didn't like the topic of the conversation at the dinner table or if a squabble broke out among the younger children, he would give us a look. If that didn't produce the result he wanted he would slowly reach his right arm behind him to the windowsill where he kept a yardstick. The whole family would become dead silent when he did this.

I don't recall my father ever actually using the stick at dinnertime, but we had felt its sting on our legs and backsides enough times to know he would. He had the power to turn us off like a radio when he reached for that stick. I could see it, the power he felt, and it made me furious. A story my father often told us was how his own father had only to close the Bible each evening after supper to send all his children to bed without a word. This story was usually preceded with, "G.D. kids these days."

After dinner, Dad always sat in "his" chair, opened the paper and read. It feels as though I spent my whole childhood trying to get my dad to put the newspaper down and look at me. I would think up reasons to interrupt his evening reading. My questions or other ploys to get his attention were usually met with a sharp snap of the paper and then he would clear his throat in an annoyed way and say "Ahem!" If I could find a question to ask that he knew something about, sometimes he couldn't resist giving me the answer. If I got him going he would get into telling me some long story that eventually branched out into a topic completely unrelated to my original question and usually bored me to death. I felt pinned under his gaze during those times. It was almost as though I was listening to the radio but I couldn't turn it off. As his deep monotonous voice droned on and on, it was odd: I had his attention but I felt invisible at the same time. This didn't stop me from trying again and again. It was as though I would forget how it would turn out and each time I got his attention I would light up like an eager little light bulb and shine all my hope on him.

In my early teens, I started to excel in sports and we lived in such a small town that my name would often appear in the local paper. He never said a word but I knew he was reading about me and it was deeply satisfying. Eventually I made the Canadian All-Star team and wherever I went in the world I always knew my dad would be reading the sports page. It wasn't enough though. No matter how successful I became, I always had an empty feeling inside.

Never once did my dad come to one of my games. And never once did I play a game without looking for him in the stands. Sometimes I would pretend he was there watching and those times I played like I had never played before. At the end of those games, when all the other dads came down and ruffled their sons' hair and gave them those rough hugs and backslaps, I remember feeling panicky, like something had broken inside me and was going to spill out. I couldn't get out of there fast enough. I would jog home in the dark rather than wait around for someone to offer me a ride.

Never once did my father say, "Good for you, son." I remember one time in particular. I was in college and I came home after my team had won the All-Canadian title. I was team captain and my picture had been on the front page of the college sports magazine. I was wearing a new suit and feeling proud of myself and I was excited to see my family after being away for over a month. I walked in the door and my dad looked out briefly from behind the newspaper. He said, "Who are you trying to impress?" Then he mumbled something about when was I going to get a real job and then he disappeared behind the paper again.

I think that was when I gave up. I started partying a lot, my grades went from bad to worse. Then I quit sports, got into drugs pretty heavy and eventually quit school. Those years are a blur. It wasn't until my early thirties when I had kids of my own that I got my life together.

Recently, I was on the phone with my dad and I told him that a close friend of mine had just passed away and that I had held him in his last moments and he had died in my arms. My voice choked up when I told him and then my throat was so tight I couldn't speak. There was a pause and then my dad said, "Earlier today I thought it was going to rain...but it's cleared up now." It was surreal. It was as though someone had just changed the channel to the weather station.

The strongest childhood memory I have of my father is a newspaper and the soles of his shoes. I am determined to have a different kind of relationship with my kids. I have two sons now and they both play sports. I go to all their games but even though I think it every day I still don't say the words "I love you" to my boys. It's like the dial's stuck and I just can't change it.

The Code
by David Hatfield, Program Director for the SafeTeen Boys' Program

Unwritten and never formally declared, a very precise code of manhood exists. It is passed down and taught by fathers, brothers, family, friends, media, the military, teachers, and coaches. Its tenets are clear, and they reveal disturbing qualities and belief systems woven into the fabric of society. Non-compliance with the code is seen and felt as a gender betrayal, and instantly invokes feelings of a parallel intensity from other men, friends or strangers alike. When unexamined at a conscious level, the code has the power to dictate male behaviour in an unceasing and lifelong manner.

The code exists to concentrate power in the male gender. Its root lies in the fact that males are generally physically stronger than females. The code defines power as an inherently masculine trait. From a physical basis, power becomes defined as the ability to control people and situations. "Power" then becomes economic, political, and sexual—in addition to physical. According to the code, men are to be fundamentally differentiated from women in those terms: women are weak, men are powerful. It defines maleness in crude and inhumane terms, and places unattainable demands on men, no matter what their age. Its tenets are simple to grasp and easy to illustrate. Popular media plays the code for laughs regularly. Implicit is the warning: we can acknowledge the code, even have a laugh at its ridiculousness, but we dare not genuinely question or challenge it. "Remember," the code tells us, "it's every man for himself, and good guys finish last."

Male SafeTeen facilitators seek to bring young men's awareness to the existence of the code, and to both encourage and challenge them to consciously measure it, and to step outside of it when it attempts to stifle their humanity. To challenge the code is a threat to the mainstream foundation of maleness. It requires time for the concept to incubate in the psyches of youth raised on the code and significant courage on their part to consider making the changes we are asking of them.

Tenets of the Code

Emotionality

The code accepts the feeling and expression of anger as powerful. When expressed with vocal and/or physical force, the code encourages respect for such power. Such "tough guys" are not to be messed with. Naturally, men who demonstrate frequent outbursts of anger are feared by other men. Thus the code causes confusion for many men, who grow up experiencing fear and believing it is actually respect.

The acknowledgement of, or expression of, physical or emotional pain is to be avoided. Expressing pain is seen as weakness, and demands instant disapproval and/or punishment from other men. The code engages all men who witness another man's pain: it is understood that disapproval of sorrow, crying, fear, incompetence and uncertainty should be unanimous, and immediate, thus placing all men under constant scrutiny and stress.

Common outcomes from men who are "codified" emotionally include a lack of ability to know their own feelings other than anger;

lack of ability in or a fear of empathy; a limited emotional range; an acute fear of feelings of pain; and a potentially volatile emotional build-up. In relations with women, codified men are at war with their own desires and humanity. They seek intimacy physically, emotionally and sexually, yet the code has taught them that such openness to another person makes them vulnerable, and therefore weak. Thus in their basic desire for meaningful communion with others, many boys and men are left fearing the retribution that years of conditioning have taught them to expect. Some men are able to recognize the emotional safety their partner can offer and gratefully let down their emotional shields, only to have to hoist them into place again in other potentially codified social situations. This "double life" is draining and confusing, and echoes the experience many men have in one-on-one relations versus group interactions where other men are present.

Physicality
The code demands that men be physically powerful: tall, muscular, adept at physical feats and physical work, athletic and sexually appealing. A man is expected to win at sports, to succeed at physical challenges, to not back down from physical confrontation and to be physically independent—that is, to not need help for tasks involving strength or stamina. Winning is expected; losing is not tolerated. A man should be sexually active, confident and competitive. And his penis, like his sexual appetite, should be huge and inexhaustible.

Men may become sexually abusive in a number of ways simply to meet the ideal of manhood the code demands—both in their own minds and in the opinions of other men whose respect they are competing for. The threat of any type of sexual humiliation becoming known in a young man's male community is profound and can provoke deep anxiety. The rejection of sexual advances, late onset of puberty, uncertainty about sexual orientation, sexual competition among guys, insecurity about penis size and sexual attractiveness can all influence a young male's attitudes and behaviours toward women. If he feels insecure in any of these areas, he can view females as either objects or hurdles he has to use or overcome in order to feel secure again. Coupled with this are the utterly human needs for meaningful contact, intimacy and sexual desire. It's a potent and confusing brew, and is greatly assisted by guidance and modelling from trusted others.

The outcomes of a codified physicality are often disastrous. Men are pitted against their own genetic inheritance. Extreme anxiety over meeting the inhumane physique of the code runs rampant. Excessive weight training, use of steroids, "involuntary" participation in sports, even the use of inappropriately loud speaking voices can be seen as attempts to take up more physical space. Those who for whatever reason choose not " to play" suffer the insults and lack of respect of other men, and the low self-esteem that inevitably follows. Arbitrary but life-long categorization can occur early in school as young men fall prey to "jock" or "loser" labelling. Both can be restrictive and damaging to a young man's self-image.

The way a man carries himself is also incredibly important in the eyes of the code. The posturing of males virtually yells out its alpha male status in excessive swaggering, stylized walking, ritualized handshakes and other very creative and complex "in" language that establishes a male's position in the hierarchy of cool. These mannerisms can enable genetically smaller men to "compete" with men they are physically no match for. The extremely baggy clothing, large, heavy shoes, short "hard" hairstyles, tattooing and certain levels of facial piercing currently popular among young men can in some degree be seen as a striving for stature and status.

My father, a physician, was a self-described "square" and was very comfortable with his own label. One day, while my mother was helping him out of bed, he blurted out that he felt like "a wimp" for requiring assistance. The moment occurred while he was in the acute stage of his leukemia, the final stage that leads to death. I remember feeling surprised that the code was so entrenched in this intelligent and deeply compassionate man, and had survived to surface intact even in the face of death.

Intellectuality

The code expects men to be ready and willing, to strive for positions of power in the world, starting in pre-adolescence. It is expected that men have the intellectual ability to meet the demands of any situation.

There are no rewards for falling behind or failing. If this weren't enough, the code also confers punishment on those who reveal too much intelligence for a given situation. Young men in SafeTeen programs are routinely harassed by their peers for giving too long an answer, or one that reveals "too much" intellectual sensitivity or maturity. The punishment is immediate and often begins before the student has even finished speaking. Unless, of course, it is one of the known tougher guys who is speaking. He can speak unchallenged for as long as he wants, even if he isn't particularly on-topic!

The guys in SafeTeen programs often define one of the codified lessons they have learned as "being responsible." They list their responsibilities as "families, friends, making money, and girl-friends"—a heady list for fifteen-year-olds. There is much respect in the room for these ideas, and the list is brainstormed quickly. Paradoxically, the name given to someone who "takes responsibility" (when a school rule has been broken, for example) when other men refuse to, is "rat." Ratting is "telling" and "squealing"—and has been disapproved of for a long time among men. Currently nothing has changed, and the code continues to send men impossibly mixed signals. Being "responsible" implies a sense of duty and personal involvement. Yet the black-and-white strokes and lack of fine print in the code "text" fail to inform young men of the leanings of morality. Previous generations offer too few role models for most young men. As a result, young men too often know "what happened" and silently struggle with the two voices in their heads: one telling them they have a personal responsibility that a man must fulfill, the other one warning them of the consequences a disclosure will bring.

Thus the code breeds another conflict within men: while young men are to be intellectually prepared to step into power positions, they are forced to "dumb down" in the process, cloaking their life knowledge and experiences in the presence of other men. Intelligence and morality have a profound ability to create anxiety among men who are trained by the code to be constantly jockeying for power. While travelling in Mexico in 2000, a twenty-eight-year-old Canadian man revealed to me that he was no longer telling other backpacking travellers his real profession. This newly graduated engineer had discovered that the interpreted status of his education was causing others to shun him. Like so many men, he "went underground," concealing a major part of his life, which he loved and felt passionate about, to procure the acceptance of others.

Spirituality
In the male world, "spirit" is commonly assigned to the sports team, or giving something "one more try." A "spirited" boy is one who bucks the system, who is "headstrong" or a "rebel"—all coveted assessments of a young man who exhibits power early on in life. He may face retribution from those his power threatens, yet even if he "loses" he may still be admired and respected for his strength of stance and not "taking crap" from anybody.

Association with a true spiritual practice can be interpreted as a grave threat to the male code of conduct. Most spiritual practices involve deep self-examination and the acceptance of alternative sources and definitions of power, all of which supersede the code in many ways. This is precisely what makes spirituality so dangerous to codified men: it dismisses the code as irrelevant, and therefore disempowers the entire codified system of maleness. The code seeks to bind men together on the basis of gender and encourages "head down" relentless competition among one another for power in all areas of life. Spirit-based practices can encourage a "head up" individual choice paradigm that supersedes that of "the tribe." Men of all ages who openly embrace a spiritual faith and practice are routinely met with the suspicion and derision of other men.

My experience with the young men in the SafeTeen workshops has turned me into a keen observer of this code of conduct. I am no longer surprised but have become quite alarmed by the intensity and unrelenting quality of this code's effects on men of all ages, including myself. In a nutshell, the code trains men to "be" only what is permissible according to code tenets, and to bury the rest of themselves or risk instant and "justified" punishment by other men.

The punitive actions I have mentioned come largely in two very direct forms: verbal and physical. Punishment is meant to be deeply shaming, an aim effectively accomplished by verbally or physically casting the man out of "the tribe" of men and into "the tribe" of women. Generally code transgressions are seen in some way as weakness, a trait the code defines as inherently female. As boys and men punish each other, they also devalue and degrade the gender of women.

When the code is challenged, the threat of its weakening demands instant action. Scornful laughter, deliberate withdrawal of compassion, exclusion from social groups and use of the words "fag," "wuss," "loser," "princess," "pussy" and "bitch" are common. Throwing objects, invasion of personal space ("stepping up" face to face), verbal threats and challenges to "step down" or fight, shoving, kicking, slapping, poking, punching and full-on beatings are all used to convey both the seriousness of the transgression and the assumed level of power the victim holds in the group and situation. Tellingly, while verbal abuse routinely includes degrading sexual references to females in general, and to boys' mothers and girlfriends in particular, it fails to include similar "dissing" of male figures.

The fear of retribution is so deep and ingrained that the code can at times function perfectly well while a man is alone and unobserved. For example, many young men understand with a knowing laugh the idea of swearing at and/or striking inanimate objects that have "caused" a moment of frustration: the lawn mower that won't start, the basketball that wouldn't go in the net, the chair leg that just painfully "struck" the shin. The momentary lack of competence felt by many men in such situations causes them to react in a codified expression of anger or violence—even when no one has witnessed their "failure." Even to experience such a "failure" alone can be distressing enough to provoke angry and violent outbursts. Add friends, teachers, coaches, parents, sexual and romantic interests as witnesses and the emotional stakes skyrocket.

For an exercise about creating awareness of the male code of conduct, see page 300.

Bill of Rights for Men

1. As a man, I have the right to show my feelings and express my fears.
2. As a man, I have the right to change and the right to choose the direction of my changes.
3. As a man, I can ask for help when I need it and offer help when I think it is needed.
4. As a man, I have the right to ask for what I want and the wisdom to know that I cannot always get it.
5. As a man, I have the right to tell people when I cannot fulfill their expectations of me.
6. As a man, I have the right to consider new ways of thinking, acting and relating to people.
7. As a man, I am not obliged to live up to the stereotypes of how I am "supposed" to be.
8. As a man, I have the right to acknowledge my frustrations, disappointments and anxieties.
9. As a man, I can choose to take responsibility for my actions and not allow other people's behaviour to push me into choices I do not want to make.
10. As a man, I have the right to show my strength by choosing not to hit someone who angers me.

(FROM THE ABUSIVE PARTNER: AN ANALYSIS OF DOMESTIC BATTERING, BY MARIA ROY)

Silent Boys /Angry Boys

The sweet little boys who hugged us and talked to us about their feelings and cried when they hurt such a short time ago are now coming home surly, monosyllabic, shut down and angry. As caring parents and educators we try to talk to them. We keep asking them what's wrong and especially we ask them to tell us how they feel. When they respond with "I don't know" or with sullen grunts and angry body language, or when they don't respond at all, it can be difficult not to become frustrated. It's hard not to take it personally.

It can be useful to understand what is likely going on for the typical teenage boy. When a young man responds to questions about how he is feeling with "I don't know" or "Nothing," he is probably not just trying to get on our nerves. It is extremely likely that he is simply telling the truth. In other words, he doesn't know what he's feeling or he feels nothing. We don't give our boys much permission to experience the full range of their emotions. It is unmanly to demonstrate any vulnerability or sensitivity or confusion, so even if they are feeling these things it is highly unlikely that they will admit it. When we ask them about their feelings and they look inside and see a big black abyss of unknown territory, they may feel afraid or inadequate. When we pressure them to talk, they may feel anxious and even more inadequate. Then anger, the one emotion that they are allowed to feel, steps in to cover for the fear and confusion. So anger is often the only emotion we see them express. It's what they're most comfortable with.

When one of our boys seems locked down tight and doesn't communicate anything at all, it may be that the angry thoughts and feelings he is having feel out of control and scary to him. He may be afraid he is bad in some way for having the angry images and thoughts he is having. He may be afraid that if he says anything, the lid will blow off and all of the angry words and actions will come pouring out. We pressure him, he locks down tighter and tighter and finally, in desperation, he explodes out of his chair and storms out the door, slamming it behind him.

Anger is what our boys know best because it is what they have most commonly seen other males model—on television, in the movies and most importantly in their personal lives. When a boy sees his dad bang his shin on the coffee table and he hears him bellow and then kick the table and curse at it as though it were to blame for getting in his way, he learns that is how males respond to pain.

When his older brother is struggling with a computer glitch, he doesn't hear him say, "I have no idea what to do. Boy, it sure is frustrating and confusing." His brother is more likely to grit his teeth and curse and groan and finally pound his fist on the desk and storm off, blaming the "stupid goddamn thing."

With his father at the wheel, this boy and his family may ride for many hours in the wrong direction before the man of the house will admit he is lost or ask for directions. All the lessons this boy has learned in the playground, in the schoolyard and in the movies are being reinforced on a daily basis by watching the most influential adult males in his life. Never show pain. Never admit you don't know. Only anger is acceptable.

We socialize our boys to be incapable of having any feeling besides anger. We teach them that being violent is synonymous with being masculine, that to ask for help is a weakness and to talk about their feelings is being "a girl." Then we act surprised when nice normal boys sexually assault women and we are shocked when ordinary teenage boys take guns to school and shoot their classmates.

It is not difficult to imagine what these boys who commit terrible violent acts must be feeling. We can imagine that they must be suffering from years of feeling deeply hurt, terribly alone, afraid and especially powerless. But we must also question whether or not they are feeling these emotions at all. It takes emotional strength and wholeness to feel our feelings. When we actually feel our pain, we are usually far too empathetic to hurt others. When boys consistently push their vulnerable feelings down time and again, year after year, we must question whether these feelings are still really in there. Many grown men will admit they are unable to cry. Do the unused feelings atrophy in the way that unused muscles wither up and become useless?

One thing seems clear. When all that pain and fear and powerlessness has been funnelled into the one emotion these violent boys are allowed to have—anger—it is highly likely that they will be unable to feel empathy. These boys are emotionally isolated and very, very angry. Is it really all that surprising that some boys strike out from this powerless and hopeless place?

Shoulder to Shoulder/Face to Face: Learning How to Talk to Our Boys

Often the most useful way to bring out conversations about real issues with our boys is while engaging in activities such as walking together or driving in the car. Even watching television and playing video games can be useful diversions during intense discussions. There are a number of things in these settings that work to make boys feel more at ease. First of all, there is another activity going on, so the boy isn't the entire focus of attention. He hasn't been asked to sit down and have a "heavy" talk. Any adolescent can feel extremely uncomfortable in a face-to-face conversation. Just making that much eye contact can be very difficult for a young person. Boys especially can have a hard time with the intimacy and openness involved in direct eye contact. "Look at me when I talk to you!" "Turn that TV off when I'm talking to you!" These are only too familiar lines from parents and teachers.

When we make these demands and the boy complies, we should not be surprised to see a stony, dead gaze or defiant glare. If we allow our teenager to stare at his feet, shift around restlessly and stare at the TV screen, we might find we'll get further than if we demand his full attention. This may be the best he can do and allowing a distraction from the intensity can serve to take off some of the edge for him, making it more possible for him to stay present.

A car ride, as long as it's to a specific location and a fairly short distance, can be the perfect setting for a talk with a teenage boy. First of all, if the adult is driving, it is impossible for any extensive eye contact or observation to happen. It is common for teens to suffer from a "spotlight syndrome"—a developmental stage where they feel that everyone notices every minute detail about their physical appearance and behaviour. It is a relief for a teen not to have someone sitting there staring at him when he feels so intensely self-conscious. As well, there is a structured time element to the talk. If the conversation starts in the car on the way to the dentist, the youth knows that in the amount of time it takes to get there, the talk will be over, at least for now. If he doesn't feel in control of when it will end, he can feel powerless and trapped.

Most parents and educators can identify with the frustration they feel when so many of these well-meaning talks end with the boy saying, "Can I go now?" It can feel to the adult that the child has been sitting there the whole time barely listening, just waiting to go. Well, in fact, this may be true. Not because the boy doesn't care but because his ability to stay focused in the face-to-face dynamic is very limited and this style of communication can produce tremendous anxiety for him. In order to achieve a release from his anxiety, he may become belligerent in order to push the adult into an anger response. If the adult becomes angry he will then have an excuse to jump up and storm out. Once again, anger is the emotion he knows best.

Remember: Boys tend to be more comfortable in shoulder-to-shoulder interactions.

The Dynamics of Power and Male Violence: The Broken Men

Although all men are exposed to the traditional masculinity rules, images, pressures, expectations and role models, the majority of men do not grow up to be abusers of women and children. Many men who were abused as children themselves get help with healing and do not pass on the abuse. However, there are many men who are deeply damaged and are unable to find the support they need to heal their wounds and they do pass their hurt on to others. These men often overidentify with traditional masculine roles. They are the battering husbands and fathers, the rapists, the abusive boyfriends and child abusers. They are the "broken men."

The psychological portraits of the schoolyard bully, the rapist, the wife batterer and the child molester all have one theme in common. The common thread is a sense of powerlessness and lack of control. The abusive male's prime motivators are power and control. This is not to say that all abusers are powerless. Sometimes people bully or assault others because they are racist, homophobic or misogynist and they deeply believe it is their right. Many abusive people have power. They may have money, expensive cars, career status, academic status or athletic status or physical power. The key is that regardless of what external symbols of power these people possess, on the inside they do not experience an authentic feeling of powerfulness. And that is the place they are acting out from.

Sexual harassment is not an expression of desire and sexual assault is not motivated by sexual gratification. The harasser and the rapist are using sex as a tool of humiliation and as an expression of their domination and ultimately their manhood. While they are exerting power over someone else, they feel powerful. Judith Herman, a well-known trauma researcher, writes, "The elevation of the self through the medium of control is a central theme uniting most forms of abuse."

This "domination dynamic" is particularly potent with males because the gender stereotype to be in control at all times is so unrelenting. The higher the standard of being in control, the more likely males will fall short and the more inadequate they will feel. This dynamic permeates every aspect of the male world to the point where men can feel it is humiliating to ask for directions when they are lost or to admit that they do not know how to fix something. To show uncertainty or vulnerability in any situation is unacceptable and perceived as weakness. This is a facade that many men live behind, and they live in fear that someone will find out the truth. The truth is that they are merely flawed human beings, both strong and fragile. Unfortunately, it is typical for males to express their increased fragility with increased aggression.

It is common for the assaultive man to construct an exterior world that reflects stereotypical masculinity. Material status symbols and a tough-guy attitude of intimidation are ways that he can build up his exterior world because his interior world is so empty. He is typically unable to access his feelings, has a very limited emotional vocabulary and is extremely emotionally isolated. Drugs and/or alcohol are often used to medicate loneliness and give a false sense of confidence—and commonly accompany violent behaviours. This man has bought the "Hollywood Hero" version of manhood.

Regardless of the strut and bravado that the "macho" man displays on the outside, his inner self is starving for the feeling of power that he has been "sold" as his right. His power may have been taken from him at an earlier point in his life through emotional, physical or sexual abuse. The abuse was not necessarily overt. Sons of absent or distant fathers are more likely to commit violent crimes. Terrence Real, author of *I Don't Want to Talk about It: Overcoming the Secret Legacy of Male Depression*, states, "Males are often offending from the victim position."

"The only time I don't feel like a victim is when I'm abusing."
—Comment by a young male offender

Understanding that crimes of sexual assault are being committed from the "victim position" makes it possible to have compassion for the lost selves of the little boys inside the perpetrators. However, the task at hand is to make all of us safe from the "broken men" that those tragic little boys have grown up to be.

In order to achieve this goal, we must give our little boys permission to have the full range of their feelings. We have to offer them ways to be powerful that aren't abusive. And we have to help them cope with the reality of the "man's world" that they have to face every day by teaching them skills that they can use as alternatives to violence. We have to help our sons redefine masculinity in a positive light. We have to show them a new way to be a man. And truly, more than any other task on this planet, this one is a job for a man.

Inside the SafeTeen Boys' Program
In this next section we will have the opportunity to be "a fly on the wall" in a SafeTeen Boys' Program workshop. David Hatfield, a Program Director for SafeTeen Boys' Program, shares a raw and powerful experience from one of his sessions with a group of grade 10 boys. In this honest and courageous account he exposes what his process is, both as an educator and as a man, as he struggles to model for the young men a new way to be a man.

It's a day like most other days. I am in a classroom standing in front of a group of grade 10 boys, asking them to examine masculinity issues and guiding them through the process of learning a new way to stand up for themselves.

For the first role-play of the day I asked Kyle to come up and work with me. He had already struck me as an intelligent young man, and was one of the few guys speaking in this fairly quiet group of grade 10s, a rarity, I assure you. In this first role-play lies the whole foundation of the SafeTeen assertiveness model, and its outcome usually dictates whether or not the boys will "buy" the skills being offered. In other words, it is a real test of SafeTeen's validity. I usually pick the most obviously dominant male in the room for this important moment—someone who has a reputation as a tough guy, to make the role-play as real and as compelling as possible. What makes it real is the brief creation of the potentially violent atmosphere young men recognize so well.

In the role-play, I set it up so that Kyle and I are both grade 10 students in the same class. I am new to the school this year, and he has been there longer. We have no history of conflict, separate groups of friends, and I sit behind him in math class. The role-play unfolds in stages.

In stage 1 I am seated behind Kyle, and I start bugging him by kicking his chair leg. He is prepped by me, ahead of time, to deal with the situation by reacting with his Tough Guy or fighter side. In short order we are both standing up, eye-to-eye, talking trash, trading insults and threatening one another. The role-play is then frozen, and after much hooting and applause is explored in terms of how the school would deal with us, and what the next step would be for Kyle and I.

The group are quick to point out that the fighter characters will take it to the next level, somewhere they won't be interrupted. They are also fast to agree that the "loser" will typically be back in a hurry to try and restore lost face, often bringing friends. They know that the conflict is not over after fighting, regardless of who "wins." Poignantly, when I engage the role-player's eyes and ask directly, "So, do you think this is something worth fighting for?" and give the chair another kick, the answer is an immediate and resolute "No." The handful of boys in the many I have role-played with who have answered "Yes" to that question often then qualify their answer. With a neutral response and no further opinion from me, they often hasten to explain: "Well if he kept doing it I would, I mean if he really doesn't stop."

In stage 2 I repeat my challenge to Kyle, and he is asked this time to show his "child side." I continue to intimidate him and when he shows no sign of being able to stand up for himself I am encouraged and my abusive treatment of him increases. It is a very difficult role-play for most guys to do. They are being asked to betray a major tenet of the guy's code of conduct: NEVER SHOW FEAR. And it is being played out in front of their peers, friends and possibly their real-life antagonists. After freezing the scene and praising the student for his ability to "act" the part, I ask the group to describe what they saw happening. The theme of power and powerlessness quickly emerges and is explored. During this time the young man who has been role-playing is taken out of the spotlight. The focus is redirected onto the group and he is given time to let go of the feeling of being taken advantage of, showing fear and nervousness. At the end of the group discussion I ask him how it would feel to come back to that math class the next day knowing what had happened and that I, the Tough Guy, would be there again. Even the toughest guys have no trouble understanding and articulating the emotions a guy who had not previously stood up for himself would be feeling: "It'd be tense." "I'd want to sit somewhere else."

In stage 3 the tables are turned, and Kyle now is instructed to bring out his fighter side again. But this time he gets to kick my chair and harass me. I, in turn, announce very briefly that I am going to show my Solid side. In this role-play, the nature of this young man's journey will be revealed. It is possible that he felt a power loss during the stage 2 role-play and I am likely to feel the intention of revenge in that first chair kick. This will mean that the intensity of his fighter will be higher than mine was. When he kicks my chair and I turn to engage him with my Solid side and our eyes meet, I am trying hard to see who is there in this moment. There is a sense in the room that something different is about to happen.

Kyle started in with me in a very typical fashion, not kicking too hard and fully expecting me to turn around. He turned out to be one those guys who just keeps kicking. Not a lot of trash talk or physical posturing, just lots of footwork. The metal bar attaching the desk to the chair I was sitting in was bashing into my left thigh in my half-turned posture, and after a few kicks it was beginning to hurt. Taking a calming breath, I dropped into my Solid side with a practised ease and delivered my message, "I want you to stop kicking my chair." At this point I hold eye contact and watch to see how the guys react. Usually a few seconds of that silent look begins to generate uncertainty, nervous laughing, and a pause in the kicking. Occasionally, a guy who is very invested in his fighter side just gets stuck. And that sure seemed to be Kyle, staring at me and really whaling away at my chair, with only an escalating intensity.

Having experienced this before I felt very calm and sure of how to handle it, although my left thigh was really starting to throb. Needing to change position to protect my thigh, and wanting to shake up the stuckness of the scene, I shifted so that I was more openly facing Kyle and I backed up a bit too. My intention was to move my chair legs away from his kicking range, to take the chair out of the scene and see how he reacted. Unfortunately, I did a poor job in two ways. I left one chair leg still within range and more importantly, this mild shift had both child and fighter posturing in it: I had backed away and squared up to him physically. His next kick was very hard. It surprised me, and I realized it was time to go to the next level, which is to give up the chair and the abuse endured while staying in it—to make a statement that I won't stay and put up with the ongoing harassment. I have done it many times and have still maintained the respect of the room by the manner in which I offer the chair instead of myself. However, I was already fully facing Kyle and a millisecond after beginning to rise I realized I was making a mistake. He was up instantly and we were then eye-to-eye, with the chairs now out of the picture. The fact that we had both stood up had raised the stakes considerably. The physicality of standing fully engages a man's body, and the qualities of height, weight, deliberate eye contact and arm's length distance had now been added into this escalating conflict.

Kyle was fully engaged in his role as fighter, and although I knew he knew it was a role-play, being up in front of his peers added a real component to the scene. I knew he had a stake in winning. He stepped up to me stating, "What you gonna bring, man? You gonna step down? You gonna step down?" His challenge was accompanied by a mild two-handed shove to my chest. The clearly stated and agreed-to rule before engaging in any SafeTeen role-plays is no physical contact. As usual, I had stated this rule and asked for agreement to the rule before we began. Kyle had consented to the rule only a short time ago and the collective intake of breath from his classmates confirmed that a boundary had just been broken. Regardless of the rule, young men sometimes get caught up in the moment and very occasionally I am shoved in a role-play. Without stopping the scene, I model taking back my original standing place before the shove had occurred, the exact place, no more, no less, and repeat what I had said just before the shove. Immediately after doing that I usually freeze the scene, and the young men who shove are asked "What was the rule for the role-play?"

One of the goals of the male SafeTeen facilitators is to never shame any of the guys for what they do or say. Instead we strive to model the right to express an opinion, and respectful disagreement. We let the guys individuate and explore the boundaries of safety we seek to create, while holding them fully accountable for their actions. It's not easy to do. The point I make with pushers and shovers is that their fighter side tends to come through their arms and hands. I ask them to note that we are only role-playing, in a familiar, well-lit place, surrounded by friends and peers, and that they know I am not truly a threat to them. I then ask them to consider how powerful the urge to shove would be if I was a stranger, or a peer who was a real threat, or perhaps if they were in an unfamiliar place, it was dark and they were alone. Young men fully understand the unwritten rule that says, If I am shoved, I have been given "permission" to respond back with physical force. The point of the discussion is for them to become aware of their own triggers and the power of the instinct to act out physically and to be aware of the response that will likely be generated by those instincts from others—especially others who have had similar conditioning to be fighters.

In the role-play with Kyle, I could feel the intense focus of the group and their investment in how real it was. I could feel them wanting it to go on uninterrupted. Wanting to see how I would handle something like this in real life. Instead of freezing the role play to re-establish a safe boundary, I chose to continue without reminding Kyle about the no-contact rule. I calmly recovered my balance and stepped back to my place. Taking my space back didn't seem to de-escalate Kyle at all, and he started repeating himself, saying, "Are you gonna step down? What are you gonna bring?" He then two-handed me again, this time with a violent intensity. I was again surprised, but hung in with the skills SafeTeen has taught me so much about. Once again I reclaimed my space. "I'm not stepping down," I stated again in a calm, clear tone, holding eye contact. It seemed the longer the confrontation went on the more stuck in his fighter side Kyle was. He now had more to lose by not "winning" and it was really showing.

At this point I was still resting on faith and the belief that this role-play would end gracefully, that my Solid side would de-escalate Kyle. When he shoved me violently a third time. he pushed me into an uncertainty I had not experienced for many years. In truth, I was no longer teaching at all. I felt targeted. I simply couldn't believe that he was doing this to me. Why weren't my Solid skills working? I had done everything I knew to do, I hadn't done anything to escalate him, and I didn't know what to do anymore. I felt fear and contempt for that fear churning in my stomach. In the absolute silence of that roomful of 15- and 16-year-old boys, I felt the pressure of their eyes watching us. I understood how badly they wanted to see this play out, and how big a test of power this had become. Dread weighed down my body and my mind went fuzzy. It dawned on me that it looked to the group as though he was just shoving me around the room, and I felt ashamed for just taking it. I had crazy images flash through my mind of how I would simply slip underneath the next shove, grab his arms and just "martial arts" him across the room. But I don't do martial arts, and I absurdly reminded myself, as I often have to with the guys, "This ain't Hollywood." During those long, sickening seconds I could only see two possibilities. Either he was going to start punching me with intent, or I would simply be humiliated, thereby experiencing one of men's highest fears: being witnessed by a group of men in a fear-based failure, losing an essential component of my maleness in one single moment. I had completely lost my earlier focus and was momentarily paralyzed by not knowing what to do.

In the intensity of the experience, I had also lost track of how far across the room we had travelled and was now unaware of the desk that was directly behind me. My visible uncertainty and loss of power seemed to increase the intensity of Kyle's forward momentum. I believe that a part of him knew he had really stepped over a big line. Like the fighter side in every man, his fighter's investment in winning had overpowered any awareness of the trouble he could get into for his actions, or sensitivity toward me he may have otherwise been feeling. "Are you gonna step down? What are you bringin'?" Kyle insisted and nailed me with a fourth two-hander in the chest. I don't know what I looked like as I flew backwards over that desk, but I know I felt completely out of control physically, and extremely vulnerable. I also heard shock and fear in the quiet exclamations of the group. As I arose, visibly flustered, Kyle stepped directly into my face and again demanded "You gonna step down? What are you bringin'?"

Kyle's unwitting gift to me was that his betrayal of the role-play rule and his unpredictable violence had propelled me to a place of authentic engagement with his challenge. I was not role-playing anymore, I was in trouble. That realization took me to a place of truth with myself. I had reached my limit, the limit I talk about with the guys, the moment when things get decided. When a man allows himself to feel his own truth, then he is ready to choose. I was ready. With a surge of renewal in my spirit, my Solid side emerged spontaneously and, stepping back to face him, I engaged him with a steady but relaxed gaze and voiced that truth in words: "This is what I'm bringing, and I'm not stepping down."

In a heartbeat, Kyle's expression shifted from a frozen and unyielding place, into a sort of surprised look. His face was a visual picture of relief. "That's good," he said, with his eyebrows raised and a half smile. It was clear that he was honouring the strength he saw in me. I had truly reached for who I wanted to be in that moment, I had allowed my certainty to clearly show and was genuinely ready to stand up for myself. I wasn't just playing Solid. I was solid.

The role-play was unmistakably over then. The tension eased, and I sat down. The room was still. I had never seen a room so still before. After a prolonged silence, where there was just no pretending that it hadn't been heavy, I turned to Kyle and said, "What was the rule for the role-play?" His face twitched with guilt, and with his fighter perhaps still trying to hold on to something, he replied, "Uh, no violent physical contact." "No," I said, "the rule was, no physical contact." Kyle's need to make physical contact despite the rule became a perfect moment to discuss the piece about the fighter's tendency to come out through the arm and hands, to shove and hit, even before the conscious intent to do so is formed. After discussing the role-play and his fighter's need for physical contact, we again switched roles. I was now asking him to show me his Solid side in response to my aggression. I played the role of fighter with intensity but of course without physical contact. He dropped into Solid very quickly, and did it well.

Fate being what it is, I found myself back at Kyle's school a few weeks later. A female facilitator and I were doing a co-ed session with a group of girls and guys who had previously taken the gender-separate programs. I hadn't realized that I would be working with Kyle's class again. I spotted him right away and I had very mixed emotions upon seeing him again, some lingering distrust, compassion and some anxiety. When I asked for a male volunteer to role-play with me in front of this large group of guys and girls, only Kyle's hand went up. The rest of the guys started buzzing immediately. I chose to trust him, and we set up the scene for Kyle to show his Solid side in response to my instigating fighting. In that eye-to-eye public yet private exchange, that 16-year-old boy could have passed for 24 years old, and I don't think I, a man in my early forties, do Solid any better than he did in that moment.

As I wrote this piece, I found myself feeling again the fear and confusion of being targeted by another man. I am grateful to have had the skills that guided me to my Solid side in a moment of genuine need. I am reminded yet again how powerful it is to be able to teach this work to young men.

Violence is profoundly disturbing and ugly. It's the worst we can be. It is the highest form of failure.

Man Made

Males have constructed a set of rules for themselves that in many ways no longer apply to their lives. It is as though they have boxed themselves into a limited humanity—in a way, painted themselves into a corner. One of the reasons I believe it is difficult for males to make the changes many of them need to and want to make is the absence of an "enemy." If there is no frontier to conquer and no enemy to overcome, males tend to be at a loss. They don't have a clearly defined oppositional force to resist and clearly defined freedoms to fight for in the way that females have had and still do have. For example, women had to fight for the right to vote and we continue to fight for equal pay. In a sense, for men, masculinity itself is the enemy and the frontier that must be conquered is their own inner world. Many males have to come to the awareness that the box they have made is too small, too limiting and they are choosing to deconstruct it and reconstruct something else—something that is still "man" but more flexible, more open—a softer place.

The following is a dialogue between the author and her father on his eighty-second birthday in April 2000:

Father: "I understand this language now. I am not a stranger to it. It's been nice to have the opportunity to live with seven women. In business I thought I had to get mad. Love is a much stronger force. I could have accomplished more with love. It's not easy to become a woman, you know. It's much easier to be a man.

Daughter: "Being a woman takes a different kind of courage, don't you think?"

Father: "It's a stage above the male stage. The world needs to hear men and women talking together about how we've changed and what new humanity we've created. It used to be natural the way it was but not anymore—we don't need the spears and arrows. We are now more intelligent and kinder and softer people.

"Women converse about their insides. Men used to say 'don't act like a woman.' Men don't even see the inside—they talk about outside things. I've been around women long enough to know that there is a warmer place to be."

Daughter: "Like when men want to have sex all the time—they are just looking for a warmer place? Is that how it is?"

Father: "After making love, I feel so complete. Otherwise we're lonely."

Daughter: "What else can you tell me about how things have changed for you as a man?"

Father: "I learned recently that there is more to me than meets the eye. I was asked to be on the board of the Canadian National Institute for the Blind. I am so used to people electing me to boards and committees because of what I look like. These people can't see me. I said, 'You can't see that I'm tall, white and handsome. Why are you electing me?'

"I realize that this is how women feel all the time. I am just learning this as a blind man."

Part IV: **BODY**

In the SafeTeen workshops we go beyond advice such as "just walk away" or "don't have sex." Through concrete body language and verbal skills, and using role-plays as the primary teaching tool, we teach youth how to access their inner wisdom and how to communicate from that place. The technique of role-playing is powerful because it provides us with a body experience of dealing with a potentially uncomfortable or threatening situation. We are far more likely to remember what to say or do during an actual crisis if we have integrated the information and skills into our body memory.

Part IV: BODY introduces role-plays, body language skills, boundaries exercises, communications exercises and the assertiveness techniques that have been so well-received in the SafeTeen programs. These exercises provide concrete strategies and address issues relevant to the everyday lives of youth: skills for managing fear and anger, how to deal with relationship violence and intimacy issues, how to respond to intimidating or threatening situations; tools to excavate inner strengths and build self-esteem. Designed to encourage young women and men to feel strong and secure in their respective identities, these exercises give teens the opportunity to practise a new way of being in the world and the skills with which to make that choice for themselves.

Chapter 10

Role-plays, Skills and Exercises

THE FOLLOWING TECHNIQUES are designed to be used in gender-separate groups of young women and men between the ages of twelve and eighteen. Some of the exercises can be adapted to gender-mixed groups and also may be effectively used one-on-one by counsellors or parents.

Exercises from Chapter 3

Getting to Know the Child in You

The purpose of this exercise is to help the individuals in the group connect with the child that they once were. Before you begin this exercise, explain to the group that the child we once were is still a part of who we are today and that what happened to us as small children can affect how we react in certain situations as adults. Getting to know the little person inside can help us figure out what we need to do in order to be strong and safe now.

Journal

Write the following sentences up on the board and ask each person to fill in the blanks on a sheet of paper. Begin by telling them: "Imagine you are a small child." Encourage them to allow themselves to write the first thing that comes to mind.

I am_____years old.

I live with_____.

What I most like to do is_____ _____.

What I am most afraid of is_____.

I feel safest when_____.

Encourage the group to find an old photo of themselves as a small child. Study it. Ask them to carry it with them for a while. Ask them to imagine that the child they are looking at in the photo is right here in front of them. Ask them if they would be willing to stand up for that child if someone were being mean to her/him. Tell them it is their job to keep that child safe.

Creating a Safe Place

The purpose of this exercise is to help the individuals in the group visualize a safe place so that they will have a place to "put" their small self when they are faced with an emotionally or physically threatening situation.

Teaching Tip: Girls and women tend to be more open and responsive than males to guided imagery as a method of learning about themselves. This is particularly true in large groups where, for young men, keeping up a "macho" image in front of their peers can get in the way of being vulnerable and staying focused. When working with groups of young men it may be more effective to do journal writing exercises. For those who do not like to write, suggest they just make a list of the things that come into their mind. In order to make it safe for both females and males, it is important to do the journal exercises in a way that ensures that they are private and anonymous. Offer an opportunity to share the writing on a volunteer basis. Sharing can be valuable for some and too terrifying for others. Participants need to feel both options are valid. A student who chooses to share can be praised for her/his courage while a person who chooses not to can be praised for her/his clear boundaries.

a. Guided imagery exercise

Have the individual or group sitting in a comfortable position, eyes closed and taking slow deep breaths. Tell them that you will count slowly to five and help them to find a safe place to put their "small self." It is important to be clear that the safe place could be a real place that they remember being safe in as a child but it could just as well be completely make-believe. Many people didn't have a safe place to be when they were children and it's crucial to assert that it is just as valid to have a fantasy place. Remember to pause in between counting to give people enough time to form the images clearly in their minds.

"*One.*" Picture yourself when you were a very small child—maybe three or four years old. Allow yourself to see this child clearly, her/his little face, hair, clothing. Now, imagine taking the child that you once were by the hand and leading that child toward a safe place. Allow whatever comes into your mind to be there and accept and trust that it's right even if it seems strange.

"*Two.*" Explore your safe place, still holding your little self by the hand if you like, and point out to her/him all the things that make this a safe place. Allow the image of your safe place to become clearer and clearer in your mind.

"*Three.*" Now, add something and/or someone to your safe place. Something that will make it feel even safer for your little child. This could be an old or current family pet, a special toy or stuffed animal or blanket, or anything at all that for whatever reason is comforting to your child. It could also be a safe person from your childhood or someone from your current life. Remember, it doesn't have to be real —it can be something or someone make-believe.

"Four." Now look your little self in the eyes and tell her/him, "This is your safe place and you can always find me here." Ask your little self if s/he would like a hug. Ask if there's anything else s/he needs.

"Five." Take a deep breath and just be there for a moment with your small self and feel what it feels like to be there, safe, in your very own safe place. Take another deep breath and then slowly open your eyes.

On a volunteer basis, invite the individual or group to share their safe place. Encourage the sharing and respect the boundaries of those who do not wish to share. It is possible that some members of a group were not able to visualize a safe place. It is very important to acknowledge this possibility and to encourage these people to spend some time thinking about their safe place. Tell them that they can borrow someone else's idea if it feels right to them or just make one up. Tell them to trust that there is a safe place and that it will reveal itself to them if they keep looking. If no one in the group wishes to share, it can be useful to describe your own and others you have heard in the past.

Some examples of safe places shared by grade 7 and 10 females are:
- In a hayloft, sun streaming in the window and I'm sitting and playing with a brand new batch of kittens. My grandpa is working downstairs in the barn.
- In a closet with the old dog I used to have as a little kid.
- In clouds with angels.
- In a field of flowers and when I'm sad or upset I just pick a flower and tell it my troubles.
- Behind a waterfall.
- In a tree fort.

b. Journal
This exercise can be used as an addition to the "safe place" guided imagery exercise or as an alternative. Make sure everyone has paper and pencil and remind the group that they will not be asked to share unless they wish to. Explain the concept of the small self and the

purpose of finding a safe place as in the guided imagery exercise above. Ask the individual or group to write a detailed description of their safe place. If they like they can also draw a picture. For those who have resistance to writing or drawing, it can be useful to suggest they simply make a list of what comes to mind. Once they have done this ask them to:

1. Imagine what would threaten your safe place and write/draw about it.
2. Imagine how you would defend your safe place, and write/draw about it.

Explain to the group the purpose of the exercise and how it applies to their real lives. Remind them that once we have a clear picture of a safe place in our mind, it is easier to be assertive in scary situations. We are less likely to smile, laugh, fidget and look away. We are more likely to be able to think of what to say and to be able to say it in a strong clear voice.

Remember: If you find yourself in a scary or intimidating situation, get your Child into a safe place.

Remember: The clearer your image of the safe place is, the more likely your Child will stay there.

Meeting Your Inner Warrior

a. Guided imagery exercise
Have the individual or group sitting in a comfortable position, eyes closed and taking slow deep breaths. Tell them that we all have a fierce side—a fighter inside us who is very brave and powerful and who would do anything to protect us. Explain that you will count slowly to five and help them to visualize a clear image of their inner Warrior. Remember to pause in between counting to give people enough time to form the images clearly in their minds.

"One." Imagine that you and the child you once were are walking down a long straight path or a long hallway or perhaps down a beach. You see a figure approaching in the distance. You know this is your inner Warrior, coming to greet you.

"Two." S/he is the physically strong, fierce part of you that will come to your defence when you are in trouble. S/he is the part of you that will fight back. S/he is powerful and fearless. Focus on the figure approaching and allow your inner Warrior to take shape as s/he gets closer. Allow whatever image comes to your mind to be right.

"Three." Now you can see your inner Warrior clearly. You can see the way s/he moves, what s/he is wearing, the details of her/his physical form. You can see her/his face. As you look into her/his eyes, you can see s/he has no fear.

"Four." Your inner Warrior is thrilled to see you. Imagine how s/he greets you. Imagine that s/he tells you she will always be there for you. See if you can sense the tone and timbre of her/his voice as s/he speaks.

"Five." Now imagine that you are walking together. You are feeling absolutely safe and protected. Allow yourself to feel that for a moment. Breathe it in. Slowly open your eyes.

b. Journal
This exercise provides an alternative method of getting in touch with the inner Warrior. Provide the group with pencils and paper and instruct them to draw or describe their inner Warrior. Encourage them to put down on the paper the first thing that comes to mind without censoring themselves. Assure the group that the exercise is anonymous and they will not be asked to share if they do not wish to.

Introduce the exercise by telling the group: "Imagine a small child that you love is in danger. Someone is threatening to hurt this child and it is up to you to save her/him. Imagine now that you have magic powers and you can transform yourself into anything or anyone that you wish to be in order to save the child."

Now write the following suggestions up on the board or verbally instruct the group to:
Describe the warrior in you.
Describe how s/he looks: Height, build, hair, eyes, clothes.
Describe how s/he moves.
Imagine what s/he would say in the child's defence.
Imagine what s/he would be willing to do in the child's defence.

Now suggest the group rewrite this exercise in the first person and encourage them to read it out loud. Once again they should not be pressured to share if they do not feel safe doing so. If they do not choose to read aloud in the group, encourage them to read what they have written at a later time to someone they do feel safe with—or just to themselves when they are alone.

Getting to Know Your Wise Woman/Solid Guy

Wise Person Skill #1: Feel and Breathe
Instruct the group to stand in a large circle, feet planted firmly on the floor, hands relaxed by their sides. Explain to them that in order to connect with our inner strength and wisdom, we need to remember to breathe. When we are afraid or angry we tend to hold our breath. When we are not breathing, no oxygen goes to the brain and we can't think!

Tell the group that when we are faced with a challenging situation, the first step is to take a moment to recognize and acknowledge how we are feeling. Taking deep breaths can help us connect with our feelings and keep our energy moving. If we identify fear (Child), we need to take a deep breath and put the Child in a safe place. If we identify anger (Bitch/Tough Guy), we need to acknowledge and validate the Warrior and take another calming breath. Once the Child is safe and the Warrior is back, we can breathe into and connect with the clear, strong part of ourselves (Wise Woman/Solid Guy).

Wise Person Skill #2: Making Eye Contact
The purpose of this exercise is to heighten awareness about the impact of body language, especially eye contact and facial expression, and to demonstrate how powerful body language is as a method of communicating.

In an open room or a classroom where desks have been moved aside and a space has been cleared, instruct the group to walk around the room at a leisurely pace. Ask them to change directions from time to time and keep them moving for a minute or two. Now, instruct them to begin making eye contact with every person they pass.

Keep the group moving and encourage them to continue making eye contact. It will soon become evident that this is an uncomfortable exercise for most people. Predictably, people will begin to laugh, smile and look away. Allow the laughter and discomfort to be just as it is and then ask the group to stop. Now, instruct them to resume walking around the room once more—once again making eye contact with everyone they pass—this time *without smiling*. Females in particular will find it difficult to make eye contact and especially to maintain it without smiling or laughing. Once again, female conditioning to be empathic, approval-seeking and polite may mean they will really have to go against the grain to be successful at maintaining eye contact without smiling in this exercise. Invite them to take a "time-out" if they are having a difficult time controlling their laughter. ("Stop, go to the edge of the group, turn your back to the group and take some deep breaths. Rejoin the group as soon as you regain your composure.") Encourage them to take their time-outs alone as opposed to taking them with a friend. Laughter can be very contagious and they may never be able to rejoin the group to try again.

As the group is walking around, encourage them to keep making eye contact and instruct them to pay attention to how it feels when the other person looks away first. Ask them to experiment with being the first to look away—or to challenge themselves and refuse to be the first to look away.

As they struggle with this exercise, encourage them to keep trying and ask them to pay close attention to how it feels. Keep this exercise going for two to three minutes or until the group has fallen into fits of giggles.

Discussion: Stop the exercise and ask the group to discuss their experience. Some questions to ask the group could be:

- Were you able to feel the power "over" someone else when they looked away first?
- Were you able to feel the loss of your own power when you gave up first?
- Did it feel rude to look at each other and not smile?
- Did you worry about the other person's feelings?
- Did you feel rejected or concerned about not being liked or approved of?
- Did you feel intimidated at any point?
- Did you feel strong at any point?
- What are some of the things you have been taught about making eye contact?

When asked how it felt to make eye contact without smiling, some typical responses are:

- It felt rude.
- It was uncomfortable.
- I felt like a bitch.
- I couldn't do it.
- It felt really weird.

It is useful to stress that you are not suggesting that they make eye contact without smiling at all times and in all situations. Remind the group that they are simply exploring the power of body language as a form of communication and that it would be useful to know what messages they are putting out and to be in control of those messages.

It can be useful to do this exercise a number of times with the same group. Once the group has learned some of the assertiveness skills and feels more connected to their inner strength, they can use this exercise as an ongoing way to practise making eye contact.

Teaching Tip: Generally, males will have an easier time with this exercise. In a mixed group where the girls are all looking away and smiling, males will usually be more successful at maintaining a strong outer appearance. As well, in a gender-same group, males tend to be able to control their facial expressions and hold the eye contact of the other males in the group. On some level this is a dominance game that males are familiar with. They take it as a challenge and will not permit themselves to look away.

However, young males who are lacking in maturity tend to act up with mock aggressiveness, arm punching, knocking into each other and glaring at each other with furrowed brows. In a gender-same group, females tend to giggle uncontrollably and may be unsuccessful at maintaining eye contact. Some females will posture in an aggressive manner much like the young men.

Teaching Tip: It is useful to be aware that participants from some cultures will find this exercise more difficult than others. Allow everyone's experience to be as it is without judgement. The purpose of the exercise is to increase awareness and to create a safe place for youth to practise assertive body language. We can simply observe the difficulty participants may have and remember that the goal is not so much to achieve anything as to experience the feelings. Encourage each student to talk about their own experience and invite them to identify the cultural differences they are aware of.

Teaching Tip: It can be useful to practise making eye contact in a mirror. Encourage the group to do this and experiment with smiling and frowning while observing the different messages the change of expression brings. It is also useful to practise in pairs, small groups and larger groups where we can benefit from the feedback of others.

Teaching Tip: It is uncommon for women to look men in the eye unless they are interested in the man in a romantic way. Because of this, it is particularly important for females to be certain that they are not smiling or looking sidelong or over their shoulder, as this could be interpreted as inviting and flirtatious. In order for the message to be assertive, the head, and if possible the shoulders, should be facing directly toward the person you wish to communicate to, and the face must be strong and serious.

Teaching Tip: It is common for both female and male participants to feel anxious about using direct eye contact as a prevention skill. The fear is that the other person will feel challenged by us and the situation will escalate. It is the quality of eye contact that makes the difference. When the gaze is neutral and calm it communicates inner strength and will not likely be perceived as a challenge. It is especially critical that the gaze be strong and consistent but without narrowed eyes, a furrowed brow or tense jaw, which could be seen as challenging. As well, watch for "attitude," which commonly manifests in a "cocky" smile and raised eyebrow.

Wise Person Skill #3: Standing Strong
Body Language
Communications experts tell us that more than 75 percent of communication among humans happens through body language. In order to demonstrate the truth of this statistic to your group, try making a strong confident statement about yourself such as, "I am very comfortable speaking in front of a group and don't feel at all nervous," while allowing yourself to fidget with your clothing or wring your hands the whole time you are talking. Now ask the group what they believe. Regardless of how strongly you deliver the verbal statement, the strongest message they will receive will be the one you communicate through your body language. Point out to the group the importance of being aware of what we are communicating with our bodies so that we can be in control of the messages we are putting out there. Imagine if we were not aware of what we were saying out loud!

Small Group Exercise
Have participants break into small groups and take turns being "speakers" and "observers." Instruct the speakers to choose a topic that is important to them and deliver a small speech to the other members of the group on this topic. Instruct them to be as passionate and confident as possible. The observers' job is to observe body language and note what signals they are picking up. They will then give this feedback to the speakers. Instruct the group to rotate roles so each member has an opportunity to be both speaker and observer.

Large Group Exercise

Have the group stand and instruct them as follows: "Plant your feet firmly on the ground, a well-balanced distance apart. Stand up straight and square your shoulders. Keep your chin level and make eye contact. Relax your facial expression so that you look as neutral as possible. It is important not to smile, as smiling can communicate a mixed message. Let your arms rest at your sides, and keep your hands relaxed and still."

Tell them: "Taking this Wise Person stance can help to connect you with your inner strength. Even if you don't feel strong and neutral, mask the fear or the anger and take the stance anyway. Remember: Body language is the most powerful form of communication. Even if you can't think of what to say, you are giving a clear strong message that you are not an easy target."

Now have the group form a large circle. Instruct them to maintain the Wise Person stance and to "ground" themselves (feet planted firmly on the ground a comfortable and well-balanced distance apart). Suggest they use an image of roots growing out of the bottom of their feet. Tell them: "When we are in the Wise Person stance, we are like a tree, claiming our space, feeling absolutely our right to be here."

Now instruct the individuals in the group to begin making eye contact with each other—to calmly look around the group and connect with other people in the group. Then instruct them to begin to walk around very slowly, continuing to make eye contact. Ask them to pay close attention to their posture, tension in their shoulders or arms or hands. Encourage them to breathe and relax and hold a neutral expression in their bodies and faces. While the group is walking, encourage them to focus on feeling the right to be strong and solid without the traditional gender stereotyping. Tell the young women that right now they don't have to think about being "female"—nice or polite or caring—just strong. Tell the young men that they don't have to think about being "male"—dominant, aggressive or having something to prove—just solid. Ask them to experience as best they can being present in the moment, comfortable with communicating just this one facet of their being: strong. Solid.

Discussion: How did it feel to do this? If the group has done the "making eye contact" exercise earlier, how was it different doing it with the strong stance?

Teaching Tip: It can be useful at this point to reassure your group that they do not have to walk around in their daily lives in a robot-like manner making eye contact with every person they meet.

Wise Person Skill #4: Speaking Up
Voice
Tell your group that the tone of voice is more important than the words they choose. Strong words timidly spoken will not carry much power. Instruct them as follows: "Speak firmly and calmly at an even level. Do not escalate in volume, especially if the person you are confronting does this. (A slight decrease in volume can sometimes strengthen your message.) Keep your voice tone neutral and relaxed. Do not 'spit out' the words or 'bite down on them.' Keep your jaw relaxed. Do not copy the other person's tone. Come from your own place of strength. Do not answer questions. Do not make statements that end in a questioning tone and do not let your voice dwindle out at the end of sentences. An assertive tone is deep and even, relaxed, matter-of-fact."

Yes/No Exercise
Have the group line up with half the group on one side of the room and the other half across from them, facing each other. Each person should have a partner approximately two feet across from them. Assign one side as the "Yes" people and the other side as the "No" people. Instruct the "Yes" people to try to convince their partner with a "yes" sentence, such as, "Yes, you are coming with me!" or "Yes, you will give me your money!" The "No" people's job is to say "No" in a variety of ways. Encourage both sides to experiment with volume, tension in their tone, question marks at the end of sentences, angry tones, etc. Remind the group that the tone is more important than the words. Ask them to try to find the strongest-sounding "No." After two or three minutes, have them switch sides so each person has the

opportunity to be both a "Yes" and a "No" person. Open the floor for discussion and ask the group what they noticed about the tone and how it affected the strength of their message. Ask them to discuss what felt strongest and why.

Words
As we've learned, body language and voice tone are more important than the actual words we use. However, there are some word strategies that can make our message stronger. Suggest to your group that they choose a message based on what it is they want/don't want and to keep their message simple.

Remind the group: Do not get tricked into losing your own message and reacting to the other person's words or tone. In emotionally or physically threatening situations take "Please," "Thank you" and especially "I'm sorry" out of your assertive vocabulary.
    Some tips to give your group are:
* Do not begin your sentences with "I'm sorry but ... " (this gives the message that you do not feel you have the right to say what you are saying).
* Do not ask for permission to speak (especially with a power/authority figure). Instead of "Can I say something here ... ?" or "May I ask a question?" try "I have something to say," or "I have a question."
* Do not ask indirect questions such as "Could you please stop shoving me?" or "Do you mind? Aren't you sitting a little close?"
* Make direct statements about what you want or don't want. For example, "I don't feel comfortable with how close you are. I want you to move."

"I" Messages
Although the exact words are not as important as the tone, it is more effective to use "I" messages when we are being assertive. Encourage your group to begin their sentences with "I" as much as possible. For example: "I don't want ... "; "I don't like ... "; "I'm not comfortable with ... " Remind them that when we make statements based on our own needs and feelings we are more likely to be heard. "You" state-

ments usually inspire defensiveness. It is much more difficult to argue with someone when they are simply stating how they feel.

Write up on the board the following examples of "I" messages and ask the group to add to them:
- "I don't like the way you're looking at me."
- "I didn't like that comment."
- "I don't want to continue this conversation."
- "I don't like playing mind games."
- "I'm not going to fight you."

We can also state want we want as opposed to what we don't want. For example:
- "I want you to stop your racist/sexist/homophobic comments."
- "I want you to stop pressuring me."
- "I want you to stop harassing me."
- "I want you to be honest with me."

Remind your group: Try not to repeat the other person's words or tone as part of your message. Find your own truth and say it. Try to keep the message simple and direct and honest. Less is usually better.

It can be useful to encourage students who have a hard time finding the courage to speak up not to be afraid to "rock the boat." Assure them that if they feel the need to speak up, the boat is probably already rocking!

The Broken Record

It is sometimes necessary to repeat our assertive message a second and even a third time. However, it isn't usually useful to repeat the message more than three times. After the third time, instruct them to follow up with "The Look": strong, consistent eye contact. In effect, they are saying: "I meant what I said." In the following section there are a list of suggested role-plays. Make sure each person has an opportunity to practise finding a strong message and repeating it like a broken record.

Assertiveness Skills: Role-Plays

Role-plays are an extremely effective learning tool because of the opportunity they provide to create a powerful visual and emotional experience for both the observers and the players. To begin with, brainstorm some ideas for role-plays with the group and then set up each scenario and ask for volunteers to act out the different roles. As the group leader, you can coach and encourage from the sidelines or play one of the roles. You should give instructions to the players to use the Wise Person assertiveness body language and verbal skills they have learned and encourage the group to help you point out the Child and Warrior behaviours when they see them. It can be useful to experiment with acting out the scenarios with the Child and Warrior first and then a third time with just the Wise Person. If the players get stuck you can invite the group to give them suggestions.

The technique of role-playing is used to provide a safe and structured place for the group to practise what they could say or do in threatening or scary real-life situations. It is important for each player to keep trying until s/he experiences some level of success. It is also important for the facilitator to recognize when the player is feeling too vulnerable to continue and to praise them for what they did right and then let them "off the hook." It is essential to create safety in the group. The safest environment for exploring sensitive and volatile topics such as violence, sexuality and harassment is in a gender-separate format. Once the young women and men have had an opportunity to practise in gender-separate groups it can be very useful to have them come together and do gender-mixed role-plays. It is important to encourage people to volunteer for role-playing while being supportive of those who do not wish to take the risk of getting up in front of the group.

The first step is to brainstorm a variety of scenarios with the group. The group could be instructed to use scenarios that are related to a specific environment (for example, school) or a specific topic (for example, intimate relationships). Suggesting specific categories such as fear/intimidation or anger/frustration can also help get the brainstorm going.

The following role-plays illuminate common elements in adolescent experience:

He wants it/she doesn't: In this role-play the person acting out the guy is sexually aggressive and shows no concern for the female's wants and needs. He pressures her persistently using guilt, anger and threats to leave her. Her job is to get her Child into a safe place, get her Warrior back and to connect with her Wise Woman. With her use of strong neutral body language and voice tone she should be encouraged to repeat her assertive message three times if necessary and to back her message up with "The Look."

Give me your money: In this role-play, a much bigger, tougher person uses intimidation and physical threats to convince a smaller person to give up their bus money.

Version 1. The smaller person says "No" and stands her/his ground.

Version 2. If the bully doesn't back off and makes physical threats, the smaller person calmly gives up the money, making good eye contact and letting the bully know s/he is making a strong choice. For example, the smaller person could say, "I don't like what you're doing but I'm going to give you my money because I don't want to get beat up over a dollar."

Power/authority: In this role-play, an adult is making inappropriate advances and using their power and authority to intimidate or pressure the young person into doing something they do not want to do. Ask the group to brainstorm some examples of people in positions of authority who could abuse that position of power. Choose one of the examples and role-play. For example, a coach who is behaving in an inappropriate way could say, "You want to make the team, don't you?" The young person's job in this role-play is to communicate a strong boundary and repeat the message three times if necessary. Instruct the person playing the adult in this role-play to persist, and instruct the young person to make a clear statement about their intent to report the incident. Encourage them to stick to their statement and not feel they have to say who they will tell.

Verbal violence: Invite the group to write down words that they have been put down with, that they themselves have used or that they have heard used to put others down. Collect the lists and write the words up on the board. With the group's help, identify which words are racist, homophobic, misogynist, gender or sexual harassment. Help the group to define which of these categories the words or phrases fall into. Encourage a discussion of the impact of verbal violence.

Version 1: Have three people role-play with one person being the target of verbal abuse by the other two players. If the words used are racist or homophobic or gender-related, encourage the player who is being targeted to name the violence for what it is when they stand up for themselves. For example: "I don't like your racist remarks."

Version 2: Once again, three people play, but this time there is only one harasser. Instruct one player to harass one of the two other players. Instruct that player to stand up for her/himself and to support her/his friend, for example with, "I don't like the way you're talking to my friend."

Version 3: In this version, two male players will be hanging out together and one or two female players will walk by. Instruct one of the male players to sexually harass the girls walking by. Afterwards have the male player who didn't say anything call his buddy on his behaviour. For example, "Hey, that's sexual harassment—it's against the law. Anyway, when you do that you make all guys look like jerks."

The fight: One person is aggressively pressuring another person to fight. The person being pressured does not want to fight and makes a clear statement asserting her/his right not to fight. Encourage the player who is asserting their right not to fight to make good eye contact and to repeat their message calmly three times. If this doesn't work, coach the player to choose to walk away by stating her/his intent to leave and then stepping slowly away while maintaining eye contact and without turning her/his back until enough distance has been established between them to do so safely. Remind the group that in some instances they may not have a choice, and begin a discussion regarding their right to defend themselves, call out for help and run as soon as they can if they are violently attacked.

The Fight Crowd

Version 1: Have two people play-act an argument that escalates into a shoving match. Instruct a large group of people to play a group of their peers and coach them to stand around and cheer them on, yelling, "Fight! Fight! Discuss the effect of the crowd on the two players.

Version 2: Have the same two people play-act an argument and instruct them to escalate as before. But this time have them leave the room briefly before the role-play begins, then instruct the group who are playing the crowd to turn their backs and walk away as soon as the escalation starts.

Discussion: Ask the group to talk about what they felt and observed in these two scenarios and how it was different. Ask them to discuss the accountability of those who stand around and cheer when fights occur. Remind them that they each have a lot of power to impact violent incidents by their participation or refusal to participate. Propose to the group that observing violence without intervening is a way of participating in violence. Invite them to comment on this point. Ask the group to brainstorm intervention methods when fights break out.

Asking for clarification: In this role-play, one player is a male who would like to take his relationship a step further. Explain to the group that the guy has been respectful and clear about what he wants and doesn't want to do anything the young woman doesn't want to do. However, the girl he is with is extremely non-assertive and has been giving him very confusing mixed messages. He is feeling frustrated. It is typical at this point for a young male to begin to pressure and use coercion to move things forward or to get angry and withdraw. There is a third option. Instruct the male player to stop and ask the female to be clear with him about what she wants—and to reassure her that he won't be angry if she doesn't want to go any further. For example, "I am getting mixed messages from you and it's really frustrating. It's OK if you don't want to go any further. I just need to know what you want." Coach the female to persist with confusing mixed messages and instruct the male player to be clear that he does not want to proceed without knowing for sure what she wants. For example, "You know, I really want to do this but I don't want to do it unless you're really sure —let's stop for now and go to that movie, OK?"

When these role-plays are being demonstrated, encourage suggestions, strategies and feedback from the group. Once the group has had an opportunity to see a number of role-plays demonstrated, divide participants into groups of three (triads). Each triad chooses scenarios that feel meaningful to them to act out. Each person in the triad has a role:

Role 1: Target
The Target's role is to choose the scenario and assign the Perpetrator (or harasser) her/his role. Then the Target acts out the scenario and defends her/himself from the Perpetrator using their Wise Person skills to the best of their ability.

Role 2: Perpetrator
The Perpetrator's role is to act out the role assigned by the Target.

Role 3: Observer
The Observer's role is to watch the Target carefully and take note of body language and verbal delivery. Look for signs of the Child, the Warrior and the Wise Person. (Watch for eye contact, fidgeting, moving away, tone of voice, "I" messages, repeating statements.) After the role-play is completed, it is important that the Observer gives positive feedback first: "The Wise Woman/Solid Guy skills I saw you use were …" and then the Observer points out whether or not they saw the Child or the Warrior, and what specific body language cues they saw. The Target should try again once the feedback has been received.

The triads can present their scenarios to the whole group once they have had a chance to practise them using the feedback from the Observers in their small groups. The whole group can give feedback at the end of each scenario. Again, instruct the group to begin with positive feedback: tell each person what they did right—list the Wise Person skills used. Then point out any Child/Warrior body language or voice tone that was observed. Have the group rotate roles so each person has an opportunity to play each role.

Although most groups of teens can come up with a variety of suggestions for role-plays, it can be useful to have a list up on the board for them to choose from. Some common scenarios that teens come up with are:

What are you looking at? (male/female).
A girl/guy who is looking for trouble walks by you on the bus and suddenly s/he's in your face for "looking at her/him."

Home alone (female).
You are home alone and your brother's friend (who gives you the creeps) comes to the door. He says he's supposed to meet your brother there and insists you should let him come in and wait.

The bad feeling (male/female).
You are sitting on the couch watching TV and an adult (or older) relative is sitting too close. You can feel this person's hand moving against your thigh. There are other people in the room and you are embarrassed and don't want to make a scene. Or, there is no one else home and you are embarrassed and don't want to accuse this person in case s/he doesn't mean to be doing anything weird. Or, this has happened many times before and you know where it will lead. You have to make a decision to tell this person you want it to stop and you need to find a safe person to tell about what has been going on.

Babysitting (female).
The family you are babysitting for is nice but when the dad drives you home you notice his fly is open. He also looks at you in a way that

makes you feel uncomfortable. You are getting a bad feeling and it happens more than once. You really need the money from this job and it's not like anything has really happened.

The bus stop (female).
You are at the bus stop. A guy sits too close and asks for the time. He starts talking to you in a friendly manner but you feel really uncomfortable with how close he is and his personal questions.

She wants it/he doesn't (male).
You are at a party and a girl whom you don't find at all attractive is really drunk and coming on to you. It seems like you are the only virgin in your grade and you feel a lot of pressure to "score." You want the admiration and acceptance of your peers. Your guy friends are laughing and cheering you on to go for it.

Drugs (female/male).
You are at a party and a joint is being passed around. Everyone in the group is taking a drag. You've never done it and you're scared. You want to stay and hang out but you don't want to do drugs. You know everyone will pressure you if you say "No."

The ride (female).
You are at a party and the ride you had been depending on has stranded you. A guy you don't feel comfortable around and who you suspect has been drinking offers you a ride home. You say "No" but he asks how you are getting home—he knows you are stuck for a ride, the buses aren't running, it's a long way and you don't have money for a cab.

The basketball game (male).
You have tickets to a big game and when you and your friend get to your assigned seats there are two guys sitting in your seat. You show them your ticket stubs and ask them to move but they laugh at you and refuse to give up the seats.

Fight over a guy/girl (female/male).
A girl/guy accuses you of sleeping/flirting with her/his boyfriend/girl-friend. S/he is threatening to beat you up and a group of her/his friends is backing her/him up. Maybe you did/maybe you didn't—but you definitely don't want to fight over it. It could be that this girl/guy has a bad reputation for being very violent and you're scared. It could be that you think fighting over guys/girls is really immature. Either way, you don't want to fight.

Exercise: The Boat Is Already Rocking

It is very common, especially for females, to be afraid to speak up because they don't want to make a scene. They don't want to "rock the boat."

In all the scenarios below, it is the men who are "making waves." And it is the girls and women who are being thrown off balance. When we stand up for ourselves, we are merely taking control of our lives and in effect "steadying our boat." A good rule for all of us to remember is, *When you are feeling off balance but you are hesitant to correct the situation because you don't want to rock the boat, tell yourself, "The boat is already rocking."*

The following scenarios can be used as role-plays. Break your group into small groups and hand out one copy of the three scenarios below to each group. Instruct each group to act out all three scenarios first non-assertively and then assertively. At the end of each scenario is a "Discussion Question" and a "Tip" on how to handle the situation assertively. Encourage the groups to use the tips as guidelines. Bring the whole group together at the end for a discussion using the questions as a prompter.

1. The Bus

A ten-year-old girl is sitting on the bus. A man sits down too close to her. She squidges over closer to the window. He opens a magazine over his lap and his hand brushes her leg and partially rests on her knee. The girl stares straight ahead. She is frozen. She is thinking, "This man's hand isn't on my leg." It is unthinkable. This couldn't possibly be happening to her.

The man's hand moves slightly. The girl's eyes widen but she doesn't move a muscle. She is thinking, "The man's hand is on my leg ... but he doesn't know it's on my leg." She turns her head and stares out the window.

The man's hand slides up her leg, lifting her skirt and then resting once more. It is sitting lightly on her upper thigh. The hand is like a giant spider, patient and sure of itself.

Discussion Question: When a girl is sitting on the bus and a man puts his hand on her leg, what stops her from looking directly at him and taking his hand off her leg? What stops her from asking for help?

Tip: Try grabbing the little finger and firmly lifting his (your role-play partner's) hand off while saying, "Take your hand off my leg." Try saying this loudly enough that others around you would clearly hear it. Now practise asking for help. You could say: "This man is touching me. Will someone please be my witness?"

2. The Party

A young woman is at a party. She doesn't really want to be here but it is a big family reunion and her parents insisted she had to come. One of her uncles approaches her and putting his arm around her upper back he steers her around the room, introducing her to other family members she has not met. She doesn't like the way he refers to her as "my beautiful niece" or the proprietary arm around her. She feels like he is showing her off as though she was something he could take credit for in some way. She feels angry and then confused because she knows she should be polite and part of her likes the attention he is giving her. As they move around the room, she realizes he is getting quite drunk and he begins to lean into her and his fingers creep under her arm at the back until they are just slightly touching the side of her breast. She squeezes her upper arm down firmly over the encroaching fingers to stop them from going any further. At the same time she is, in effect, holding the fingers in place. She feels frozen with anxiety, begins to sweat profusely and the whole while she continues smiling and chatting with the relatives she has just been introduced to. She feels trapped but she doesn't want to say anything. She doesn't want to make a scene.

Discussion Question: When a girl at a party is walking around ignoring the fact that a man's hand is on her breast, what stops her from turning to face him and saying, "I appreciate the introductions, Uncle Jack, but I'm not comfortable with the way you're holding me and I want you to let go"?

Tip: Try turning to face him (your role-play partner) and using your STOP hand while you deliver the message.

3. The Movie

A fourteen-year-old girl and her friend are sitting in a movie theatre. It's not very crowded so the girl gets a funny feeling when a man sits down right next to her. There are so many other seats all around them that he could have chosen. She crosses her legs and moves a little closer to her friend. The lights dim and the movie starts and she becomes caught up in the story and forgets about the man. Then she feels a rhythmic jiggling motion at her elbow and she looks out of the corner of her eye and sees that he is masturbating. She is filled with shame. She feels somehow that she has caused him to do this. Her body goes rigid and she closes her eyes and waits for him to finish. When he is done, he gets up and leaves but before he goes he leans in toward her and says, "Thanks, sweetheart." The girl's friend is momentarily distracted from the movie and asks, "What was that? Did that man say something?" The girl says, "No, but I feel sick, can we go?" She goes to the ladies' room on the way out and throws up. She doesn't tell her friend what happened. She doesn't tell anyone.

Discussion Question: When a teenage girl is in a theatre and the man sitting next to her starts touching himself, what stops her from standing up and saying as loud as she can, "THIS MAN IS MASTURBATING!"?

Tip: Try standing up and making this statement loud and clear.

Exercises from Chapter 4

Transforming Fear Exercise for Females: "Waking the Warrior"

In groups of three or four, ask each female to tell a story of a time when she felt afraid. Write on the board or flip chart all the places, activities and people involved in the fear stories using the headings Where / When / Who. Read the list back to the group and ask each individual to say in one or two words how she feels. The most frequent responses are: overwhelmed, more afraid, hopeless, anxious, numb and sad.

The purpose of the next step in this exercise is to awaken the dormant anger and release the fierceness of the inner Warrior. In awakening the Warrior, we are not saying "let your anger rule." We are saying that it is important that the inner Warrior be alert and prepared.

In order to re-script their stories, have each individual repeat their story in its essence (a shortened version with just the key points). Now instruct them to end their stories with the words, "I was really angry." Discuss how changing the ending of the story affected the experience for the group. Were they able to connect with the underlying anger?

Transforming Anger Exercise for Males: "Awakening the Child"

The purpose of this exercise is to teach the inner Warrior to step aside, thereby releasing the humanity of the child-self.

In small groups of three or four, ask each male in the group to tell a story of a time when he felt angry. After the storytelling, write up on the board or flip chart all the places, activities and people involved in the anger stories under the headings Where / When / Who. Read the list back to the group and ask each individual to say in one or two words how he feels. The most frequent responses are: angry, pissed off, annoyed, frustrated and more angry.

In order to rescript their stories, have the males retell their anger stories. Now instruct them to end their stories with the words, "I was really afraid." Acknowledge that this may feel uncomfortable or even "wrong." Ask them to do it anyway—as an experiment. Discuss how changing the ending of the story affected the experience for the individual and for the group. Did the anger stories have a subtext of vulnerability? Were the participants able to acknowledge the underlying feelings?

In awakening the Child we are not saying it is wise to be vulnerable at all times. We are saying that when we awaken the dormant fear we awaken the gentleness and compassion of the child-self, thereby encouraging our boys and men to be more whole human beings. In the words of psychologist Aaron White, "Our boys are in trouble. We need to hold them to their humanness."

Remember: Anger is your ally. Anger defends your boundaries. We can't banish our anger but we can transform it and carry it with us as energy.

Releasing Anger: Unsent Hate Mail

Anger is an enormous source of energy. When it is unexpressed, it can "leak in" and act as an emotional poison that can deaden the spirit and make us bitter. It can also "leak out" and poison our relationships with others. Also, repressed anger can erupt faster than thought and become violence. Having a safe place to put anger can be a life-or-death survival skill. It is also important to know who is and is not safe to express our anger to directly. The following Hate Mail exercise provides a safe place for us to put our anger when we can't speak up about it directly. Provide your group with writing material and give them the following instructions:

a) Make a list of all the people you are angry with. You are going to write letters to these people. Date each letter and write across the top: UNSENT LETTER. Each letter should be folded, placed in an envelope and addressed ... and then filed and reopened at least three days later. Do not mail.

b) Begin: "Dear _____" Fill in the name of a person who is on your list. Continue writing and let everything that comes to you be right. Do not censor yourself—tell yourself you can say anything and everything you feel.

c) If you feel you are unreasonably angry at someone—that the intensity of emotion is too extreme for how long you've known the person or what they have done—try putting in someone else's name and then re-reading the letter. Keep trying until you find a fit. Remember: The current anger you are feeling now might be loaded with the weight of anger you have been carrying for years. Identifying who you are really angry at can be very powerful and freeing.

As a follow-up, you can encourage the group to tear their letters up, or burn them in a ritual ceremony. Another alternative is to suggest they start an "Unsent Letter" file and keep their letters in a safe and private place. Reading these letters weeks, months and even years later can be illuminating. It is important to warn them about the seriousness of sending an angry letter and advise them to think carefully about the consequences.

Safe and Unsafe Anger Actions

The following exercise can be done as a brainstorm. Ask the group to suggest ways that we can express anger without hurting ourselves or others. Break them into small groups and have each group come up with some anger actions that are safe. Instruct each group to write their list up on the board.

Some examples of safe actions are: angry pushing (on a wall/door/person who agrees), running, stomping, tearing/scrunching paper, punching and kicking a pillow/punching bag, biting towel/blanket, writing an unsent letter, drawing pictures and tearing them up, making play-dough figures and then squishing them, sticking pins in a doll, play-acting a puppet show with stuffed animals or socks on your hands, starting a petition, writing a letter to the press, yelling, swearing, role-playing what we would want to say—in the mirror, with another person or even an object representing the person we are angry with.

Remind your group that it is important to make sure we are in a place that is safe for us and for others when we express our anger.

Now ask the group to suggest unsafe ways of expressing anger. Break them into small groups and have each group come up with some anger actions that are unsafe. Instruct each group to write their list up on the board.

Unsafe actions could include: kicking doors, punching walls, writing on books/desks/walls, hitting people, swearing at people, name-calling, yelling at people, pushing people, physically blocking someone from leaving, grabbing/holding/restraining someone, directing anger at self: hitting forehead, banging head on wall, biting lip, punching legs, pulling hair, cutting/suicide.

Brainstorm examples of using anger constructively. Some examples are:
a. Harriet Tubman got angry and freed hundreds of slaves.
b. Susan B. Anthony got angry and won women the right to vote.
c. Environmentalists get angry and protest the destruction of trees and wildlife.

d. Women who fight back when they are attacked.

Invite the group to discuss personal examples of using anger safely, unsafely and constructively.

Exercises from Chapter 5

"Snipping Your Sorries"

This exercise is particularly relevant to females. It is extremely common for North American females to overapologize and it is one of the most common ways for girls and women to give up their power. Inform your group of the importance of getting the word "sorry" out of their assertive vocabulary and give them the following exercise as a way of building their awareness and cutting back on their inappropriate apologies.

Instruct your group as follows: "Count the number of times you say the word 'sorry' for one whole week. While you're busy counting, imagine having an imaginary pair of scissors and, using two fingers in a snipping gesture, 'snip' each unnecessary 'sorry' when it slips out. Make it a game with a friend to listen for your own and each other's 'sorries' and snip them for each other as well."

Some examples of inappropriate "sorries" are:
a) Saying "sorry" when you bump into an inanimate object.
b) Jumping in to apologize when two people are clearly equally at fault.
c) Apologizing when "oops!" or "Do you need to get in here?" would suffice.
d) Apologizing when it is not your fault.
e) Apologizing profusely: one sincere "sorry" is usually enough.
f) Apologizing when a situation is completely out of your control.
g) Using "Sorry" instead of "Excuse me" or "Could you please say that again? I didn't hear you."

Encourage your group to try very hard not to feel bad about how many "sorries" they have to snip in one week. Remind them that they have had a lifetime of learning to be nice and only a short time of practising a more assertive way of being. Tell them: "If you catch yourself slapping your forehead and saying, 'Oh god, I am so pathetic!' you're being too hard on yourself. Calling yourself names only means you get to be pathetic *and* sorry!" Tell them to give themselves credit for hearing each "sorry." Noticing your inappropriate "sorries" is the first step toward change. Encourage them to take it lightly, have fun with it and watch for the moment when they are able to snip that "sorry" before it escapes their lips!

Remember: It is important to give ourselves lots of time to work on getting rid of the word "sorry" and not to shame ourselves (or others) for slipping up.

Exercises from Chapter 6

Boundaries Exercises

In the following Boundaries Exercises, we will deal with three types of boundaries: Space, Talk and Touch. Describe the concept of boundaries to the group as outlined in Chapter 6. It is important to make clear guidelines for the group as it is possible for participants to have a boundary invaded during one of the exercises. Be clear that people should stop when told to, not answer questions they don't feel comfortable with, and be specific about what kinds of touching is allowed. Strongly encourage participation but support those who does not wish to participate and praise them for having strong, clear boundaries.

a. Space Invaders/Space Defenders
Participants line up on either side of the room, facing a partner across the room. On one side are the Space Invaders, on the other are the Space Defenders. Have the Space Invaders walk slowly toward their partners while making eye contact. The Space Defenders must put

their hand up and say "Stop" when they feel their "boundary" (when they feel their partner is too close for comfort). It can be interesting to ask partners to step back a fraction just to see if the comfort level improves. If this is the case, the Space Defender has probably said "Stop" a little too late. Ask the group to try it again, this time anticipating the boundary and stopping partners sooner.

Teaching Tip: When we are first learning about our boundaries, the tendency is to assert a boundary once it has already been invaded. This is because the "No" feeling is more distinct once the line has been crossed. In these exercises participants should be encouraged to anticipate the boundary by paying close attention to how they feel and to say "Stop" before their boundary has been crossed.

b. Word Invaders/Word Defenders

Participants pair up into partners and "interview" each other. The Word Invader should think up four questions that are increasingly personal. Brainstorm with your group what kinds of questions they would find too personal. Common topics are sex, body image and money. Some examples of personal questions might be:

"Do you have a boyfriend/girlfriend?"
"How far have you gone?"
"How much money do your parents make?"
"How much body hair do you have?"
"Do you masturbate?"
"Tell me who you like and what your fantasy is about that person."
"What's your most embarrassing secret?"

Remind your group that you all understand that they would not normally ask these questions and that the purpose is to ask invasive questions in order to reach a boundary quickly.

The Word Invader should ask increasingly personal questions until they get to the Word Defender's boundaries. (If their partner keeps answering the questions they may have to stop and respect their own boundaries!) When the Space Invader has crossed the Space Defender's verbal boundary, the Space Defender says "Stop" using a raised hand and good eye contact. She/he refuses to answer the question.

Teaching Tip: The Word Invader may have to cross her/his own boundaries in order to ask such personal questions. S/he should be encouraged to do so for the sake of the exercise but supported if s/he chooses not to. Offer the group the option of pointing out the question they wish to ask from the list written up on the board. Ask the group to pay close attention to how uncomfortable it feels to cross one's own boundaries and ask them to think of times when they have given personal information too freely in the past. Point out that we have to be aware of when we are crossing our own boundaries as well.

c. Touch Invaders/Touch Defenders

Participants pair up and contrive non-sexual ways of touching each other by pretending to examine clothing or jewellery. When the Touch Defender feels her/his space is being invaded, s/he says "Stop" with a raised hand and good eye contact.

Teaching Tip: There are no right and wrong places for the boundaries to be. They are where they are and it is up to the participant to experience the exercise and to decide if s/he wants to make any boundary changes.

Healthy Ways to Express Disagreement

Write these three healthy and assertive ways of expressing disagreement and anger up on the board. Break your group into small groups of three or four and ask them to role-play common relationship conflicts and practise expressing disagreement assertively using all three examples. Encourage them to demonstrate their role-plays in front of the large group.

1. Strong "I" statements: Using "I" statements is good communication and defuses defensiveness. For example, "I don't feel comfortable with how much you flirt when we go out together."

2. XYZ statements: (When you do "X", I feel "Y" and I want "Z".) For example: "When you ignore me and flirt with other people (X), I feel humiliated and really insecure/angry (Y)and I want you to be more sensitive and respectful of my feelings when we're out together (Z)."

3. Boundary statements: "I'm feeling really angry right now. I want some space and I need you to leave." Or, "I don't want to hug yet. I'm still too angry."

Unfair Fighting

In order for your group to identify what are "Fair Fighting Rules," it can be useful to have them brainstorm a list of examples of unfair fighting. Do this brainstorm with the whole group before they break into small groups to develop their Fair Fighting Rules. Help them out by writing up a few examples of both unfair and fair fighting on the board.

Examples of unfair/fair fighting:

- **Unfair:** "You are such a slut."
- **Fair:** "I hate it that you slept with someone else and right now it feels like I will never forgive you for it."

- **Unfair:** "What is wrong with you? How could you be so stupid? Can't you ever do anything right?"
- **Fair:** "I see you've put a dent in my car again! I don't want you to borrow my car anymore until you get this fixed."

Fighting Fair

The purpose of this exercise is to help individuals develop their own personal list of Fair Fighting Rules. Tell your group that there may be things that they feel strongly about that are personal to them and their life experience. For example, leaving (or refusing to engage) can be a form of abandonment and a power trip. It could be frustrating for anyone to have this happen. However, if you had a parent who "walked out" on you, it might be unbearable for you to have a partner who walks out when s/he is angry. In that case, you might want to add the rule "No Walking Out" to your list.

Break the group into small groups and ask them to brainstorm a list of Fair Fighting Rules. Invite them to share the lists with the whole group. Learning what other people's feelings are regarding what is fair and unfair can help us feel strong about our own personal list.

Going Too Far

The purpose of this exercise is to help your group define behaviours that are going too far. Tell your group that every relationship should have clear boundaries about certain controlling or abusive behaviours. Brainstorm with your group some examples of things that would be going too far in a friendship or intimate relationship. Start them out with some examples:

Example 1: You know your partner was sexually abused and when you are feeling frustrated with her/his unwillingness to go any further sexually you refer to the sexual abuse as the problem in a mean way.

Example 2: If you have a car and your partner doesn't, it would be going too far to leave your partner stranded without a ride home just because you had an argument.

Example 3: Tearing up your friend's important essay that is due the next day, because you are angry.

Example 4: Planting drugs in your friend's locker and then informing the school, to get back at her/him for something s/he did to you.

Example 5: Refusing to bring your partner home at curfew because you are having a good time and don't want to leave the party.

Example 6: Reading your partner's/friend's personal journal because you feel shut out or suspect s/he is hiding something from you.

All of these things are going too far, no matter how angry or upset you are. If one person has the power to cause the other to lose her/his job, get kicked out of home/school, fail a class—and they abuse this power—that is definitely going too far.

Safe and Unsafe Relationships

This exercise will help individuals define the qualities of a safe relationship and help them be aware of what to watch out for in unsafe relationships. Break your group into small groups and ask them to make a list of safe relationship qualities. Ask them to make a list of unsafe elements in a relationship as well. Have them share their lists with the large group. Afterwards, provide the following list for them and see how many of these points were covered and if there were any new ones added.

Some things to look for in a safe relationship:

Acceptance
A person's behaviour may be in question but who they are is not.

Encouragement
When you do well there isn't a sense of threat and competition. Both partners will be encouraging of each other's successes and feel excitement and pride in each other's achievements.

Support
You are there for each other. You can cry together and hold each other when you need to be held. You will be there for each other for career decisions and changes, loss of a loved one through death or divorce, school stresses and successes. You care about each other and support each other and it's not a one-way street. Both people give and receive support.

Laughter
You both have the ability to see the humorous side of things. You can laugh at yourselves without putting down one another. You can laugh at life without putting down other people.

Comfort
In a safe relationship there is an easy feeling. You recognize that there's a comfort in the relationship that you may have missed in other less-healthy dating situations. You'll find that you aren't afraid to say what's in your heart, to disagree, to suggest where to go on a date, or to comment on something in the news.

Some things to watch out for in a relationship:

The Rush
A feeling of ease can only exist in a relationship when there is no violence or threat of violence, including sexual abuse or verbal or emo-

tional abuse. In an abusive relationship, there's often a tension—a "walking on eggs" feeling—because you sense the potential for abuse or you've already been abused. It is common for young men and women to think they are attracted to someone because they get a "rush" when they are around that person. The intensity that they are experiencing is often interpreted as "love." When examined closely, it is usually exposed for what it is: a rush of adrenaline that is simply fear. If you constantly have a knot in your stomach when you are with your partner, it is not love. It is your body telling you that you are not safe.

Dead Space
The relaxed feeling in a safe relationship is different from a flat or "dead" feeling. In some unhealthy relationships the depressed energy between the two people can create a "dead space" between them. In this kind of relationship, both people's energy is absorbed by the effort it takes to repress their true feelings, which they are too afraid or too unskilled to express. If you are reluctantly spending all your time together sitting around watching TV or hanging around doing nothing, you are in an unhealthy relationship. Both people in this situation are waiting for the other person to take charge and make them feel alive.

Emotional Abuse
When we talk about safety we are not just speaking of physical safety. When we talk about abuse, we are not only talking about physical abuse. Over time, emotional abuse can chip away at your self-esteem and result in severe depression, drug and alcohol abuse and even suicide.

Getting High
If you are spending much of your time together figuring out how to score alcohol or drugs and getting high together, you and your partner may have substance addiction problems. When drugs and alcohol take centre stage in your relationship, they are in control, not you. If this is the case, you are probably in a co-dependent relationship that is more about keeping your addictions fed than it is about each other.

The Hook

When abusive people are remorseful they can be extremely convincing. This can be a very big "hook," especially for women. It is a very strong part of female conditioning to be overly compassionate (feel other people's feelings instead of their own) and to emotionally rescue (he needs help and I will be the one to "save" him). The rule is: If your partner is acting abusively, s/he is abusive. Period.

Assessing Sexual Attraction

Who we tend to be attracted to can be based on either healthy or unhealthy patterns that were modelled for us when we were children —usually by our parents but also strongly influenced by popular media and even childhood fairy tales. In the following two exercises, you will assist your group in becoming aware of their personal patterns. It is important for the group to know that the types of people they are attracted to is something they can change if they find they are stuck in an unhealthy pattern.

a. My Ideal Mate

The purpose of this exercise is to assist young people in examining the types of people they tend to be attracted to and to assess whether or not they have healthy or unhealthy attraction tendencies. Creating a list of the qualities of an "ideal mate" can help them identify and choose healthy people to be with.

Instruct your group as follows: List the qualities you want in a mate. Begin the list with: "I deserve to have a partner who..." Make the list as long as you like and then make a short list of qualities that you are not willing to do without. Begin this list with: "I am not willing to do without ..." If you're in a relationship with someone, check their qualities against your list. You will be able to either reaffirm or question why you are with them. If you are not in a relationship, each time you find yourself attracted to someone, check your list and see if your attractions align with your ideals.

b. To Have Sex or Not

This exercise can help young people become clear about their values and boundaries regarding entering into sexual activity in relationships. Tell your group it is essential that they have a clear vision of what they do and do not feel ready to do before they find themselves "in the moment." Stress that they have the right to choose to stop having sex if they have already entered into sexual activity with a previous or current partner and they discover that they do not feel they are ready to be sexually active.

Instruct your group as follows: Make a pros-and-cons list about beginning a sexual relationship. Whether or not you've had sex before doesn't matter. Whether you're with someone right now or not doesn't matter. Just start where you are now and ask yourself:
"Is this something I choose at this point in my life?"
"Do I know for sure that this is something my partner also wants?"
"Do I trust myself (and my partner) right now?"
"Do I feel emotionally and physically safe with myself and her/him?"
"Am I prepared to deal with the changes in myself and my
    relationship?
"Am I doing it to feel less lonely? To keep my partner's interest?"

Guys in Trouble: Feeding the Beast

We know that teens are in trouble when they drink or do drugs or choose to have unsafe sex. It is obvious that when a girl is being sexually assaulted or hit, she's in trouble. What is not so obvious is that the guys who are doing the assaulting are also in trouble. It is not only that they are potentially in trouble with the law if they get caught, but they are in trouble because the moment they hurt someone else they are supporting the part of themselves that is violent and unhealthy. They are abandoning their more human side. The more they "feed the beast" the bigger and hungrier it gets. As the unhealthy side of them gets stronger, they will feel less and less in control of their violence. They will feel more and more powerless and shut off from themselves and close relationships with other people. If this cycle continues, they will become the beast. Eventually, what you do becomes who you are.

With a group of guys, brainstorm examples of when guys are in trouble. If the group doesn't identify committing violence as a way of being in trouble, add it to the list and discuss it.

"Stud Status": Will the Real Man Please Stand Up

Males often feel they have to pretend they are as stone-hearted, fearless and virile as the men in the movies. They posture and brag and lie about their sexual conquests. The sad thing is that they believe each other. How is one grade 10 boy to know that he is not the only virgin in the class? In one SafeTeen workshop, a grade 10 boy blurted out: "OK, I'm still a virgin, is there anybody else in this class who is still a virgin?" All but one or two of the hands in the room went up. The relief was palpable on the boy's face. To ask that question took real courage.

For the most part, it feels life-threatening to boys to reveal what they truly feel. This exercise provides them with the opportunity to do this in a way that is safe and with no risk of being personally exposed. The power of this exercise is that it exposes the "stud" and reveals the real (hu)man.

Ask boys to put "Yes" or "No" on a piece of paper in answer to the following questions:
1. Have you cried at any time in the past year?
2. Have you felt afraid at any time in the past year?
3. Are you still a virgin?
Instruct them to write answers and pass the papers up front. Shuffle the papers and redistribute them. When each person has an anonymous paper, go over the three questions. Ask individuals to stand if their paper says "Yes" and remain seated if it says "No." This will indicate how many in the group said yes/no to each question.

Group Discussion: Why do guys feel they have to pretend they don't have feelings? Why do guys pretend they have more sexual experience than they do? Why do guys tend to avoid intimacy but want sex so badly? Why do guys seem to be able to cut off their feelings so well and just use girls for sex? Who does it hurt? How does it feel to be used?

Redefining Masculinity

Because it can be difficult to "sell" the concept of the Solid Guy to young men as a viable method of resolving disputes, it is useful to mention powerful sports heroes who model assertive rather than aggressive behaviour. For example, hockey players are employing a new way of asserting themselves during conflict on the ice—rather than the violent tradition of beating each other's brains in when they are in conflict we can see them "facing off" with each other. In a demonstration of powerful self-control they stand and make eye contact for a brief but significant period of time. It is clear that they are saying, "I am choosing not to fight, but I am not afraid."

Another good example of powerful men modelling a different way of being strong is evident every time an NBA player goes to the free throw line. Highly skilled basketball players don't posture and strut and pound their chests before they shoot. We can see them focusing deeply, blocking out all attempts from the opposing team to distract them. They take a breath, ground themselves and then shoot. When "talking trash" or losing their temper could cost these men tens of thousands of dollars, it is interesting to see how much they rely on body language and especially eye contact to let each other know they are not afraid. When we compare athletes who lose their tempers with athletes who do not, it becomes clear that the men who feel they have something to prove and cannot control their violent impulses have self-esteem issues.

Have a group of boys brainstorm about male figures they admire. Write the names on a board as they come up. Then go back over the list and write down the quality or qualities that are admired about this person beside each name. Initiate a discussion about the admired qualities. Are they negative or positive qualities? Do they reinforce or redefine notions of masculinity?

Now have each boy write down one quality they admire about

themselves. Ask them to do so anonymously—they should not attach their names to the papers. Have them pass the pieces of paper to the facilitator, who then reads these qualities aloud. Discuss the similarities to, and differences from, the qualities of "admired males" discussed previously.

Girls Valuing Themselves

If we do not value ourselves, we will not stand up for ourselves or keep ourselves safe and healthy. Learning how to give less attention to negative feedback and take in positive feedback is something that improves with practice.

Have each participant think of something they like about themselves and write it down at the top of a page. Instruct them to put their name on the back of the paper and put it face down in the centre of the group. Now, each person in the group adds something positive to every other person's list (remind the group to stay with "essence compliments"). If there are ten people in the group, each person will end up with ten positive comments. This is the start of a list that they can carry with them and add to each day. By handing the list to other people they see throughout the day or just making a mental note when they hear something positive, they can add at least one each day.

Encourage them to think of one positive thing to add to their lists each day. Keep the lists going for at least one week. Encourage them to share the lists by reading them aloud either in the group or to someone they feel safe with.

Encourage them to counter negative feedback from self and others with the comments on their lists. If you think a bad thing about yourself or someone says something mean or critical to you, repeat the good things in your mind or out loud.

Redefining "Good Girls"

Discuss with a group of girls what the label "a good girl" generally means. Why is it that "a good girl" is nice, quiet, polite and does everything she's told? Brainstorm how the word "good" is used when applied to other things. For example:

A good truck is one that holds up on a bumpy road.
A good story is one that stays with you for a long time.
A good meal is full of nutrition.
A good job is one where you make lots of money and feel that you are contributing something to the world.
A good leader is a strong leader.
A good voice is a skillful voice and a powerful voice.

Once you have a long list, apply the list to what makes a "good girl." Have individual members of the group stand and say, "A good girl is … " (fill in any word from the list).

Redefined, a "good" girl is:
a girl who doesn't fall apart during bumpy times;
a girl who is a friend that lasts;
a girl who is healthy;
a girl who makes lots of money and contributes something meaningful to the world;
a girl who is strong;
a girl who is powerful.

What Females and Males Want from Intimate Relationships

The way males tend to posture around sex and intimacy we could think all they are interested in is sex, sex and more sex. Using a safe and anonymous method, this exercise exposes the difference between the way males posture and what they really feel. In doing so, females and other males get to see the truth. This exercise can be a strong bridge in the gender gap, bringing an openness and understanding of the similarities between what females and males need and want from each other. This exercise also makes it difficult—and less necessary—

for the males in the group to "posture" in the future. This exercise is effective in a gender-separate group and can be done in a mixed-gender group as well. If in a mixed-gender group, instruct them to put "female" or "male" on their paper or give males and females each a different colour of paper.

Ask participants to list four things they want most from an intimate relationship in order of importance to them.

Stress that they should keep their lists private and answer anonymously and then ask them to fold the papers and pass them up front. Shuffle the papers and redistribute them. Now, ask them at this point, before they look at the piece of paper they have in front of them, to predict what will be number 1 on the list. It is common for most groups of males to predict "sex" as the most likely number 1 item. Now have them look at their lists and reveal the truth about what guys really want from intimate relationships. In the vast majority of classrooms the results will be the same. The fist item on the list is rarely "sex." Have the group demonstrate by a show of hands how many have "sex" as the first item on the list. Qualities such as "trust" and "love" are usually listed as the most important. Instruct each group member to read aloud the list they have. Discuss the difference between what they predicted and what was revealed to be true. If the exercise was done in gender-separate groups of youth who know each other, bring them together in a co-ed group and reveal the results of both genders' lists. Discuss the differences and the similarities.

Exercises from Chapter 7

Gender-Specific Insults

The purpose of this exercise is to bring an awareness of the use of gender and sexuality as a form of verbal violence and how these words are used against females and males.

Break up into small gender-mixed groups. Brainstorm words used as insults—have one person write a list. Bring the group back together and write the lists up on board.

Divide the words into gender groups:

a) examples of words used to insult males:

sissy, wuss, homo, fag, girl, pussy, jerk off, asshole, bitch, bastard, loser, pig.

Point out that many of the insults used against males are homophobic. They say "you are gay" (and therefore like a woman), which is the worst insult for a man.

b) examples of words used to insult females:

slut, whore/ho/hooker, cunt/hole/pussy, bitch, fat, dog, lez.

Point out that many of the insults used against females are related to their sexuality or their bodies.

Discuss how the words for the two genders are the same or different and how people feel about them.

Teaching Tip: Homophobic comments are used to insult both females and males. These comments are not always necessarily intended to imply that people are actually homosexual—anything can be called "gay": a person's clothing, choice of music or hair style. Point out how the word "gay" is almost exclusively used in a negative context and that it is still homophobic to use words such as "gay" or "lez" or "queer" in this context regardless of intent. Define homophobia for your group and stress that it is about fear as well as hatred. Adolescents may claim their right to "hate" gay people but they will rarely admit that they are afraid. If they think making homophobic remarks will label them as afraid, it may inhibit them from using them.

Self-Esteem and Media Images of Females

This exercise will help young women identify why they may feel both seduced by and offended by images of women in media. It can be very confusing to have these mixed feelings and very liberating to expose the ways that female bodies are used to manipulate and market everything from cars to cigarettes. This exercise can be effective in female-only or mixed-gender groups.

Break into small groups and pass around fashion magazines. Have small groups examine the magazines and report to the main group on the images of girls and women and how they make them feel. Write up on the board and discuss ahead of time the following things to look for:

Infantilizing: words like chick, babe or baby, kitten, doll or doll-face, cute or cutie pie. Females portrayed as both childlike and sexy. Images of adult women that are dressed or posed in childlike ways: little or no pubic hair, ponytails, little-girl shoes and socks, body language such as finger in mouth, toes turned inward, pouting, etc.

Violent images: insinuations of violence, women who look afraid, stalking images, torn clothing, bruised faces and bodies, pale faces with dark hollows under the eyes, black eyes, vacant stares, images of insanity (such as tearing out hair, scratching face or body, tearing at own clothing), evidence of needles, drug use.

Anorexic images: girls and women who look too thin and pale, women with sunken eyes and ribs showing who look like they are starving to death.

Death images: half-dressed or naked women who are lying as though they are dead, washed up on a beach with staring eyes, posed in coffins, etc.

Power-over images: males standing over females, males restraining or grabbing or choking females, cruel-faced males nearby or standing too close, uniformed males with passive females, women tied up or restrained by males, males with large dogs, males in threatening poses with cornered females, whips, chains, leather, guns and hunting images with females portrayed as victims or prey, etc.

Objectifying images: males looking at females as though they are objects, females in come-take-me poses, females in sexual poses around cars and boats and other male "toys," females in liquor ads being overly attentive to males, women undressing in windows, segments of women's bodies (legs, breasts, pubic area, lips or bums) as the focus of images.

Encourage group discussion with the following questions:
Who has the power in each picture? What are the messages in the images and the text saying about females? What are they saying about males? Why are women's bodies so exploited? Are the women who pose nude liberated? Are prostitutes or women who do porno films liberated? Why do some female athletes pose nude? Are there ways that they could pose differently that would be more powerful? Is it the nudity that is offensive or the way the bodies are posed?

Girls' Body Images and Self-Esteem

No matter how "perfect" other people may see them as, most girls and women feel unattractive and even ugly sometimes. Most females feel shame about their bodies and hide their body flaws from each other. By grade 6, girls have become skilled at the art of undressing for gym class without exposing one inch of skin. The only naked bodies that most females see are the ones in the magazines—and they are air-brushed and computer-altered into society's version of perfection. Because of this, many young females think they are the only ones who have flaws. For instance, most females have stretch marks somewhere on their bodies—even young women who have never had children— or body hair where they don't think they should have it. These are well-kept secrets. This exercise provides an opportunity for girls to share with each other, without exposing themselves personally, how imperfect (and therefore normal) all their bodies are.

1. Rating body image: Individually and privately on a piece of paper ask the girls/women to rate their body image on a scale of 1 to 10. Pass papers to the front and redistribute. Read the results aloud anonymously.
2. Ask participants to write a list of their body flaws and read the lists aloud anonymously.
3. Ask participants to write a list of their body pluses and read the lists aloud anonymously.

Ask the participants in the group to raise their hands if:
a. they do *not* have any stretch marks anywhere on their bodies;
b. they have *never* felt they were too fat;
c. they are completely satisfied with their body exactly as it is and wouldn't change a thing.

Encourage a group discussion with the following questions:
What is a "perfect 10"? Does it exist? Why is what we look like so important? Is it less important for guys? Why? Why aren't women allowed to have body hair? How skinny is too skinny? Why is it so important to so many of us to be noticed by guys? Do we want to be noticed for who we are or what we look like? Should we depend on male assessment to determine how we feel about ourselves?

Building Self-Esteem: A Letter Worth Sending

The purpose of this exercise is to help young people build their self-love. Provide the group with writing materials and an envelope and if possible provide a stamp for each member of the group. Tell them they are going to write a love letter. Tell them to try not to think of any one person in particular—even if they feel they have someone in mind that they would like to send a love letter to. This letter is to "an ideal love." The exercise is in two parts. Instruct your group as follows for the first part.

a) Begin: "Dear _____" Leave the name blank for now. Write a letter to an ideal love. Use qualities that you admire in a number of people and praise your beloved for these qualities. Focus on inner beauty rather than physical beauty. Be romantic and fearless in your adoration and appreciation. Acknowledge the goodness and worth in them and tell them why you are grateful they are in your life. Reassure them that you will be true and loyal and never abandon them. Sign it.

Once your group has completed their love letters, instruct them as follows:

b) Fill in the _____ with your own first name. Put it in an envelope, seal it, address it, stamp it and take it out and mail it to yourself. When it comes in the mail, go someplace private and read it.

Teaching Tip: Young people who have low self-esteem may feel embarrassed by this exercise and may forget or refuse to mail their letters. You may wish to collect the letters and mail them yourself. If providing stamps for large numbers of students is a problem, you can ask your students to bring a stamp with them ahead of time.

Compliment or Insult?
It can be confusing for young women to define the difference between when they are being complimented and when they are being insulted. Stress to your group that the way they feel should be the determining factor. The purpose of this exercise is to define the difference between being objectified and being complimented. Have the group brainstorm a list of objectifying comments and a list of "essence compli-

ments" (comments that praise based on inner qualities).

Some examples of objectifying comments are:
"You're sexy when you're mad!"
"You look hot! Now what was that you were saying?"
"Nice dress—and I like what's in it too."
"You really are quite an attractive girl—if you'd only wear your hair down."
"You are a babe!"
"You turn me on."

Examples of "essence compliments":
"I like the way you do your hair."
"You have such a confident way of speaking."
"You are funny—you make me laugh!"
"Watching you run, I feel so inspired."
"Your whole face lights up when you smile."
"Your choices show integrity."
"I love how playful you are."
"You have a unique sense of style."
"Your strong spirit is awesome."

Arrange your group in a large circle. Have each participant turn to the person on their left, choose an essence compliment from the list or think up a new one and deliver a compliment to the person next to them. Instruct the person receiving to respond with an assertive "Thank you" and then turn to the person on their left and so on until everyone in the group has had an opportunity to give and receive.

Powerplay Exercise

The purpose of this exercise is to increase awareness and to create empathy among males for the loss of power that females so often feel when they are objectified or not taken seriously.

In gender-mixed groups of two, instruct the male participant in each group to prepare to deliver a one-minute speech about a topic that is very close to his heart with all the passion he can, aiming to educate his partner on his point of view. Take the female participants aside and privately instruct them to interrupt their partner at the point when he is most sincere and make a comment on his appearance. For example: "Excuse me, John, but I couldn't help but notice your hair, the way it falls over your forehead ... it's just so adorable. I'm sorry, continue—what were you saying?" Or, "Excuse me, John, but I just have to say, the shirt you are wearing, well, I don't mean to offend but you're a nice-looking guy—you have such a nice build. You would look so much better in something more fitted. Anyway, what was that you were saying?"

When the male stops and reacts, instruct the female to say, "What's the matter, can't you take a compliment?"

Follow up with group discussion. Point out that it is not the intent that is relevant but the experience of the person who is receiving the comment. A well-meaning guy can inadvertently offend if he is not aware of how his "complimentary" comments may be received.

Consent Defined: Yes Means Yes

The following exercise is most effective if done in small gender-separate groups and is geared toward males. The purpose is to expose attitudes regarding consent and to clarify both personal values and legal realities of what defines consent.

Break your group into groups of three or four. Provide each group with the list of questions below and paper to write on. Instruct as follows: "One person from each group reads the questions aloud. Go through each question slowly and carefully. Jot down notes if you want. For each question, answer Yes or No. When you get to the last question, you must come up with a definition of consent that everyone in the group can agree with."

1. Is there consent to have sexual intercourse if the woman says nothing but pushes the man away with her hands?
2. Is there consent if the woman is smiling while she is saying "No"?
3. Is there consent if the woman is too intoxicated to say anything?
4. What if she had been drinking a lot and says she wants to have sex?
5. What if both people have been drinking a lot?
6. Is there consent if at first she says "I'm not sure about this" but then is silent?
7. Is there consent if she says nothing at all?
8. Is there consent if at first she says she wants to, but then changes her mind?
9. Is there consent if the woman lets the guy pay for everything on the date and then doesn't try to stop him?
10. Define consent. (Be specific. How could a judge know that consent was given?)

Articulating Yes/No Feelings Clearly

This exercise is geared toward a female-only group. The purpose is to help young women articulate what they want and don't want regarding sexual activity with a partner, what their fears are regarding communicating clearly and how to turn a mixed message into a clear message about mixed feelings. Have the group break into small groups and come up with some possible messages that include all of what they could be feeling in a situation where they are being pressured for sex. When we are able to see the mixed messages as a clear communication that a female has mixed feelings, we may be able to see that she is in fact saying both "Yes" and "No."

Here are some examples:
• "I do feel attracted to you and find you almost irresistibly desirable and I don't think going ahead with this is a wise choice, right now. I don't want you to think I don't want to be with you, because I do."
• "I don't know you well enough to know if I want to have sex with you but I don't want you to leave me before I have a chance to find

out. I'm afraid if I say 'No' right out, you won't stick around."
- "I know I want to be with you and I also know I need time to heal from the hurt I suffered in my last relationship. I want you to care enough about me to wait until I'm ready."
- "I want to fool around and experiment sexually but I don't want to go all the way. I don't want to say 'No' to everything but I don't want to say 'Yes' to everything either. I'm not sure what I feel comfortable with yet."
- "I know we went all the way once before but I've changed my mind. I don't think I'm ready to be in a sexually active relationship but I still want to go out with you."

Drawing from the previous examples and from the results of the small group brainstorm, have the groups role-play making these "mixed message" statements in an assertive way to their "partners." Invite them to act out the scenarios in front of the large group.

How to Handle Disclosures

This exercise is for adults. The purpose of this exercise is to give educators and parents practice in handling disclosures of abuse. In groups of three (with one person acting as observer) each person should have an opportunity to role-play both the young person disclosing and the adult who is handling the disclosure and also have a turn at being the observer. The observer's role is to cue the adult player—making sure all five points are covered—and give her/him feedback afterwards. The group should familiarize themselves with the information in chapter 7 on disclosures and have the following Disclosure Outline written up on the board or on a sheet of paper to refer to:

Disclosure Outline

Five things to say when you receive a disclosure of sexual assault:
1. "I believe you."

2. "I'm sorry that this happened to you."
3. "I'm glad you told me."
4. "It's not your fault."
5. "I'll help you to get help."

Teaching Tip: Try to cover all five points in a way that feels and sounds natural to you. They do not necessarily have to be in the order presented in the above list. Make certain you are aware of the legal responsibilities involved.

Remember: It is common to end a session where a disclosure has taken place feeling that your help has been inadequate. Do not underestimate the power of the simple act of listening and believing.

Remember: If you find yourself emotionally triggered, overwhelmed or going into denial while receiving a disclosure, get help. Tell another adult and pass on the responsibility to insure that the young person gets the help and support they need.

Exercises from Chapter 9

Creating Awareness of the Male Code of Conduct

Ask a group of guys to brainstorm "Who teaches us how to be a man?" Who do we watch as young men to learn how to carry ourselves, react to pressure, how to act in a crisis, etc.?

Typical answers include: fathers, brothers, family, TV, media, friends, teachers, coaches, women, films, heroes, idols, mentors.

What do these people teach us? What are the do's and don'ts? What are we supposed to look like, be good at, be interested in, do with our lives, not be interested in, not do, not look like?

Typical answers include: muscular, tall, good at sports, be responsible for girlfriends/families, don't back down, don't cry, don't be gay, don't watch ballet, know how to fix cars/things.

The facilitator then stops the brainstorm to make the following points:
"The reason we are doing this is to build an awareness that the code exists. The more awareness we have of the code, the more choice each of us has as an individual to choose to step outside of the code when it is getting in the way of who we really are. So we can choose our own way of being in the world instead of having it dictated and decided for us.

"By understanding how the code works, we can also prepare ourselves for the way the code may try to punish us for breaking it. In fact, we are all breaking the code right now just by talking about it. What happens to guys who break the code? Say a grade 10 guy comes to school with painted fingernails; crying because he was cut from a sports team; the day after backing down from a fight? How will other guys react to him? What will they say/do/not say/not do?

"So the code is real, you guys are giving me really concrete examples of how it works. Let's leave this idea open now, and move on. And while we are talking today, I invite anyone to point out moments when they think the code is in action. Just so we can keep understanding how strong it is, and how it works."

Teaching Tip: The brainstorming reveals the inherent truth about the code's existence and its workings in the lives of young men. Honest facilitation includes the male facilitator's openness in noting that the code has affected and does affect him too. It's not just something young men wrestle with. Typically, youth are reluctant to point out codified behaviour in a group. But the invitation to do so is important as it does invite young men to begin, or further, the validation process of choosing their own behaviour, attitudes and depth of self-expression.

Teaching Tip: Any further moments of visible code adherence in the group—and there will be lots to choose from—can be calmly and neutrally pointed out by the facilitator. "OK, so you just called him 'gay' for saying he thinks respect is more important than sex in a relationship. What does the code say about how highly we are supposed to value sex in a relationship?" Highlighting the code as the culprit allows facilitators to hold young men accountable for their actions and attitudes with impact, yet without shaming. The "open door" nature of this exercise inspires the idea and leaves the group with the encouragement to continue evaluating the code and its impact on them personally. Ideally, acknowledgement and discussion of the code becomes part of school culture, empowering young men to create themselves in accordance with their own internal truths.

Teaching Tip: Some tenets of the code can be, and are, interpreted by some men in healthy ways. It can be useful to brainstorm with your group some of the positive things the code teaches about being a man. A feeling of physical well-being and strength, for example, is possible and can be helpful in building a healthy sense of self-worth. Pride in one's ability in sports, music or rebuilding transmissions can be a basic source of positive self-image and validation by one's peers. However, it also important to note that the code lacks any type of measurement of how much self-esteem is enough, and it leaves many men and boys in a never-ending competition for more.

A Final Word: Physical Skills and the Right to Defend Ourselves

When girls and women contemplate standing up for ourselves in a direct and powerful way, we often fear we will make the situation worse. "What if I make the guy even more angry and then he kills me?" This is the most commonly expressed fear in the SafeTeen girls' program workshops. This fear can, and does, stop us from speaking up. In order to neutralize this fear, and because there is no magic answer, no perfect response that guarantees we will be able to prevent a violent attack, in the SafeTeen programs we offer a physical self-defence component to young women as a "back-up" to the assertiveness skills. The result is an integration of the power in the body and the power of the spirit. This integration is profoundly transforming.

It is every woman's right to learn how to defend herself. To see self-defence skills incorporated into the Physical Education curriculum for girls in elementary and secondary schools is my lifelong dream. I also encourage parents with sons who are vulnerable to being bullied to enroll the sons in a martial arts program—one that is committed to the traditional, spiritual, non-violent teachings.

Coda

In honour of all the girls and women who have survived assault.

In honour of all the girls and women who got away.

In memory of all those who did not.

Index

abuse, 145–46, 157–59, 183–87, 233–35, 280–81
abusive relationships, 158–59, 283–84
acceptance in relationships, 137–38
acquaintance rape, 121–23, 149–52, 175–82
addiction, 283
advertising, sexism in, 291–93
aggression, 35, 91–92, 119
alcohol, risks of, 124
Allen, Lillian, 21
anger, 25–26, 79–80, 89–99, 223, 230, 231; "acting in," 93; acting out, 91–92; constructive, 274; exercises, 271–72; expressing, 96–98, 102, 274; and fear, 85, 88–89; healthy, 90, 104, 278–79; physical contact and, 66–67; physical signs of, 135; in rela tionships, 142–45; releasing, 35, 272–73; repressed, 90–91, 93, 94, 95–96, 100, 1o1, 103–4; "safe" and "unsafe," 274–5; as survival skill, 89–90, 93; "triggers," 96; unhealthy, 90–93; and violence, 94–95, 97, 98, 99; working with, 93–99
anonymity in exercises, 6, 286, 289
apologizing, 20, 117–18, 259, 275–76
approval-seeking behaviour, 20, 42, 59–60, 108, 154, 201–2, 205, 253
assault, 3, 47–48, 171
assertiveness, 23–25, 32, 64–66; definition of, 35; language

exercise, 259–60; in role-plays, 261–71; skills, 66, 67–72, 79–81
authority figure role-play, 262–3

Bill of Rights for Men, 229
Bitch, The, 44–49, 52; exercises, 250–52
bodies, 197–200, 203–5
body image exercises, 293–94
body language, 29, 43, 47, 54, 62–63, 253–58
body reactions, 135
boundaries, 122, 123–24, 125–26, 130, 134, 141, 165; exercises, 276–78; reconstructing, 136
boundary statements, 279
Boys' Program, 4–7, 235–42
breathing exercise, 252
Broken Record technique, 67–68, 260, 262, 263
Bully Mirror technique, 70
bullying, 21–22, 29–30, 32–34, 70, 154–55, 167, 214–19; role-play, 262, 266; scenarios, 72–74, 215–18

"Cave or Kill" dynamic, 25, 38
"chameleon" behaviour, 138
Child, The, 41–43, 73–74, 84, 85; exercises, 246–47, 248–50, 272
circumcision, female, 198–99
Code of Conduct, male, 300–2
communication, 70–72, 113, 135, 232–33
compliments, 170, 295–96
compromise in relationships, 141
confidence, female, 59–60. *See also* self-esteem

About the Author

ANITA ROBERTS was the third child in a family of six girls. Her childhood was one of chaos , crisis and violence, and Anita was both a witness to and a subject of the violence. When she became an adult, she created "SafeTeen," an internationally recognized violence-prevention program for adolescents. It developed out of Anita's own need to learn how to be strong and safe in the world.

In the early years, Anita taught a physical self-defense program based on the Martial Arts. A transformational moment for both Anita and her work came when she learned that her Karate instructor, a powerful and highly skilled woman who had won the British Columbia Championships three years running, was terrified to stay home alone at night. Anita began to study the socialization of women, the dynamics of power and gender, and the psychology of assault. Through a combination of research and experiential testing, she developed a highly effective assertiveness model that has become the focus of her prevention programs for youth.

The girls' program was born out of her commitment to making girls and women safer in the world. She developed the boys' program because she believes that boys and men who feel good about themselves don't hurt other people. Anita believes that both genders need to learn how to stand strong without violence: "Teaching our children how to make choices from a place of inner wisdom can be the best prevention strategy of all."

Anita Roberts lives in Vancouver, British Columbia. She is the author of one other book, *The Last Chance Cafe* (Polestar).

For more information on Anita Roberts and the SafeTeen violence prevention program, visit the SafeTeen website at www.safeteen.ca

Praise for *Safe Teen: Positive Alternatives to Violence*:

"*Safe Teen* is written in clear, enjoyable language accessible to teens, parents, and educators... The author has designed the curriculum with profound respect for the challenges confronting adolescent males, while remaining frank about the prevalence of violence against females. The material is sensitive to needs of both bullies and victims, boys and girls. The book and program provide the concepts and practical tools for teens to make safer choices, to change destructive dynamics in relationships, and to be effectively assertive."
— *Quill and Quire*